PROFIT
PATTERNS

30 Ways to
Anticipate and
Profit from Strategic
Forces Reshaping Your Business

ADRIAN J. SLYWOTZKY AND DAVID J. MORRISON
TED MOSER, KEVIN A. MUNDT, JAMES A. QUELLA

TIMES BUSINESS

RANDOM HOUSE

Photo credits on page 424.

Value Migration® and Strategic Anticipation® are proprietary trademarks of Mercer Management Consulting that have been registered with the U.S. Patent and Trademark Office.

Library of Congress Cataloging-in-Publication Data

Slywotzky, Adrian J.
    Profit patterns : 30 ways to anticipate and profit from strategic forces reshaping your business / Adrian J. Slywotzky.
        p.   cm.
    Includes index.
    ISBN 0-8129-3118-1 (alk. paper)
    1. Success in business.   2. Corporate profits.   3. Competition.
  I. Title.
    HF5386.S6362   1999   98-31337
658.15′5—dc21

Random House website address: www.atrandom.com

CONTENTS

WHAT THIS BOOK IS ABOUT AND WHO IT'S FOR

HOW DO WE LEARN from experience?

By learning patterns.

Great physicians combine the art and skill of diagnosis, based not only on their brainpower and education, but also on their intuitive use of experience. Great doctors are adept at pattern recognition. They see the whole picture. They connect symptoms to causes, and use that insight to develop powerful, on-target analyses and prescriptions to help their patients.

The same is true in business. Great managers are skilled at strategic pattern recognition. Every industry is reshaped by patterns of strategic change that can drastically shift profit and power across the landscape. Sometimes the patterns build slowly, sometimes they move rapidly—but change is always occurring. The ability to anticipate how and why a company's strategic landscape is changing, connect symptoms to causes, and then create strategies that lead to significant, sustained profitability is an art and a skill everyone in the world of business and investment can profitably cultivate.

The ability to anticipate strategic patterns helps managers see beyond the surface complexity to the underlying drivers of customer and economic behavior. This ability, which we call Strategic Anticipation is not about 100 percent prediction—it is about being *prepared* to exploit change, and making informed decisions as to the best moves and countermoves for your business.

When change and complexity increase, patterns occur more frequently. Pattern recognition becomes more important. It moves from "nice to know" to "need to know."

*   *   *

This book equips the practitioner with a set of tools that will increase their odds of success in the new game of business. The type of change occurring in business—the focus of Part I—calls for a new skill set. The level of complexity and rate of change have grown quite rapidly in the past decade, and will continue to increase for the next several years. We are unlikely to return to the "good old days," to the rules that defined how business was done through the 1980s. There is great advantage to be gained from learning the new rules of the game, and the ability to recognize key patterns will help us play the game much more effectively.

Part II is the heart of the book and provides managers and investors with thirty patterns changing the landscape of every industry. As you learn them, you will begin to build a repertoire of moves and countermoves that will be invaluable allies as the marketplace continues its process of continual transformation. The art of identifying, understanding, and exploiting patterns needs to become part of the mental process of every decision maker interested in creating sustained profit growth.

Part III is a "how to" guide. Through stories and techniques for applying patterns, it shows how to identify key patterns that are changing your corporate landscape. The next step is energizing the organization to act, and act early. Part III also addresses the key issues that often stand in the way of initiating the right changes within your organization.

The conclusion to Part III, Chapter 14, is a workbook designed to help a team of managers systematically apply pattern thinking to their business situation.

Finally, we have included an appendix that delves a bit deeper into several valuable dimensions of the analogy between chess and business.

Profit Patterns is a book that is designed to help develop a way of thinking about business strategy that builds on the cumulative experience of decades of business design innovation. Throughout the book, we have included references to a Web site, www.ProfitPatterns.com, that provides additional data and perspectives to expand and further develop this thought process.

* * *

Patterns have multiple applications. They are clearly a tool developed for managers to improve the effectiveness of making major strategic moves, allocating resources, and managing strategic risk. But investors, customers, and star employees can also put the power of pattern thinking to work in making smarter investment decisions, smarter supplier decisions, and smarter career decisions.

The increasing volatility of the market makes things harder for manager and investor alike. For the investor, the turbulent waves disrupting the surface of the investment ocean make it increasingly difficult to see the underlying currents of genuine value growth.

Knowing patterns does not guarantee success in this erratic environment. But patterns can help return focus to those underlying customer and economic movements that lead to both opportunity and obsolescence.

As equity prices rise and fall with greater rapidity, it becomes even more important to ask fundamental questions about the companies you have invested in. For example:

1. Am I investing in a company using an outdated business model? Will a new value leader soon appear? If so, how can I identify that company?
2. Am I investing in a "no-profit" industry? What are the chances that structural profitability will return to the industry?
3. Are the companies I'm investing in ahead or behind in the skills required to be an industry leader? To be a survivor?

Investors can take each one of the thirty patterns and convert them into the right set of questions to determine how comfortable, or uncomfortable, they should feel with the business designs of the companies making up their equities portfolio.

Investors have to decide about investments. Customers have to decide about suppliers. Making the right supplier decision can have a tremendous positive impact on a customer's economic performance. Strategic pattern recognition can help customers make smarter supplier decisions.

Every single pattern can be translated into a set of questions from the customer's perspective. Just as suppliers need to anticipate patterns to move to the right next business design, customers can anticipate patterns to understand what their best supply options will be tomorrow.

Knowing patterns can also help star employees work up to their full potential, by empowering them to:

1. Deliver extraordinary value to the company by helping the company "get" the key changes occurring in its business as early as possible.

2. Determine which companies are most likely to create the type of value growth that will provide the greatest return on their own performance.

For example, being a great executive inside a company that finds out its supplier will begin to compete effectively for its customers is probably not an uplifting experience. Nor is working in a narrowly product-centric company, when all the value has shifted to solutions, necessarily a high-reward situation. In both cases, patterns of strategic change are rendering the business model obsolete. Obsolete business models do a poor job of rewarding great performers.

At a time when all employees have to take greater responsibility for creating and managing their own career progression, an awareness of the major patterns reshaping tomorrow's opportunity can be a useful cross-check on the career decisions we make.

* * *

The material in this book builds on and extends the ideas and research from two previous books: *Value Migration* and *The Profit Zone*.

Value Migration identified a dramatic shift in the business landscape as new aggressive companies defeated established giants—not through new products or innovative technology, but superior business design.

The Profit Zone told the stories of twelve reinventors whose profit strategies created over $700 billion in market value for shareholders. In both books, patterns that were changing the corporate landscape were implicit in the analysis but not identified to nearly the breadth and depth to which they are in this book.

The Profit Zone explained why some very successful companies (GE, Disney, and Intel, for example) have been so consistently profitable. It contained stories of "the generals"—Jack Welch, Michael Eisner, Andy Grove—their campaigns, and their repeated victories. *Profit Patterns* is the "codebook": the specifics of how to identify the shifts taking place in your market so that the performance of your company, your division, or your small business can be raised to a level similar to that achieved by the reinventors.

It's also useful to think of *Profit Patterns* in the way that most fans see professional football on television: three-hundred-pound people running in different directions, trying to demolish each other. It's not until observers like John Madden start drawing instant diagrams after key plays that most of us understand the pattern that a few seconds ago seemed almost incomprehensible.

Today's business market can also seem incomprehensible. Things are changing so quickly that it's tough to keep up with what's going on in the game. The thirty profit patterns in this book will help you see through the chaos and determine what needs to be done so that your company, and not your competitor, emerges as the winner.

Learning patterns and using them to create sustained profit growth will not happen without effort. As in chess, one does not become a grand master overnight. However, the early learning rate is very high, and mastery of the basic rules and patterns leads to dramatic performance improvements in a surprisingly short period of time.

ACKNOWLEDGMENTS

THE FIRST CHAPTER of this book uses Gary Kasparov's battle with Deep Blue to introduce the importance of patterns thinking. Just as chess requires the ability to recognize patterns on the board, dealing successfully with the dynamism and complexity of today's business environment requires a fundamentally new skill set—that of strategic pattern recognition. However, there is another key learning illustrated by the Deep Blue story: Gary Kasparov was not defeated by a machine, but rather by a team who codified their own knowledge, and that of hundreds of other players, into a patterns knowledge base.

Today, all managers and investors face a painful combination of greater complexity and less bandwidth for dealing with it. This "bandwidth crisis" plagues more and more decision makers. Tougher decisions have to be made in less time. One way of dealing with this challenge is to learn aggressively from past strategic errors and triumphs—to know the smart moves our predecessors made in anticipating change, and profiting from them. However, that is easier said than done. There are hundreds of companies in multiple industries from which to learn. How can an individual executive gather, learn, and apply all of this knowledge? The answer is often unclear. What is clear is that forming a team of people who can bring their own patterns experience to the table can provide the necessary expertise to build the knowledge base required to solve today's strategic issues.

Because of the importance of the new skill of strategic pattern recognition, strategy is becoming a team sport. The team can be dramatically more effective if its work is leveraged by a knowledge base of past patterns, their triggers, and the moves they lead to.

Constructing a knowledge base of strategic patterns—how they work, why they happen, how to profit from them—is a complex and challenging task. It requires building on, and integrating, the experience and knowledge of dozens of specialists whose expertise derives from industry knowledge, functional excellence, and a broad range of business and economic disciplines such as customer science, organizational analysis, and others. This is not a static process, but a continuous one. The patterns Web site (www.ProfitPatterns.com) is designed to keep the knowledge base current and evolving, with new examples, new patterns, and potentially new categories.

The ideas and examples in this book have relied on an extremely broad knowledge base at Mercer Management Consulting—a knowledge base formed from experience across the company, focused on detecting and dealing with fundamental strategic changes in dozens of industries. Just as today's executive requires a team of people to bring these ideas together, we have relied on Mercer's diverse industry expertise to gather a deeper understanding of the key strategic patterns reshaping the major industries in our economy. We would like to thank the heads of our practices and their teams: Bob Fox in CIE (communications, information, & entertainment), Scott Birnbaum in Financial Services, Peter Baumgartner in Manufacturing, Hugh Randall in Transportation, James Bonomo in Energy and Process Industries, and Kevin Mundt's team in Retail Consumer and Healthcare for their insight into the patterns playing out in their industries. In addition, we would like to thank our partners Charlie Hoban, Rick Wise, Ed DiGeronimo, Nancy Lotane, and Matthew Clark, who were especially helpful in furthering the development of our concepts.

This book is the product of the same organizational and intellectual energy that generates insights for Mercer's clients. We would like to thank those clients who have inspired us to develop a deeper understanding of strategic change—what triggers it, and how to take advantage of it—by asking us tough questions and providing us the opportunity to work with them on confronting their most pressing strategic issues. As a result of this constant challenge, we have identified these patterns of strategic change and have characterized the repertoire of best moves and countermoves to be used when a company is caught in the midst of a pattern of fundamental change.

Profit Patterns is a visual book, and many thanks must go to the production staff at Mercer for their graphics advice and assistance. In particular, we would like to thank Vicki Bocash for her assistance and expert artistic advice throughout the process. Without her effort, there would be no book today.

Thanks also go to Patrick Wolff, a Mercer Associate and two-time U.S. Chess Champion, for his help in building the metaphor between chess and business found in the Appendix.

We would like to thank John Mahaney at Times Books for his coaching, encouragement, guidance, and feedback as the manuscript was developed. His ideas shaped the approach we took, the level of insight and specificity required, and the balance between framework and example.

Finally, we would like to recognize the entire team at Mercer who shared their research, their ideas, and their enthusiasm. Without the support and investment from Peter Coster, Chariman of Mercer, and Jim Down, Vice Chariman of Operations of Mercer Management Consulting, we never could have collected the organization's knowledge or integrated it into a useful framework and manuscript. A big thank you goes to the core team—led by Jack Kolodny and including Mark Copelovitch, Isha Archer, Kang Ahn, Matt Stone, Adriaan Zur Muhlen, and Martin Stein. They gathered the research material on the patterns from which the book was constructed and helped to shape the thinking and direction of the manuscript. Special thanks go to Jack Kolodny, Mark Copelovitch, and Isha Archer for their efforts in manuscript development and support of the editing process. Their insights and energy were critical to moving this project from start to finish.

Picasso

In the classic world of strategy, it was easy to see what was going on.

Picasso

Reality was recognizable;

Picasso

even though sometimes fuzzy, the picture was understandable.

Picasso

Then things started to look funny . . .

Picasso

harder to recognize,

Picasso

. . . disjointed.

Picasso

You could still tell what was going on,

Picasso

but it was getting harder . . .

Picasso

and harder.

Finally, it became impossible . . .

Picasso

to see what was going on . . .

Picasso

by looking at things in the conventional way.

Picasso

man _woman_ _group_

Our job is to figure out the pattern that lies hidden underneath the apparent chaos on the surface,

Picasso

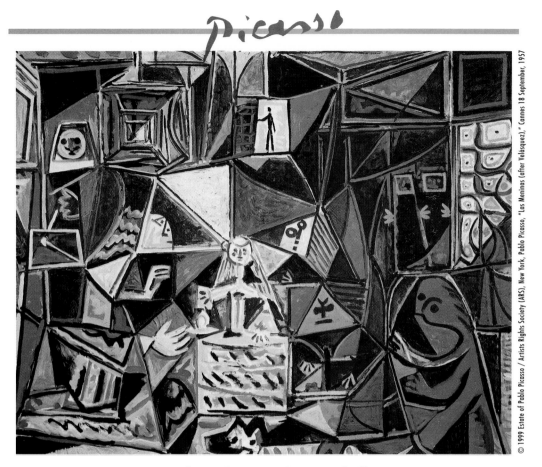

to see through Picasso's outer shell . . .

to the Velázquez that lies behind it.

PART I

THE NEW GAME OF BUSINESS

CHAPTER 1
GETTING IT

I N MAY OF 1997, Gary Kasparov—arguably the greatest chess player alive—was defeated by Deep Blue, a computer program written by IBM scientists. In the aftermath, pundits rushed both to declare and to decry the ascendancy of machine over man.

We see a different lesson in Deep Blue's victory.

Chess is a game of patterns; patterns about how the game has unfolded, about where the game stands at the moment, and, most importantly, about where the game is heading. In chess, the player with the best skill at pattern recognition has a critical advantage.

Gary Kasparov was not beaten by a machine. He was beaten by a team of IBM employees who took patterns so seriously that they invested several years and millions of dollars to build a machine that could recognize and manipulate all of the patterns that they had learned.

The IBM team had three advantages which ensured that it was only a matter of time before Deep Blue won:

- The real contest (learning and applying patterns) was played out between dozens of very smart individuals vs. one genius, long before the physical contest occurred. In the long run, bet on the team.

- The IBM team approached patterns with incredible discipline. They cataloged and set up relationships between every pattern that matters in chess—even Kasparov-specific patterns.

- The IBM team used computing power—which never forgets a pattern and is fast enough to review all necessary patterns before the next move—to create cumulative learning.

In the end, Kasparov found himself facing a far more dangerous foe than he had anticipated. He knew it, and his tirades at the end of several games betrayed his frustration.

Deep Blue's victory was not a case of machine over man. It was a case of teamwork, of systematic dedication to knowing patterns, and of cumulative learning, over genius. It was a human victory. And it was a parable for business managers and investors everywhere.

PATTERN THINKING APPLIED TO BUSINESS STRATEGY

Deep Blue's victory was an event that provides a window on the future to every senior manager and investor. With a little imagination, we can see how the IBM chess experience is an early indicator of a critical tool that we will all use to do business and investment strategy in the future.

We propose that any company that makes a pattern investment similar in direction (not in cost) to that of the IBM chess team—a combination of management teamwork, systematic pattern development, and cumulative learning—will generate superior innovative strategies, and superior sustained long-term returns. This book aims to help any company jump-start the development of its own database of patterns, thus minimizing both investment and time to payback.

An investment in patterns can empower executives to win in the game of business where—unlike chess—the rivalry never ends. For at the heart of business strategy is pattern recognition. Patterns of how the game has unfolded to date, where it stands today, and where the game is headed.

Masters of business pattern recognition are accustomed to staring at what looks to the newcomer like chaos. Instead of seeing chaos, they see the strategic picture unfolding within the complexity, and discover the pattern behind it all. They "get it."

"Getting it" is all-important. It is like putting on infrared vision goggles on a cloudy, moonless night. It helps you see danger three moves early. It helps you see where the pathway to opportunity lies, and what moves and combinations will turn the game in your favor.

"Not getting it" has all the opposite effects. Blindness to danger, blindness to opportunity, playing the game on the run, reacting rather than creating.

That is why those who know the power of pattern recognition in business play so intensely and study so hard. Those who "get it" use their experiences to build their strategic skills and raise their game to the next level. Those who don't "get it" lose and fall further behind.

PATTERNS ARE NOT A NEW PHENOMENON

The good news is that all businesspeople are already engaged in pattern thinking. From CEOs to middle managers to securities analysts, we already traffic in patterns as basic tools of our work and our strategic thinking.

Many managers can describe and apply the "consolidation and shakeout" pattern. Many can articulate the characteristics and consequences of the "commoditization" pattern, the "disintermediation" pattern, or the "deregulation" pattern.

Similarly, most players can recognize the "power shift" pattern as power moves from manufacturer to distribution channel. They've seen it with Wal-Mart, Home Depot, and Toys "R" Us. They can anticipate what is likely to happen with CarMax, AutoNation, or Amazon.com.

Strategic patterns are neither new nor mysterious. We use them all the time. They are a critical shortcut for capturing and highlighting the essential economic characteristics of a complex, changing picture.

Compared to the late 1980s, the number and complexity of the patterns required to know and understand business have grown. Back then, we all operated, explicitly or implicitly, with a dozen or so strategic patterns at our fingertips. Today, we need to know several times as many. And what we have to know about them, particularly about buyer behavior and how profit really happens, implies a more detailed and nuanced understanding than was sufficient for effective performance ten years ago.

PATTERN PROLIFERATION—AND IMPORTANCE—IS INCREASING

For most of the twentieth century, the idea of understanding value patterns was irrelevant. Things did not change very quickly. Everyone

PATTERNS AND "GETTING IT": A SIMPLE EXAMPLE

The contrast of new vs. experienced chess players provides a striking illustration of the power of pattern thinking.

If two individuals are looking at a chessboard, one a novice and the other a grandmaster, the two will see very different things. The novice sees pieces on a board. The grandmaster sees patterns within a strategic space.

Consider the arrangement of chess pieces in the top part of Exhibit "Board A." View it for fifteen seconds, then cover it. Take thirty seconds to reproduce it on the blank chessboard.

How many of the twenty-four placements did you reproduce correctly?

Now look at Exhibit "Board B." Follow the same procedure. Look at it for fifteen seconds, then cover it. Take thirty seconds to reproduce it. How did you do this time?

Board A is a random arrangement. Novices and grandmasters score about the same: roughly nine correct placements out of twenty-four. Board B is an actual game. Novices again score nine out of twenty-four. Grandmasters, however, score sixteen (or more) out of twenty-four (see *Thinking, Problem Solving, Cognition* by Richard E. Mayer, pp. 387–414). Why?

BOARD A

Grandmasters know how games unfold. They look at the chess pieces' locations and recognize the patterns. Over time, they learn and store over 50,000 patterns, or chunks of information. They look at a situation, tap their mental library to find the pattern, and get to the answer faster. They "get it," and they "get it" quickly. The novice sees only a random arrangement of pieces.

The same process is at work in business, but with some important favorable differences. A chess game takes two to four hours and requires dozens of moves. A competent chess player must learn thousands of these sequences. Grandmasters may spend ten years learning all of the essential games.

A business game—with patterns of changing competitive and customer behavior— might last two to ten years and involve only four or five key moves. A competent "business chess player" must learn 300 to 400 of these games, and draw from them thirty to forty critical patterns. This is not an easy task, but it is manageable. (This number of patterns is fewer than the patterns and plays an NFL team must learn to master in its preseason practices.)

BOARD B

knew the fundamental formulas for success, because the formulas were straightforward in nature.

In manufacturing, the key pattern to understand was that profit was a function of relative market share. The strategic tools and thought technology needed for this universe were straightforward and extremely useful. The growth/share matrix, the experience curve, Total Quality Management, and a solid knowledge of core competencies all served us well. Many manufacturers became experts at playing the relative market share game.

But today, we see more and more contradictions to these rules, such as smaller automakers being consistently more profitable than much larger automakers, or Starbucks being more profitable than much larger coffee companies. We are not even surprised by the idea that Dell is the most valuable PC maker, even though it doesn't manufacture its own core products—paying a point or two more to outsource key components because its overall business design saves ten extra points of cost in the way it goes to market.

In retail, another simple pattern reigned: location, location, location. Location closest to home, location in the best shopping malls. In that world, there were no destination superstores, no e-commerce, no kiosks, almost no branded retail, and no "entertainment-while-shopping" to confuse our thinking.

Services also had their own pattern. Good service meant personalized service by someone you knew, someone who called you by name, someone who put a personal touch into everything they did. In that world, there was no remote service, no 24-hour, 7-day-a-week service, no self-service for a lower price, no service via an intelligent agent.

As the above examples begin to show, knowledge of traditional patterns is no longer adequate. The modes of analysis that developed them—linear, logical, two-dimensional, bottom-up—also don't work. Even worse, they can fail in spectacular fashion. Traditional market share leaders doing traditional strategic analysis donated $700 billion in shareholder value to newcomers in the past decade and a half.

Traditional patterns are not always wrong—they are just no longer right all the time. They should be treated as one value pattern of many, not as our North Star or our compass. There are now many other patterns that supplement them and that explain much of the new value creation in business today. There are companies that break the old rules to their benefit, and in doing so create new rules that can be exploited by others via pattern thinking.

PATTERNS AND LEADERSHIP

Most science fiction fans are familiar with the light-speed travel depicted in movies such as *Star Wars* and *Star Trek*. With the flick of a button, our hero's spaceship hurtles into hyperspace and escapes from the clutches of the enemy. The audience sees an incredible stream of light rushing past. Viewers' visual and auditory senses are flooded with an overload of impressions.

Any diligent reader of the current business press will also experience a sensory excess, a broad stream of data rushing at us at Mach 2. The psychological effects are confusion, overload, and chaos. Managers today face hyperspace without a map. New and old customers are changing their priorities. New business designs are emerging from all angles, and old competitors are resurfacing as challengers in entirely new ways. Thousands of "inputs" crowd into managers' decision process, and they have no way to parse them to find the most useful nuggets.

Input overload can lead to chaos in our organization, a sense that everything is changing around us, but a lack of clarity about what to do next. Such chaos is typically a prelude to failure, to shareholder value destruction, and to a black mark on an otherwise successful management career.

Strategic pattern recognition is all about navigating through the onrushing hyperspace (how the world presents itself to us) and working to see the patterns underneath the surface noise. If these skills are gained soon enough, they can help us to make better decisions and take more effective actions. The flood of information can overwhelm decision making. Seeing patterns—superimposing a structure on the chaos—allows us to map the landscape and direct our strategy toward the most profitable opportunities.

Pattern thinking is a manager's best tool for communicating as well as making sense of chaotic change. Via patterns, management can communicate to others that it has a grasp on how to turn change into opportunity, that it is worthy of employee and investor trust. Establishing such a leadership profile can pay handsome dividends in retaining critical talent and investor enthusiasm.

To those who work for, invest in, or buy from a company, the flood of information can feel even worse. These players may have less direct control over the situation than the manager does. In these cases, pattern thinking is even more important. Understanding the key strategic patterns playing out in an industry can help investors, customers, and employees make more informed decisions and more astute choices (see pages ix–xiii).

HOW STRONG IS YOUR PATTERN GAME?

It's 1999. It's your industry. Does your company "get it" or not?

Get what?

The patterns of change that describe how the strategic landscape is deforming itself from yesterday's topology into tomorrow's. The patterns that describe which business designs are becoming economically obsolete. The patterns that describe which business designs are becoming customer-relevant—even customer-compelling—and extremely profitable.

There are dozens of examples of "getting it" and "not getting it." Those described in Chapters 4–11 are but a few. In each case, several very specific, well-defined patterns were unfolding. Some players "got it," while others did not. "Getting it" allowed the winners to make the strategic decisions that tapped into the enormous economic energy released by the patterns. Those who didn't "get it"—who didn't see the patterns—failed to make the right moves, and destroyed enormous shareholder value as a result.

How was Nokia able to exploit the "product to solutions" and "product to brand" patterns in order to surpass Motorola and Ericsson as the leading innovator and value creator in wireless communications? What did the founders of SAP "see" years earlier than its established competitors that enabled them to anticipate and take advantage of the "knowledge to product" pattern? How did two consultants foresee that the "product to customer knowledge" pattern would transform the credit card business, and how did they craft a business design that allowed Capital One to become a financial services powerhouse? How did Bang & Olufsen alter its business design to capitalize on the "product to brand" and customer redefinition patterns? We will explore the answers to these questions in Chapters 4–11.

Unfortunately, hindsight is 20/20. In order to succeed, a company must "get it" *before* the competition, not years later. In case after case, those companies that "got it" earlier than the competition have created the most value growth and the greatest degree of strategic control in their business.

In your industry today, there are probably between two and five discrete patterns playing out. Shifts from old profit sources to new. Shifts from old business models to new. Does your company "get it?" Do you see and understand the patterns? Can you anticipate how the patterns will unfold to create opportunities and threats? Do your competitors "get it?" Which of you is responding more quickly and accurately to exploit the unfolding patterns of customer and economic change?

PATTERNS AND PROGRESS

Learning patterns and using them to create sustained profit growth will not happen without effort. As in chess, one does not become a grandmaster overnight. However, the early learning rate is very, very high, and mastery of the basic rules leads to dramatic performance improvements in a short period of time.

Patterns might seem like a daunting subject to tackle to the reader just starting this book. But it is worth remembering that pattern recognition is an approach that has been applied in many fields to anticipate uncertain futures. Among them are:

Seismography	Where's the oil going to be?
Meteorology	What's the weather going to be?
Medical diagnostics	How is the patient going to be?

When we systematically exploit pattern recognition technology in business strategy, this is the challenge we face:

Business strategy   Where's the value going to be?

Sorting through the vast data flow from the evolving business landscape is a task very similar to anticipating the weather or approximating the location of oil reserves. Meteorologists and sonar experts work with powerful computer programs that apply patterns to the current data set. As business strategists, we must apply the pattern-trained thinking of our management teams. The human mind is capable of accomplishing this activity effectively. Strategic pattern recognition is a skill that can be learned, but requires a different way of thinking than we've been accustomed to, and a different way of building experience.

By investing to learn strategic pattern recognition, you will acquire the basic skills necessary to discern the most important patterns and their implications for the new game of business. With this new skill set, you will be better able to map out a profitable course for your unit or your company in spite of a seemingly chaotic corporate landscape. In fact, superior pattern recognition skills will help you to transform this apparent chaos from a liability to a distinct advantage in the next business game you play.

POLARIZATION

VALUE PROPORTIONALITY: BIGGER IS BETTER

HISTORICALLY, THE PRESCRIPTION for business success was to be the largest player in your industry. The formula was based on the fact that companies that sold the most moved down the experience curve the fastest, and attained a cost advantage. Lower costs resulted in superior profitability. Superior profitability resulted in a superior ability to invest, which drove costs even lower. In addition, customers were willing to pay more for the reputation of the market leader, and the best talent wanted to work for the biggest firms. The key to industry leadership was to capture a larger share of the market than your competitors.

When looking across various industries, the correlation of size and market value held true. The market rewarded companies that achieved the highest revenues with the highest market value.

The evidence of this reward was overwhelming. Across a broad cross section of industries, including computing, automobiles, consumer goods, steel, airlines, and financial services, the same scenario was playing itself out. During the era of proportionality, winning the market share game led to winning the value game.

VALUE MIGRATION: BUSINESS DESIGN INNOVATORS
CREATE NEW VALUE THROUGH PATTERN RECOGNITION

In the past two decades, many fundamental characteristics of the business landscape have changed. A fundamental shift has occurred in how business is done and what determines business success. We have all seen the turmoil of the 1980s and 1990s. Once mighty giants are mighty no longer. "Big" and "entrenched" have become associated with "troubled" and "failing."

In the past decade and a half, hundreds of billions of dollars of market value have migrated from old business designs to new. The highest valuations now go to those that have the most effective business designs, and they are not necessarily the largest companies. These new players have positioned themselves in the "profit zone" of their respective industries. That position may include size, but the real value driver is a powerful new way of doing business that creates or exploits new rules of the game. The hallmarks of a great business design include:

- High customer relevance
- An internally consistent set of decisions about scope (products offered and value chain activities performed)
- A terrific value capture mechanism or profit model
- A powerful source of differentiation and strategic control that gives investors greater confidence in future cash flows
- An organizational system that is carefully designed to support and reinforce the company's business design

Pattern recognition is one of the most effective ways to be the first to identify a new opportunity—to redefine the rules of the game, and to create a great new business design.

For General Electric, the pattern was "solutions," where the company moved from selling a traditional product to offering the product *and* services such as financing, insurance, consulting, and management.

For Microsoft, the patterns were "deintegration" of the value chain, emergence of a "de facto standard," and "cornerstoning" (from operating system, to applications, to browsers, to content).

For Coca-Cola, the pattern was "reintegration." In order to succeed in its own steps of the value chain (syrup sales and advertising), it had to intervene in a value chain step that it had traditionally left to others (bottling and distribution).

WHY MIGRATION? THE VENTURE FACTOR

In the late 1940s, there were a few venture funds in the United States. In the late 1990s, the number approaches 1,000. This is the single most important factor driving the phenomenon of value migration.

Without the intense activity of these funds, where would all the talent and genius be? Embedded in the structure of large corporations, complaining about slowness and about managers who don't "get it."

Where is all the talent and genius today? In *thousands* of new businesses, creating new value for customers, stock price growth, excitement, jobs, competitive instability, anxiety among incumbents, a magnet for new entrants, and many colossal failures.

The venture factor is going into its next major phase in the United States as the powerful seeds of business design innovation and value growth spread from the venture sector to the corporate sector. A rapidly growing number of Fortune 500 companies are making venture investments and setting up organizational units to play the game.

The venture factor is now spreading geographically as well. Europe, Asia, and Latin America are entering the first phase of venture culture development. In the next several years, each of these economic regions will begin to change and new waves of entrepreneurs will emerge.

Why? Because they will have to. The venture entrepreneurial mode will be a critical element of competitiveness for every major economy that aspires to be relevant and competitive on the global economic stage.

Although the full force of the venture factor has not yet hit Europe, the process of business design innovation has already begun. Recently completed research has identified a sample of "European Reinventor" companies that have created extraordinary returns through business model innovation (see Exhibit "The European Reinventors").

As Europe completes and emerges from its current "reengineering/restructuring" phase, and as venture activity in Europe expands, we can anticipate a significant increase in business design innovation in the European economies.

When business design innovation intensifies, value migration accelerates. The venture wave coming to Europe, Asia, and Latin America will not only replay many of the patterns that first occurred in the United States, but will develop many new ones. The number of patterns available to us to enrich our decision-making process will increase significantly in the next several years—providing great advantage to those who know patterns, and disadvantage to those who don't.

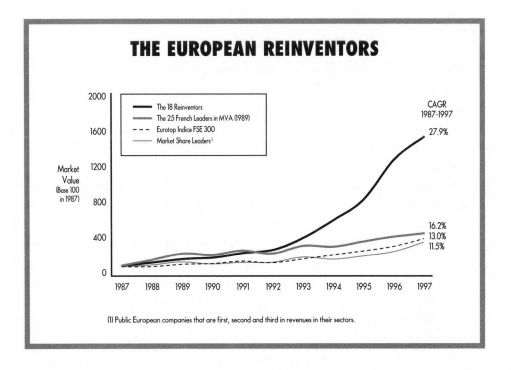

THE EUROPEAN REINVENTORS

Market Value (Base 100 in 1987)

- ——— The 18 Reinventors
- ——— The 25 French Leaders in MVA (1989)
- – – – Eurotop Indice FSE 300
- —— Market Share Leaders[1]

CAGR 1987-1997

27.9%

16.2%
13.0%
11.5%

1987 1988 1989 1990 1991 1992 1993 1994 1995 1996 1997

(1) Public European companies that are first, second and third in revenues in their sectors.

For Nike, the key patterns were "outsourcing" and "new branding." The company moved beyond traditional 60-second ads for their shoes to 60-minute celebrity product demonstrations (Michael Jordan in basketball, Tiger Woods in golf, Ronaldo in soccer, etc.).

Thanks to the power of pattern recognition and business design innovation, the traditional formula of proportionality has begun to fail. New value growth winners are emerging. Hundreds of billions of dollars in market value have been redistributed from old business models to new in computing, retailing, materials, and numerous other industries. The paradigm has shifted away from those with market share and toward those that are capturing the greatest share of value. More innovative players focused on the customer and on the key dimensions of business design, particularly profit models and strategic control, have captured leadership positions.

VALUE POLARIZATION: THE BEST OF BOTH WORLDS

Take the quiz shown below. What's the market value of each of the following companies?

Market Value ($ billions)			Market Value ($ billions)	
Microsoft	____	vs.	Apple	____
Coke	____	vs.	Pepsi	____
Cisco	____	vs.	Bay Networks	____
GE	____	vs.	Westinghouse	____
Nike	____	vs.	Reebok	____
Yahoo	____	vs.	Excite	____
Mattel	____	vs.	Hasbro	____
The Gap	____	vs.	The Limited	____

In polarization relationships, the "winner" combines a new business design with dominant market share to win in a very, very big way. The reason? Investors believe that the combination of superior business design, strategic control, and super dominant share not only make the leader able to achieve high profit in the current cycle, but also position it to lead the next strategy cycle.

In these situations, the value that migrates to the gold medal performer leaves the second place player gasping for breath.

The process of value polarization typically unfolds in two phases (see Exhibit "The Polarization Phenomenon"). In phase I, multiple competitors try to position themselves for success by making investment and business design moves that they hope will match customers' priorities most effectively.

While in phase I, competitors appear to be at parity as legitimate contenders for leadership. Beneath this surface lies a different reality. One competitor sees the few key patterns unfolding in the industry—the others do not. One competitor "gets it." That competitor responds to emerging changes by crafting a small number of key moves designed to tap into the energy of the pattern that is starting to reshape its industry.

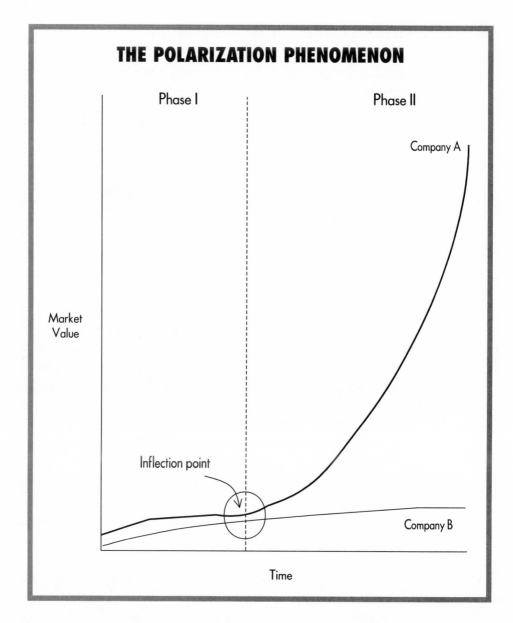

THE POLARIZATION PHENOMENON

Phase I   Phase II

Market Value

Company A

Inflection point

Company B

Time

At some point in time, all of the triggers and conditions that precipitate the pattern fall into place (like cylinders falling in place to open a locked safe) and phase II begins. Now the moves of one competitor begin to pay off in significant ways. At this point, that competitor begins to compete intensely for mindshare of customers, investors, and talent (Chapter 3 describes this investment). The result is that momentum builds for the competitor that "got it" first, and its market value explodes. Value is no longer proportional; it has polarized. The gold medalist's value is several times greater than the value that goes to the silver medal position.

Consider the examples on the following pages. And keep in mind that each set of moves that produced a gold medal winner was first stimulated by explicit or implicit pattern recognition on the part of the gold medal management team.

POLARIZATION: THE VALUE OF "GETTING IT" EARLY

In each of the illustrated cases, the leader was able to take full advantage of the patterns at work in its industry. The other competitors either failed to see the patterns or responded too late.

Detecting a pattern of change that is reshaping your landscape is much more important than it used to be. The positive power of the polarization effect can create previously unimagined results. The silver medalist—which may be doing a fine job and finishes second—finds itself increasingly disadvantaged. Polarization has increased the stakes.

Polarization demands a different strategic mindset from company management. The nature and value of time have changed. In the proportional world, market share battles were fought over a span of years. Competing with roughly similar business designs, companies could afford planning and investment cycles at a rhythmic pace set by the industry. That industry calendar has become irrelevant.

Value migration demands that companies look at the market differently, and respond to discontinuities in customers' priorities or to new competitive business designs. Value migration requires companies to begin a continuous and broad-scale scanning of competitors and the

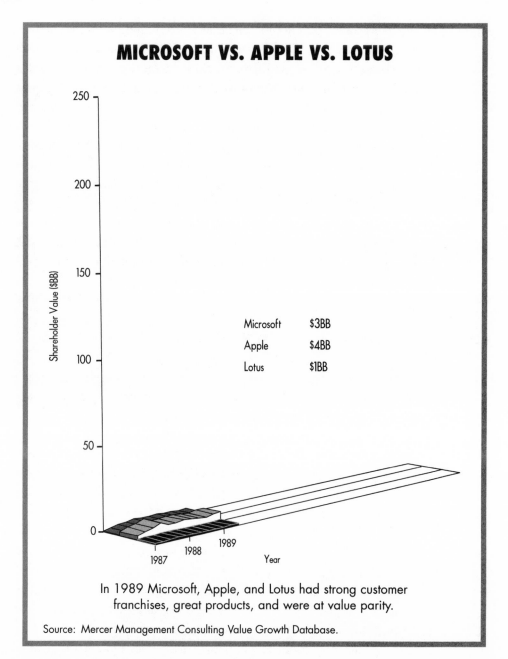

MICROSOFT VS. APPLE VS. LOTUS

Microsoft	$3BB
Apple	$4BB
Lotus	$1BB

In 1989 Microsoft, Apple, and Lotus had strong customer franchises, great products, and were at value parity.

Source: Mercer Management Consulting Value Growth Database.

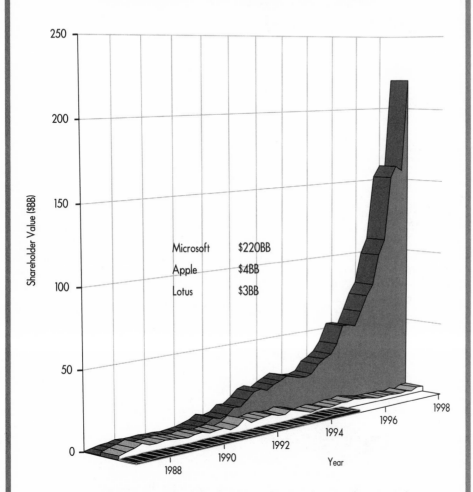

MICROSOFT VS. APPLE VS. LOTUS

Shareholder Value ($BB)

Microsoft	$220BB
Apple	$4BB
Lotus	$3BB

Year

Since that time, Microsoft's business design changes harnessed the energy of several different patterns to create a gold medal position vastly more valuable than the silver and the bronze.

Note: Values as of Q3 1998.

Source: Mercer Management Consulting Value Growth Database.

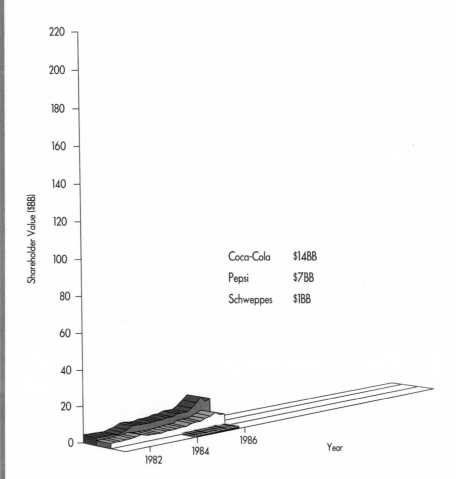

COCA-COLA VS. PEPSI VS. SCHWEPPES

Coca-Cola $14BB

Pepsi $7BB

Schweppes $1BB

Coke battled Pepsi and Schweppes to a standoff in the grocery store. In 1986, the value gap between Coke and number two Pepsi was $7 billion.

Source: Mercer Management Consulting Value Growth Database.

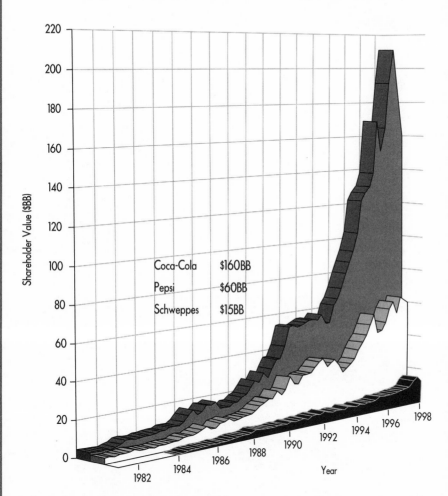

COCA-COLA VS. PEPSI VS. SCHWEPPES

Coca-Cola $160BB

Pepsi $60BB

Schweppes $15BB

Coke understood and exploited several key patterns in its business, reinvented its business design to take full advantage of those patterns, and created over $140 billion in new value, producing a value gap of $100 billion relative to Pepsi.

Source: Mercer Management Consulting Value Growth Database.

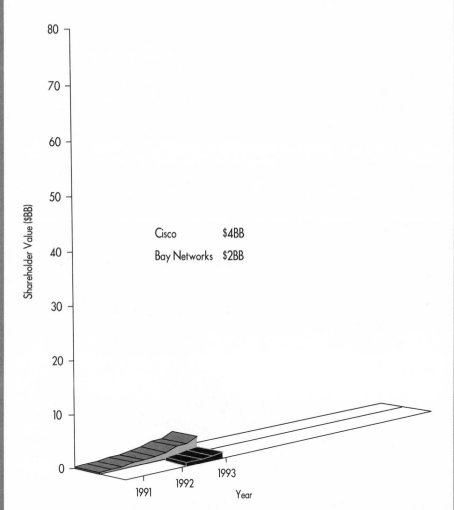

CISCO VS. BAY NETWORKS

Cisco $4BB

Bay Networks $2BB

Together, Cisco and Bay Networks were the founders of data router technology; in 1993 the value gap between Cisco and Bay Networks was $2 billion.

Source: Mercer Management Consulting Value Growth Database.

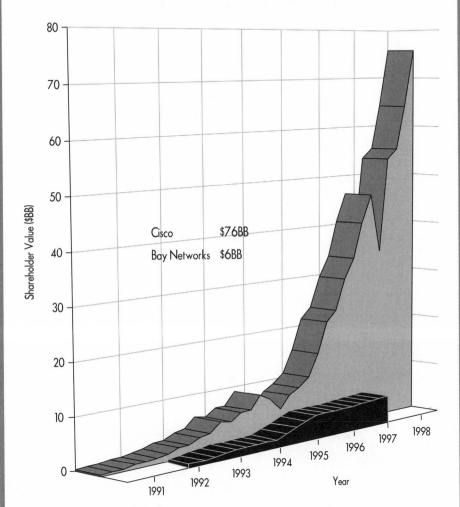

CISCO VS. BAY NETWORKS

Cisco $76BB

Bay Networks $6BB

By capitalizing on the patterns in its fast-moving industry,
Cisco was able to create a market value many
times greater than that of its competitor.

Source: Mercer Management Consulting Value Growth Database.

GE VS. WESTINGHOUSE/CBS VS. UNITED TECHNOLOGIES

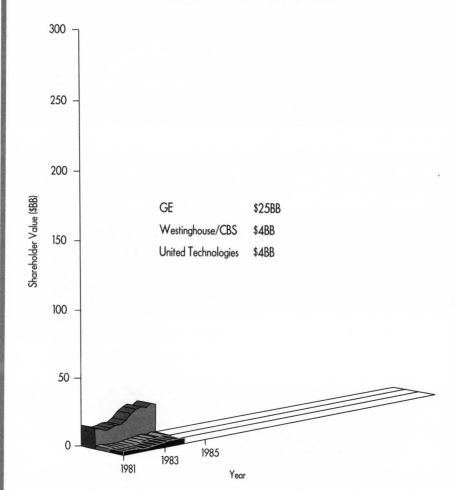

GE	$25BB
Westinghouse/CBS	$4BB
United Technologies	$4BB

In the early 1980s, these companies considered themselves world-class industrial product manufacturers. In 1984, the value gap between GE and its peers was $20 billion.

Source: Mercer Management Consulting Value Growth Database.

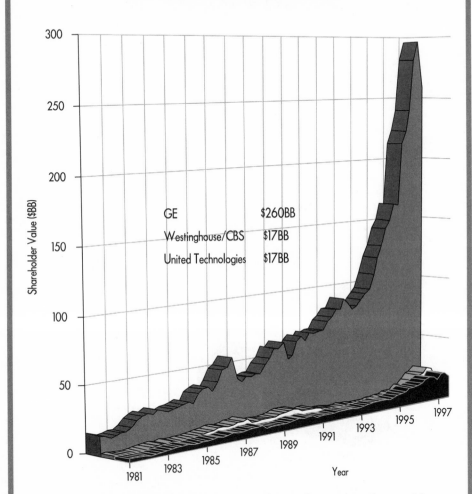

GE VS. WESTINGHOUSE/CBS VS. UNITED TECHNOLOGIES

GE	$260BB
Westinghouse/CBS	$17BB
United Technologies	$17BB

After multiple reinventions of its business design that exploited several key patterns in its industries, by 1998 GE increased the value gap to $240 billion.

Source: Mercer Management Consulting Value Growth Database.

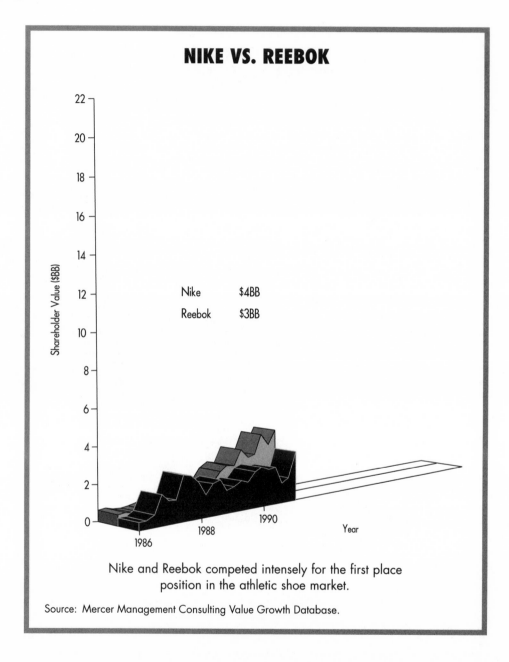

NIKE VS. REEBOK

Nike $4BB
Reebok $3BB

Nike and Reebok competed intensely for the first place
position in the athletic shoe market.

Source: Mercer Management Consulting Value Growth Database.

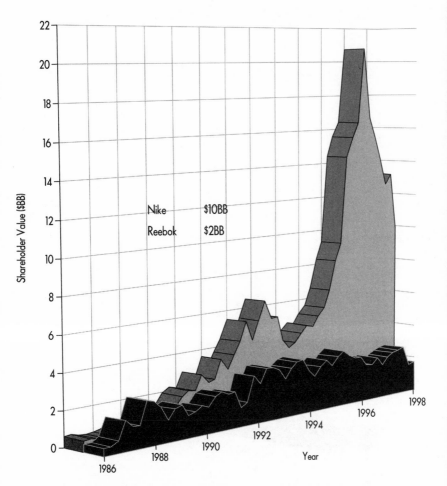

NIKE VS. REEBOK

Nike $10BB

Reebok $2BB

The "swoosh" company exploited a set of patterns that created shareholder value several times greater than Reebok's.

Source: Mercer Management Consulting Value Growth Database.

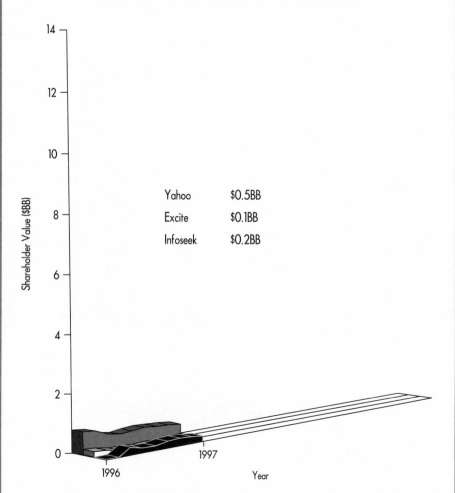

YAHOO VS. EXCITE VS. INFOSEEK

Yahoo	$0.5BB
Excite	$0.1BB
Infoseek	$0.2BB

As the Internet unfolded, three companies competed to become the leading catalog/search engine.

Source: Mercer Management Consulting Value Growth Database.

YAHOO VS. EXCITE VS. INFOSEEK

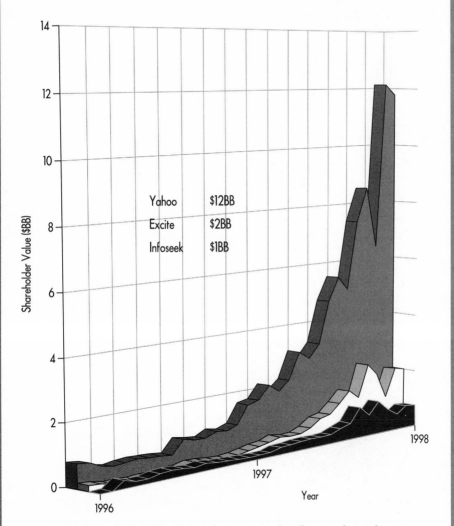

By the end of 1998, Yahoo has emerged with a market value
many times greater than that of Infoseek and Excite combined.

Source: Mercer Management Consulting Value Growth Database.

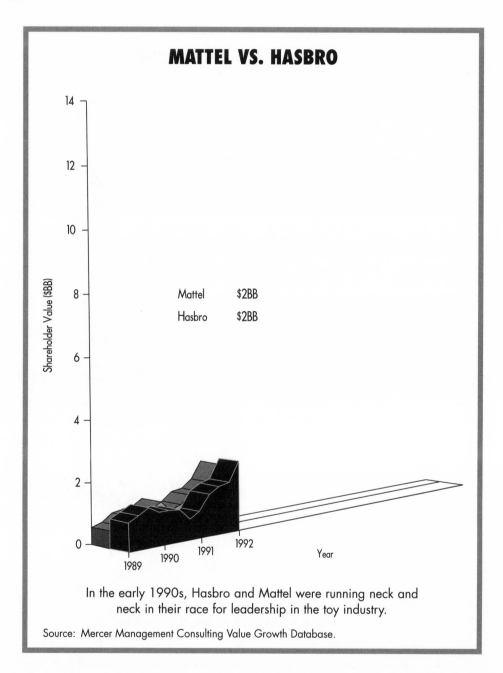

MATTEL VS. HASBRO

Mattel $2BB

Hasbro $2BB

Shareholder Value ($BB)

14

12

10

8

6

4

2

0

1989   1990   1991   1992

Year

In the early 1990s, Hasbro and Mattel were running neck and neck in their race for leadership in the toy industry.

Source: Mercer Management Consulting Value Growth Database.

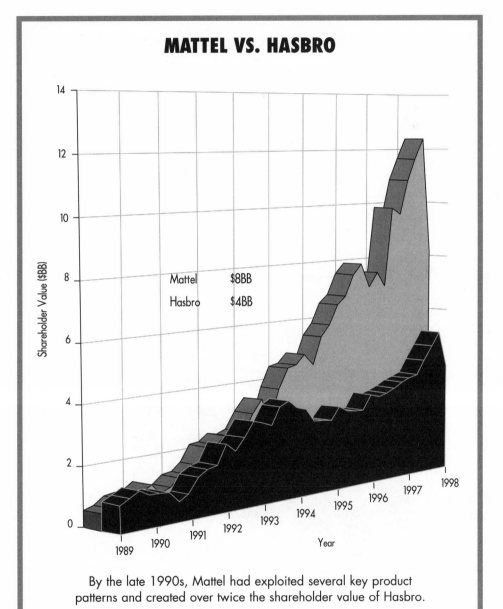

MATTEL VS. HASBRO

Shareholder Value ($BB)

| Mattel | $8BB |
| Hasbro | $4BB |

Year

By the late 1990s, Mattel had exploited several key product patterns and created over twice the shareholder value of Hasbro.

Source: Mercer Management Consulting Value Growth Database.

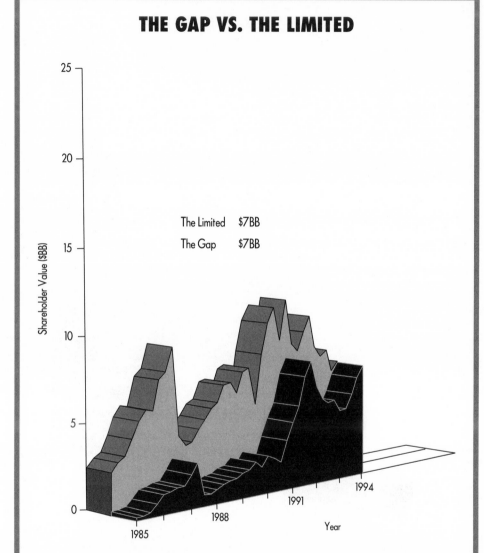

THE GAP VS. THE LIMITED

The Limited $7BB

The Gap $7BB

In 1994 The Gap and The Limited were fighting for leadership in the specialty retail clothing market.

Source: Mercer Management Consulting Value Growth Database.

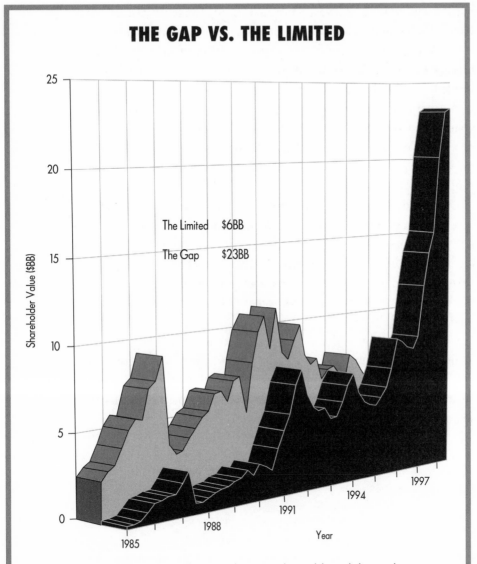

THE GAP VS. THE LIMITED

The Limited $6BB

The Gap $23BB

Within a few years, The Gap became the gold medalist in the
industry, creating four times as much value as The Limited.

Source: Mercer Management Consulting Value Growth Database.

market, and to process a vast set of new inputs to identify those causal factors that would signal new opportunities and new threats.

Value polarization adds a new dimension of urgency. Reacting nimbly to discontinuity is no longer enough. Today, the key skill needed is Strategic Anticipation and focused, rapid investment in the next generation business design. In the era of polarization, the rewards go to those who identify the key patterns early, and act on those insights *one year sooner* than the competition. Being first to establish the trajectory of success translates into being the winner in the polarizing environment that follows.

In industry after industry, polarization is redrawing the competitive map. In some cases, such as those highlighted earlier in this chapter, the winner and the value stakes are already clear. In others, the second phase has not yet occurred. Companies that can see the patterns first—that can "get it" before the competition—will be in a position to think through and execute the moves it will take to capture the gold medal position.

Consider the industries represented on the following page. Which competitor will win the polarization game? Which companies will "get it" first? Are the winners already positioning themselves to take advantage of the unfolding pattern? How will these pictures look in five years? How does *your* industry's picture look?

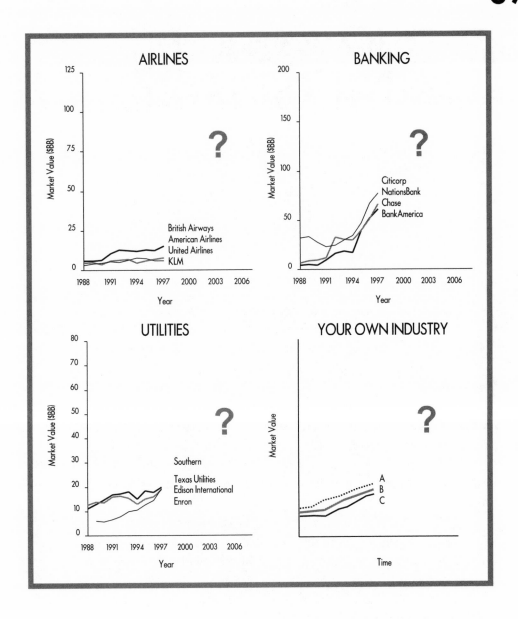

AIRLINES

Market Value ($BB)

125
100
75
50
25
0

?

British Airways
American Airlines
United Airlines
KLM

1988 1991 1994 1997 2000 2003 2006
Year

BANKING

Market Value ($BB)

200
150
100
50
0

?

Citicorp
NationsBank
Chase
BankAmerica

1988 1991 1994 1997 2000 2003 2006
Year

UTILITIES

Market Value ($BB)

80
70
60
50
40
30
20
10
0

?

Southern
Texas Utilities
Edison International
Enron

1988 1991 1994 1997 2000 2003 2006
Year

YOUR OWN INDUSTRY

Market Value

?

A
B
C

Time

CHAPTER 3
MINDSHARE

COMPANIES THAT HAVE become value growth leaders through pattern recognition have the opportunity to become value polarization winners. The key to moving from rapid value growth to value leadership is winning mindshare with key customers, investors, and talent.

That's why the focus of competition in more and more industries is competition for mindshare. Get the early mindshare lead, and people will buy, will recommend to others, and will create the foundations for an upward spiral. At the critical market juncture—the inflection point—winning the mindshare game has become management's top strategic priority.

This new investment activity is most successful when it is crafted as a three-part strategy: (1) mindshare with *customers* makes it hard for the number two player to catch up, (2) mindshare with *investors* provides resources to stay ahead of competitors, and (3) mindshare with *talent* raises the likelihood of near- and long-term leadership (see Exhibit "Components of Mindshare").

Capturing all three positions leads to a chain reaction that releases enormous economic energy. Early wins create positive self-reinforcing cycles. Get the early mindshare lead with a powerful new business design. Others will buy, invest, and join. Word of mouth or economic necessity will do the rest.

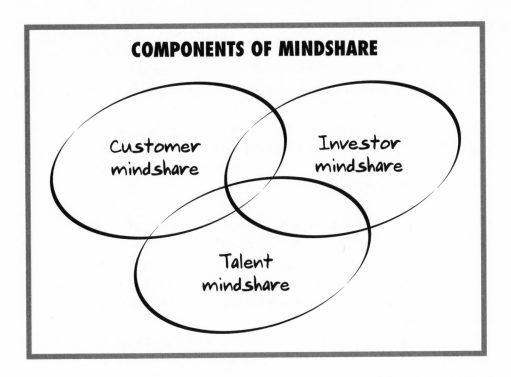

COMPONENTS OF MINDSHARE

Customer mindshare

Investor mindshare

Talent mindshare

CUSTOMER MINDSHARE

Winning mindshare with customers while you are first to market with a new business design enables you to win the close calls, the "50/50" decisions, after the second competitor mimics your design. The impact of mindshare is the creation of a self-reinforcing "customer wins" cycle that allows the business to accelerate its rate of value growth. In many markets, initial success also begets a cycle of increasing returns. A business that is able to establish an early leadership position can increase its value by successively larger amounts with each additional market victory to create an accelerating economic position that competitors are unable to emulate. America Online (AOL) has recently achieved this kind of effect by creating sufficient critical mass to change both the economics of its operation and its value proposition for the customer.

These changes affect the profit line dramatically, attracting investors to your position.

INVESTOR MINDSHARE

Today's stock markets are characterized by a frightening degree of transparency. Success and failure are incredibly visible to everyone. The intensity of media scrutiny, the proliferation of research services, and the increasing appetite for new stories all combine to create a state of hyper-attention that surrounds many competitive situations. The vast success of some investors has everyone—amateurs and professionals alike—looking for the next big win. This investment mentality has even extended to the job market, where increasingly equity-focused compensation packages stimulate employees (future and current) to search incessantly for the next great "ground floor deal."

This psychology is manifested in the response to polarization. When a winner seems to be emerging from the pack, a "piling on" effect begins. Momentum snowballs and dramatically affects the way a company is perceived.

The winning becomes self-reinforcing, as thousands of investors turn their sights on the early emerging winner. The stock of the company rises as buyers pour in and the perception that the company is successful is reinforced. The increased stock price focuses even more media attention on the company, and it is declared to be the winner.

A critical cautionary note is needed here. A rising stock price represents a valuable perception (see Exhibit "Perception and Reality"). It gives a company a strong currency, which the company can either squander, or use to cause reality to catch up with perception. If it doesn't catch up (Case A), perception will crash. If management causes the reality to catch up (Case B), it gets the chance to keep creating further value growth. Its credibility and track record cause the stock price to go even higher.

TALENT MINDSHARE

Managing the stock price trajectory gives the company yet another priceless advantage: a rising stock price curve attracts the very best talent in the market. The "high scrutiny" investment culture has extended

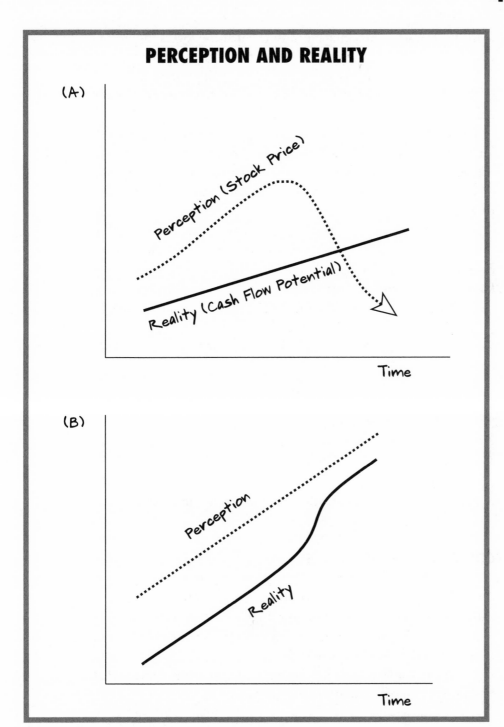

PERCEPTION AND REALITY

(A)

Perception (Stock Price)

Reality (Cash Flow Potential)

Time

(B)

Perception

Reality

Time

to the job market, stimulating the most talented employees (future and current) to search for the next best value growth opportunity.

When a company achieves mindshare with customers and investors, the "winner mentality" becomes a part of the company's culture. Turnover drops with marketplace wins. High achievers send in their resumes as the stock market begins to recognize a company's potential. The culture strengthens around the elements of success, and alignment within the organization tends to increase dramatically. These factors boost organizational energy, morale, productivity, and competitive performance.

The best talent joins the company to learn (more is to be learned from winners than from losers) as well as to make money. The best talent fills its days coming up with new ideas that create yet a better deal for the customer and investor.

This leads to more customer and investor mindshare, and the upward cycle repeats itself. Before you know it, five years have gone by, and the gold medalist is worth several times more than the silver medalist.

HOW POWERFUL CAN MINDSHARE BE?

Take the quick quiz shown on the opposite page. For each category, list who is #1, who is #2, and how great is the mindshare distance between the two competitors (neck and neck, a small distance, or a huge distance).

PATTERN RECOGNITION AND TIME'S TWIST

A major mindshare investment will not make any difference in a company's market value unless the company has first identified and exploited a specific pattern of strategic change that can alter the basis of competitive advantage in an industry.

The potential of winning the contest for mindshare means that "getting it" soonest has become all-important.

Getting what?

CATEGORY	#1	#2	DISTANCE BETWEEN #1 and #2
Gourmet Coffee			
Internet Bookselling			
Internet Search Engines			
Girls' Dolls			
Enterprise Resource Planning Software (ERP)			

Getting the next twist in market time. A twist that reveals a different customer buying behavior, a different profit model, a different dimension of competitive advantage. A twist that opens a new cycle of value growth. In other words, a new pattern.

A new pattern that says what we're now doing, what we're now good at, is less important than it used to be because the market has started to move in a different direction (see Exhibit "Time's Twist"), creating a new market opportunity and a new battle for mindshare.

Browser mindshare. Bookstore mindshare. Digital broadcasting mindshare. Gourmet coffee mindshare. E-commerce mindshare. Printer mindshare. Cellular phone mindshare.

Timing, therefore, is worth getting right. "Getting it" sooner than others enables your company to prepare and execute a series of moves that will give you an early lead that can then feed on itself. An

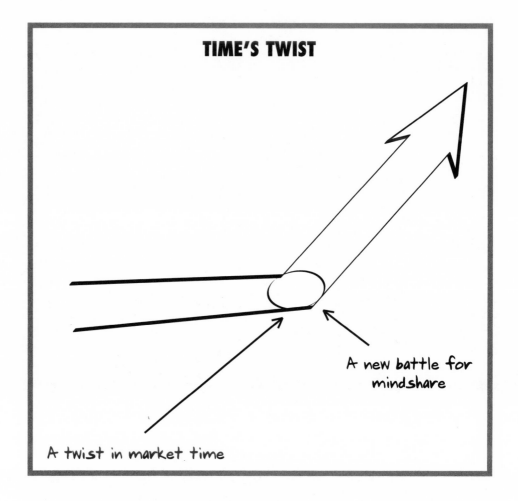

TIME'S TWIST

A new battle for mindshare

A twist in market time

early lead in one dimension (customer, investor, or talent) will spill over to the other two.

On the other hand, failing to see the twist in market time—failing to "get it"—can be extremely expensive. Early, accurate pattern recognition can make all the difference for the company, its customers, and its most important long-term investors.

Consider the exhibit titled "Time's Twist: Getting it." How long is the time between when companies should "get it" and when they do "get it?"

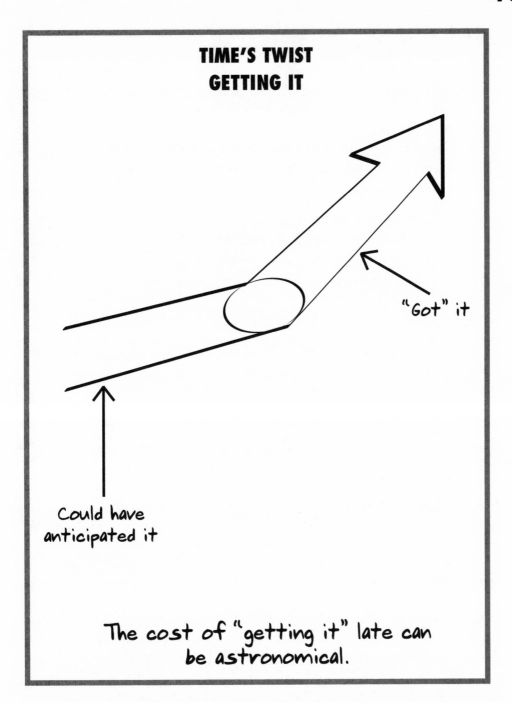

TIME'S TWIST
GETTING IT

"Got" it

Could have
anticipated it

The cost of "getting it" late can
be astronomical.

- One to two years?
- Five years or longer?

Sometimes companies "get it" relatively soon, but then take too long to act on it. Caught in the spread between "getting it" and "acted on it" are fortunes beyond measure.

How can I know sooner? How can my company "get it" sooner? There are several attitudinal, behavioral, and knowledge characteristics that can help:

1. Be paranoid.
2. Talk to people who see things differently than you do.
3. Be "out there" at street level, searching for change.
4. Build a patterns search engine that extends beyond yourself and your management team.
5. Know patterns better than your rivals.

The whole point of patterns is to see time's twist sooner than the competition. To give us the maximum runway for winning the triple mindshare game—with customers, with talent, and with investors (see Exhibit "The Reinforcing Nature of Mindshare").

Practice in patterns helps us take one more step backward in time. It helps us to "get it" just a little bit sooner, which could make all the difference. Companies that are good at pattern recognition begin to develop a new, priceless skill. They begin to *anticipate* the next twist in time. They build themselves an even longer runway for winning the mindshare game.

INVESTMENT INTENSITY

Early recognition and early action are necessary, but they are not enough. The third variable is intensity: pouring it on; parallel processing; doing what it takes to capture, protect, and expand the early mindshare lead.

If companies tend to err during the mindshare investment period, they err on the side of underinvestment. There are many powerful

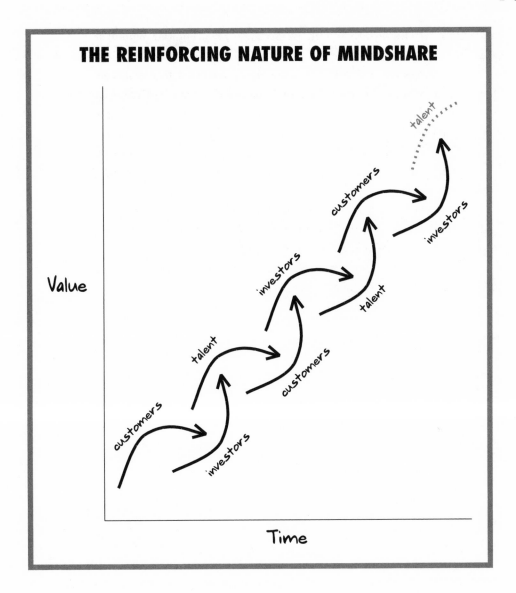

THE REINFORCING NATURE OF MINDSHARE

psychological reasons for this error. It is quite possible that the business design receiving investment during this period is "destroying" shareholder value according to EVA accounting standards. It may well be cash negative due to investment needs. To sidestep this trap, companies must keep in mind that EVA is a lagging indicator of value, not a leading indicator. If a company recognizes that it is in a mindshare game, and that it will be rewarded with extraordinary shareholder value if it succeeds, it should consider the total value creation potential of a mindshare investment. Think of Oracle pouring it on with its sales efforts. Think of Starbucks pouring it on with its store openings. Think of Cisco pouring it on with acquisitions. Think of Worldcom pouring it on with network acquisitions.

First. Fast. Furious. Pouring it on puts you on the right side of the polarization process, and gives you a higher platform for searching for the next cycle.

Patterns open our eyes, our thinking. They give us clues. They tell us what signals to look for. A properly managed head start of seven to ten months can deliver a polarization gold medal position of enormous value to your company. Well worth the time of study it would take to learn the thirty patterns we already know.

PART II
THE THIRTY
PATTERNS

OVER TIME, changing strategic market conditions create a migration from one set of customer priorities to another. Existing business designs become obsolete, and new business designs must be invented to deliver new value to customers. Some senior executives understand this phenomenon and reinvent their company's business design—they exploit the value opportunity. In contrast, other senior executives miss the value migration. Their company becomes a value donor as its value is lost to new, more customer-relevant business designs.

Experienced players can detect similarities between movements of value at different times and in different industries; they can detect patterns. Most patterns can be grouped into several major categories that pertain to the key dimensions along which these patterns play out.

Chapters 4 through 10 describe seven of these categories: *Mega, Value Chain, Customer, Channel, Product, Knowledge* and *Organizational.* Each unit describes several examples and offers a set of questions designed to apply the experience to your own business situation.

In reading patterns, it is useful to keep in mind three of their characteristics: Multiplicity, Variants, and Cycles. It is also valuable to keep in mind a diagnostic set of questions that will help develop a deeper understanding of why patterns happen, and how to profit from them.

MULTIPLICITY

Some business situations confront strategic change that can be characterized by a single pattern. Most business situations aren't so simple. Most are multidimensional, complex, and characterized by several patterns occurring simultaneously inside the boundaries of a single economic neighborhood.

Just as a company typically uses three or four different profit models simultaneously, a competitive environment is often being reshaped by three or four patterns at the same time.

An excellent example is computing. In the past decade, the industry has been transformed by the following patterns:

- Deintegration of the value chain
- Collapse of the middle
- Channel multiplication (e.g., value-added resellers, Integrators, direct mail, Internet, superstores)
- A shift from products to solutions
- Channel compression (e.g., Dell)
- De facto standard

Each pattern illuminates a different facet of the complex strategic landscape on which computing is unfolding, sharply defines a strategic issue, and articulates a specific set of options and action implications.

It's hard to keep track of so many patterns simultaneously, and to keep making the right decisions time after time. That's why there are so many failures, errors and disasters in that industry.

A much more straightforward industry is steel. Even here, however, there are several major patterns at work:

- Convergence
- A shift from products to solutions
- Deintegration of the value chain

Perhaps it is true that industries with slower growth present a less complex picture to the strategist. We wouldn't bet on it. It is more likely the case that even apparently "slow" and "simple" industries are being reshaped by several patterns at once.

Each pattern is a different lens through which to see a complex reality. Each pattern is an organized way of looking that helps us understand more of the picture, more of what's going on. Each pattern sensitizes us to a different aspect of the strategic challenges our companies are facing, to help us see the key movements, to define more options and get to more profitable decisions sooner.

Not surprisingly, the larger and more complex an industry, the more patterns there will be at work. Healthcare, a trillion-dollar space, will have more patterns at work than pharmaceuticals, a $200 billion subset of healthcare. Computing, a half-trillion-dollar space, will have more patterns than PC computing, its $200 billion subset.

The great value of patterns is that they stimulate us to keep expanding our field of vision, to look beyond pharmaceuticals to healthcare, beyond banking to financial services, beyond PCs to computing and further still to communications, content, and so on.

And that expansion of perspective is critical, because the number of industries that are totally immune from what's happening in neighboring economic domains is getting smaller and smaller.

That's a very different situation compared to two decades ago. Twenty years ago, 90 percent of what a banker needed to know took place inside banking. Ninety percent of what an insurer needed to know took place inside the insurance industry. Ninety percent of what a broker needed to know took place inside the brokerage industry.

That's true no longer. The area of the average competitive circle has undergone a tenfold increase in the past two decades. On the surface, this leads to chaos. It's precisely for that reason that patterns are important. Using patterns helps us to cut through the chaos more quickly.

We should not expect most situations to be solved by the application of a single pattern. Sometimes, we may need as many as five or six patterns of change to fully characterize the strategic issues facing an industry. Patterns also give us perspective, clues, and answers. They trigger our creativity by suggesting new options or hinting at unconventional solutions.

Is there an organized way to put patterns to work? The first and most natural is to characterize an industry situation in a way that triggers references to the patterns you have in your own personal or company database. Another way is to develop a set of tools to help you analyze patterns more effectively. Chapters 12–14 provide a process for doing so.

VARIANTS

Patterns do not always play themselves out in the same way. A pattern can have several major variants, versions created by the differences in their development and the creativity with which they are exploited by forward-looking players in the industry.

The "product to brand" pattern has numerous variants depending on the customer, the product, and the creativity of the supplier. So too with reintermediation; the value added by Schwab is quite different than the value added by Rosenbluth (see pp. 167 to 171).

There are also, for example, many variants in the organizational pyramid to network pattern. The experiences of ABB, Virgin, and Thermo Electron in exploiting this pattern are quite different.

However, in all of these cases, the core idea of the pattern is maintained. In the network pattern, it is the focus on maximizing employee exposure to customers, investors, and profit accountability.

In the reintermediation pattern, the focus is on the creation of a new-value added step to open an extra space in the value chain for a new intermediary. In the "product to brand" pattern, it is the movement of profit opportunity from the product itself to the brand built around it.

The variants are important because they reflect the strategy and creativity of successful players. Studying these variants—their similarities and differences—will expand your own repertoire. It will help you figure out what will (and what won't) work for you in your own business situation.

CYCLES

Some patterns are like big wheels that turn slowly. Others, like small wheels, turn over much more quickly. Deintegration, reintegration, and convergence tend to be long cycle patterns. Others (like channel multiplication, product to brand, or skill shift) can develop more quickly.

The rate of pattern development is determined not just by the nature of the pattern but by its customer and industry context. In aerospace, the skill shift pattern might occur over a decade. In computing, it might happen every three to four years.

As you read through the patterns in Chapters 4 through 10, keep asking yourself about cycle time. How quickly does this pattern usually unfold, and how quickly will it play out in my industry? (Chapter 13 provides several perspectives on how time works differently in various industries.)

QUESTIONS

As you study the patterns profiled in Part II, it may be useful to ask a diagnostic set of questions about each pattern you've read:

- What triggers the pattern?
- How quickly does the pattern play out?
- What are the options available to the players?
- What is the best move to make?

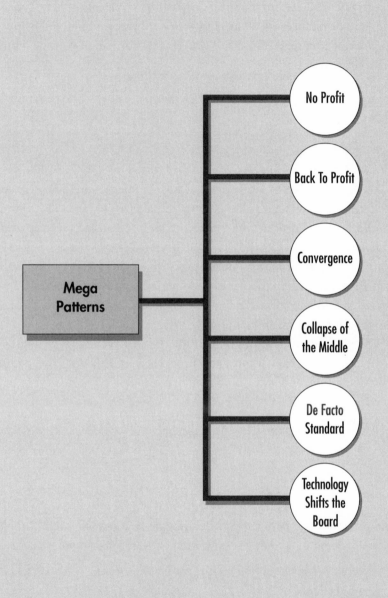

CHAPTER 4
MEGA PATTERNS

MANY PATTERNS PERTAIN to specific dimensions of business activity—the value chain, the customer, the channel, and so on.

Certain patterns, however, cut across and transcend these categories. They can be found within numerous industries as well as in large, multi-industry patches of the economy. They earn the label "mega" because of their impact and their scope. They cut across long, often multi-decade, periods of time.

The classic examples discussed herein include convergence, the collapse of the middle, the creation of de facto standards, and technology shifts.

We begin with perhaps the most insidious pattern of all: the evolution to a no-profit industry. We then look at its mirror image: the back to profit pattern, in which strategic imagination and business model innovation bring profit back to the economically lifeless terrain of a no-profit zone.

No Profit

The total absence of strategic imagination drives profits away.

In the "no profit pattern," once profitable businesses become profit-less. There is no profit in the industry, no value to be captured. Even the leaders in a no profit pattern find the rewards of a leadership position to be bittersweet. Yes, they are number one. All that means, however, is that their losses are smaller.

The no profit pattern is not established by one bad year. It is established when the sum of profits from the "good" years in an industry minus the sum of losses in the "bad" years yields zero or negative profit. It is measured over the entire economic cycle from peak to peak, or trough to trough.

Two preconditions lead to the no profit pattern. The first is an overabundance of the same business design within an industry. Every player competes the same way, leading to deteriorating economics and commoditization. Because everyone is competing in the same way, the only avenue left open for differentiation is through price. Each player tries to lower product price to increase market share. Competitors, rather than doing the hard work of business design innovation, return the favor.

The second precondition is the unexpected removal of the profit crutch or profit support system that the industry's players had been counting on to compensate for the fact that they all used the same business design.

These profit supports have traditionally come in several forms. One form is the "all boats will rise" crutch. Examples include: the whole housing industry waiting for interest rates to go down; the whole consumer electronics industry waiting for the Next Big Product launch; the whole retail industry waiting for the next fashion trend to take hold.

Another type of profit support is the hope that "costs will keep going down." It is the banking industry hoping that the next mega-merger will still be allowed by regulators and will still achieve cost synergies. It is the company which, on its third round of re-engineering, hopes that it can wring out yet another layer of costs without cutting core.

A third type of crutch is the "avoid true competition" crutch, in which competitors hope that another year of price management, another year of foreign anti-dumping restrictions, or another year of government regulation will protect the industry's profitability.

A fourth crutch is the hope that somebody will leave the business. According to this attitude, even if all players are competing in the same way, even if that is leading to industry losses, "the weakest players will drop out soon." Their exit will give the industry some temporary respite from the no profit pattern.

The fifth and final crutch is that of the "reasonable customer." In the past, suppliers could count on customers to agree with the following statement: "In return for world class products and service, every supplier deserves to earn a sustainable profit."

Today, such agreement is not assured. Wal-Mart does not act as if suppliers deserve such profit; Volkswagen does not act that way either. (These customers at least do not act as if suppliers should profit at a level that sustains the supplier's stock market value or, in some cases, enables them to remain an independent company.)

Once these crutches are removed, the normal action of commoditized business designs drives all the profit away.

For most of this century, these crutches were strong and the no-profit pattern was a rare occurrence. Commoditized business designs existed in numerous industries, but a no profit result rarely occurred.

Then came agriculture, the first widespread no profit zone. As production methods improved, far fewer farmers were needed to meet consumer demands. Many farmers did not make the transition to a new industry, and continued to raise crops or livestock. Acreage did not drop despite the growth in capacity. The sheer continued excess supply stripped value away from the industry.

There was nothing mysterious about the decline of value in agriculture: too much supply in the face of slowly growing demand. But there weren't many people who expected this pattern to play out in other industries. In the 1950s and 1960s, no profit farming was joined by no profit rail passenger transportation. Just as in farming, government subsidies were called to the rescue.

Then, in the 1980s, one of the classic laws of business strategy—"every industry makes money, but the leaders make the most money"—collapsed. The no profit pattern began to occur with increasing frequency.

The airline industry was the next major example. Over the past 10-, 20-, and 30-year cycles, it has produced no profit, let alone profit in excess of the cost of capital. Between 1990 and 1993, the U.S. airline industry lost more money than it had earned in the previous four decades. Deregulation cleared the way for natural pricing mechanisms that drove the industry's cumulative profitability to zero.

The no profit pattern is at times a paradox: the combination of incredible technical sophistication, diligent investment, and the total absence of economic reward.

Consider the manufacture of memory chips. The process involves some of the most sophisticated technology in the world, with incredible quality controls, clean room environments, and highly complex manufacturing techniques. The investment requirements are prodigious. The industry consumes enormous quantities of capital, with new factories costing one to two billion dollars.

Yet, the industry is profitless. Once every five or six years, when supply is tight, a ray of profitability appears from behind the clouds. Then the clouds close in, and the industry loses money for years, with no prospect of structural profitability in sight.

Sometimes, there is no way to reverse the situation. Sometimes, the best course of action is to walk away. That's the decision Intel made in 1985.

Intel recognized and was willing to acknowledge the bitter reality of life in a no profit zone. It had excellent engineering talent, worked exceptionally hard, competed successfully with the Japanese, invested enormous amounts of capital—and made no money. In fact, it lost $200 million in 1985. Worst of all, there was no action that Intel could take to reverse the situation, nor was there any prospect that circumstances would improve. Intel confronted the reality of the no profit pattern and made the toughest decision in its history—it walked away.

Today, there is a long roster of looming no profit zones in our economy. It includes large parts of consumer electronics and the personal computing business, homeowners' insurance, memory chips, environmental remediation, and a growing list of others. Waiting for a place on the no profit list are automobiles, many classes of chemicals, traditional banking, and many utilities.

Why is the no profit pattern increasing now? Stronger forces than ever before have been kicking the "crutch" out from under an increasing number of industries populated by commoditized business designs:

- The globalization of competition has eliminated one of the primary weapons that manufacturers used to manage no profit conditions for the past century—price management. As long as there were only 2–3 major players competing for the same geographic customer, all coming from the same culture (and sometimes from the same town), it was relatively easy to maintain pricing discipline. Now, with 10–15 worldwide suppliers competing for the same customer (some from industrialized economies and others from developing economies) and with price quotes available by internet and fax, such discipline is becoming much harder to maintain.

- Customers have become incredibly more aggressive. Corporate customers have professionalized their purchasing functions. They have also computerized, internationalized, and created global supplier management processes that are extremely effective.

- New and innovative business designs often attack an industry's leaders by "cherry picking" the profitable subset of customers who have meant the difference between profit and loss. With this customer set gone, the leaders are left with an unprofitable business.

Still, corporations that have come to rely on traditional profit support systems may find trends that offer "new crutches" to lean on. These new supports hold out hope to those who want to avoid the hard work of redesigning the business:

- In recent economic cycles, the ratio of good to bad years has improved, and many think this trend will continue.

- Competitors in industries threatened by the no profit pattern are engaging in "swaps" to lessen the intensity of competition. Airport hub swaps, chemical factory swaps, and cable company metro area swaps are all mechanisms to slow down the advent of the no profit pattern without rethinking the business.

- The recent Asian crisis may have thrown into chaos a number of the new Asian government-supported competitors who were threatening the profitability of traditional market leaders.

To depend on any of these events as the way out from a no profit zone is tempting, but ultimately high risk. It will only allow the product-centric mentality that has produced the no profit pattern to remain in place. And it could put the company's future at risk once the new crutch is removed.

HOW TO PROFIT?

Walk away. Or invent a new way of doing business.

- Is my industry in danger of becoming a no profit zone?
- Do all players in my industry use the same business design? If so, what crutch or profit support system has maintained profitability in my industry to date?
- Is a major segment or customer in my industry a no profit zone?
- Where will my company be allowed to make profit in this industry?
- What is it about how the customer is changing that redefines the opportunity?
- To capture and protect profitability, what next generation business design must I build?

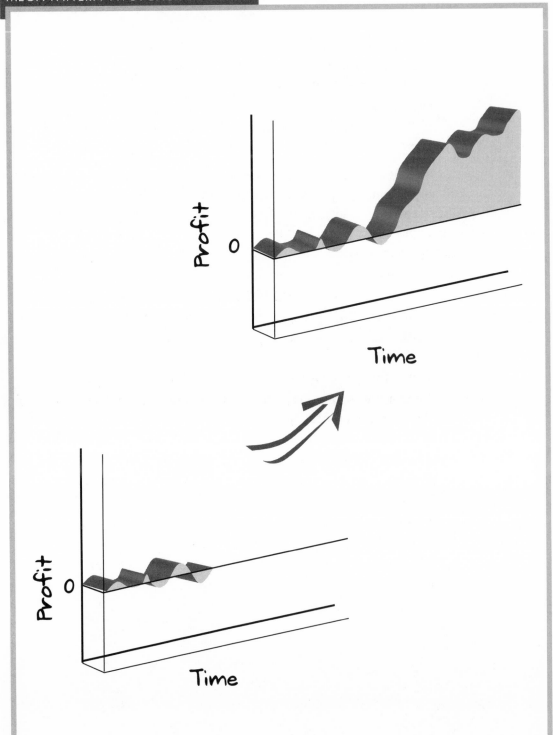

Back to Profit

Business design innovation strikes back—and profits return.

The past decade has seen dramatic growth in the number of actual and potential no profit zones in the economy. This growth has been caused by new levels of economic pressure applied to industries full of me-too business designs whose traditional profit support system, or crutch, may no longer effectively support industry participants.

The back to profit pattern has occurred far less frequently than the no profit pattern. This emerging pattern might grow significantly in the next decade—and, in doing so, dampen the growth of no profit zones—depending on choices made by industry participants. The back to profit pattern has already occurred in coffee, watchmaking, grocery distribution, and filmmaking. In each of these cases, business design innovation brought the business back to sustained profitability. In each of these cases, at least one player created a paradigm shift, a change in the rules of the game, in order to create new kinds of value that had not previously existed within the industry.

In retail coffee, Starbucks redefined coffee from a beverage to an experience. It then built a business design around that idea, replacing a model that had made coffee a profitless commodity. Using its cafés as its cornerstone, Starbucks built a high end brand without the aid of 60 second advertising that was the heart of the "old" coffee business (see pp. 183–185, New Branding). It then exploited that brand image through restaurant, kiosk, and other high margin channel distribution.

In the early 1980s, Swiss watchmaking went beyond "no profit." It went bankrupt. Nicolas Hayek's brilliant "product pyramid" business design, built around Swatch plus a dozen other Swiss watchmaking brands, brought profitability back to the industry and created double-digit profit growth for over a decade. Swatch was the firewall brand and volume builder; the high-end brands were the profit zone.

Grocery distribution had been a proverbial "1 percent margin" business until several astute grocers understood how customers' priorities (for convenience, quality, and variety) were being ignored by the industry's traditional business model. By changing their business designs to cater efficiently to the customers' unmet needs, these grocers created real convenience for customers and meaningful margins for store owners.

In all of these cases (coffee, watches, grocery), the traditional suppliers assumed a sameness about customers that was inaccurate. They *under-recognized* the significant differences, the extreme variability in what was important to different customer groups. In coffee, there were not only the traditional price buyers. There were also time-rich quality seekers willing to spend a half-hour in a café, and time-pressed quality seekers willing to spend fifty cents more on a great cup of coffee on the way to work.

In watchmaking, there were not only luxury buyers and "accurate timepiece" buyers. There was considerable untapped whimsy in the customer base, as well as a sense of fun, fashion, and willingness to buy not one watch, but twenty.

In grocery, customers looking for low prices were not the only type of customer in the market. Other customers sought service, convenience, and time saving.

In each of these cases, customer variability provided enormous opportunity outside the mental box of the traditional business model in the industry.

Success in the back to profit pattern hinges on inventing new ways of doing business to meet customer priorities. Astute business model innovators search hard for these undiscovered priorities. When they find them, they create a business design that matches them perfectly—and very cost-effectively. They invent completely new ways of doing business which, in turn, create new benefits for buyers (and channels) and new profits for suppliers.

The back to profit pattern continues to grow. Consider Coca-Cola and the 20-ounce plastic bottle. In grocery distribution, colas are a loss leader, a major no profit zone for the grocer, the bottler, and the brand alike. In response to this decades-long profit headache, Coke invented a new way of doing business: the 20-ounce plastic bottle. This innovation consists of three elements: a larger package, a reclosable package (in contrast to the can), and a package that is available only in coolers at the checkout counter. Cans standing on shelves elsewhere in the store sell for 2 cents per ounce. Plastic bottles, kept cold at the cash register, sell for 5 cents per ounce, bringing more profit to grocers and bottlers alike.

Finally, a major new wave of the back-to-profit pattern will be triggered by digital business design (see Chapter 10). Digital business designs have already brought enormous profit improvement to previously commoditized activities like cement and trucking (for an example, see the Cemex case, on p. 257). Astutely applied, digital business designs will be able to restore significant profitability to several of the major no profit zones that have emerged in the past decade.

Which direction will the future take? No profit? Back to profit? The deciding factor will be business design innovation—in autos, airlines, PCs, consumer electronics, and in many other industries.

Consider a thought experiment: Design a business model that would bring back sustained profit growth to the above four arenas (autos, PC's, etc.) of economic activity.

What other no profit zones are candidates for the back to profit pattern? What type of business design innovation would be needed to trigger the back to profit pattern in these arenas?

HOW TO PROFIT?

Look harder at the customer base. See the undiscovered or unmet needs. Build a new business design to meet those needs.

- How much variation in customer needs exists in my market?
- What are the most important unmet or undiscovered needs in the customer base?
- What type of new business design would address those needs effectively *and* be cost-effective enough to be profitable?

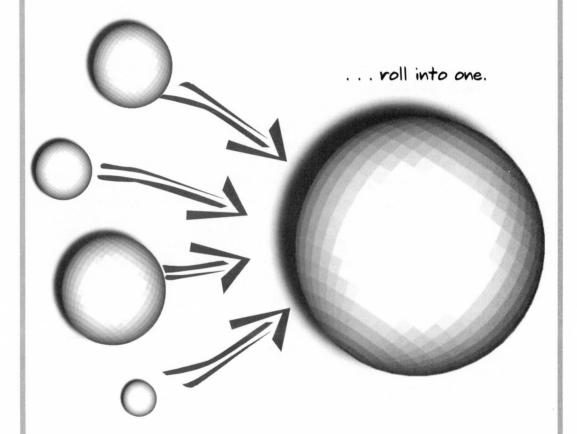

. . . roll into one.

Several different
industries. . .

Convergence

Frontiers fall. The rules of competition change.

Competitive boundaries are evaporating. Previously solid competitive walls are disintegrating in industries as varied as materials, financial services, life sciences, and retail.

In the convergence pattern, competitors from previously distinct industries start competing for each other's customers.

A company that finds itself in the midst of a convergence pattern faces several strategic challenges. The first is to expand its radar screen to identify the full set of competitors who are starting to compete for the company's customers. That set may be 2–10 times larger than the narrow cluster of traditionally defined competitors.

A second challenge is to develop and exploit a new formula for competitive success. This second challenge is so difficult because the way to win a convergence contest is always different than the way to win in the "home market." Most companies only experience convergence once or twice in their corporate histories, so there is little internal knowledge to exploit. And human nature being what it is, most companies tend to fight a convergence battle as if it were a traditional one.

The American Revolution provides a powerful image of the effect of convergence on competitive strategy. The better equipped British army, accustomed to European warfare rules from its "home market," fought in a straight line, on bended knee, in a clear space in a large meadow. The American army, less equipped but hardened in its fighting techniques from countless Indian battles, stood behind trees at the edge of the meadow and fired at the British in the open field. We know the rest of the story.

How can a company that finds itself in a bet-the-company convergence struggle find the right competitive approach with no prior experience? Patterns can help.

Pattern thinking helps discern that there is not one monolithic type of convergence pattern. In fact, there are three distinct types of convergence contests, each has its own characteristics and its own set of competitive rules. Understanding which type of convergence battle you face is a good place to start.

The three types are:

1. Supplier convergence
2. Product convergence
3. Complementor convergence

SUPPLIER CONVERGENCE

Supplier convergence occurs when regulatory change or a customer desire for bundling (often driven by a desire for simplicity and transactional efficiency) enables suppliers to create a one-stop shop for customers. Suppliers who traditionally have provided one part of the one-stop shop all try to expand their offerings simultaneously. The result is a vast excess of suppliers, each having a strong historical competence in one part of the one-stop shop, but typically being weak in the remainder.

Financial services convergence is such a contest. Customers once had checking accounts at banks, traded stocks through brokers, and bought insurance from insurance companies. Cash was deposited into savings accounts, and banks controlled most personal assets.

Then came deregulation. Retail banks found themselves competing with insurers, brokers, and mutual funds. Chase, First Chicago, and Citibank found themselves fighting for customer assets against companies named Schwab, Fidelity, Merrill Lynch, and Prudential.

In this supplier convergence battle, three competitive success factors are important. The first is to define the scope of the offering correctly—on a customer segment by segment basis. If you don't define the scope of offer correctly, the customer excludes you from the rest of the conversation. The second principle is to identify and own a differentiated position on the "high ground" activity within the bundle. Not all supplier activities are created equal in the eyes of the customer. For the customer, typically one activity is the hardest to do well (not all suppliers can perform it equally well), and the most important to do well because it provides the greatest customer benefit. The customer will determine the one-stop shop choice on this high ground activity. The third principle is not only to offer but also improve on the "low ground" activities in the remainder of the bundle.

Who might be best positioned to win the financial services convergence battle? Surprisingly, one of the smallest players—Charles Schwab—has constructed the strongest position for future consumer financial services. Why? Schwab's offer is as broad as it gets—Internet broker, tele-dial broker, discount broker, mutual fund manager, insurer, credit card issuer, and banking service provider. Customers can choose as few or as many services as they want. Second, Schwab is known for being best at the "high ground" activity—helping customers manage their equity investments, either through its own systems, or its extensive affiliated network of financial planners. (The high net worth individual—the one who contributes the vast majority of profits in financial services—typically has 60 to 70 percent of all assets in equities.) Third, Schwab offers improved "low ground" activities in the bundle, such as banking and insurance. Finally, its mutual fund program offers not only Schwab mutual funds, but 1,400 mutual funds from other companies in a no-fee "switchboard" offer.

PRODUCT CONVERGENCE

A different competitive dynamic occurs in the second type of convergence pattern, substitute product convergence. In this pattern, the functionality of two different products or technologies evolves over time to the point where they overlap and address the same customer need. There is no issue about supplier substitution—both suppliers are still needed. The question is how important each product will be in the future customer purchase mix.

The materials industry provides an excellent example of product convergence. In 1960, steel was the leader in the world of materials, and the integrated steel mill model was worth $60 billion. Steel was the material of choice for the majority of high-profit applications. Within three decades, as others contributed better ideas, the value of the integrated steel model had declined to $12 billion.

If steel was a convergence loser, plastic (in autos) and aluminum (in beverages) were convergence winners; plastic and aluminum are clearly lighter than steel, a major consideration for customers concerned with fuel economy. How could steel have responded differently?

Steel could have employed several competitive strategies that are effective for product convergence battles. They include influencing the customer's perspective—directly or indirectly—on which criteria matter most; becoming expert in applications thinking in order to better measure and articulate systems economics benefits to the customer; investing for high rates of product performance improvement; and being willing to co-opt competition in order to remain in control of the customer relationship.

Overall, steel carried out none of these steps; with additional fear, imagination, and action, it might have significantly reduced its convergence losses.

Steel did not actively influence the choice criteria of its auto OEM customers—and their predominant criterion was lower weight. Steel may have changed this by enlisting the help of others in the economic landscape. For example, we know auto consumers are concerned about crash safety, particularly for cars that regularly carry children. Nothing prevented steelmakers from communicating to the consumer the importance of steel in maximizing safety, or creating an "X% steel inside" as an awareness-heightening labeling system. Nothing prevented steel companies from turning to medical insurance companies to seek differential rates based on the structural strength of the car (and carrying out the research to back up the request). Instead, steel allowed weight minimization to remain its customers' unchecked top priority for decades.

Applications research, combined with new product and process development, would also have enabled steel to defend certain parts of the car that were lost to plastic. However, it was the convergence attacker—plastics—who invested most aggressively in applications research. Steel remained product and manufacturing centric.

In addition, steel underfunded product and process performance improvement at a critical moment. Aluminum and plastics did not start with a superior technology position, but ultimately achieved it through focused investment and a higher rate of improvement. In the 1980s, steel had the highest cash flow, but aluminum and plastics had the highest improvement rate. Eventually, it was high enough to coax the value away from steel and toward aluminum and plastics.

Finally, no leading steel maker chose to create a multi-materials company in order to develop hybrid applications. At least one player— if not more—could have better exploited and retained its customer relationships from the beginning of the convergence cycle through such a business design.

COMPLEMENTOR CONVERGENCE

The third type of convergence pattern is complementor convergence. Sometimes, this complementor convergence is nothing more than the joining of two products. (In fiber optic electronics, for example, Uniphase is acquiring fiber optic telecom component makers. Uniphase integrates these components into modules that save Uniphase's customers—very busy telecom systems houses—from having to do the integration work themselves.)

More often, complementor convergence has a high-end/low-end aspect to it: biotech converging with pharmaceuticals, strategy consulting converging with information systems, investment banking converging with global corporate banking, smart card chips converging onto magnetic stripe banking cards.

In these cases, there is no zero sum game, no need to rationalize suppliers or products. The key in this type of convergence pattern is to create positive synergies.

Two principles drive competitive success in this complementor convergence. Both principles apply to the "low-end" partner, because it is usually that partner who has the resources to acquire the "high-end" complementor, and who is ultimately responsible for value creation. First, act early and aim to partner one step higher than your rank in the

THE CONVERGENCE CURVE

Industries aren't converging at the same speed, nor are they at the same stage in the process. The diagram of the convergence curve indicates the status of various industries.

Companies at the bottom of the curve compete primarily in their own industry, safe from the chaos and uncertainty that await them higher on the curve.

As industries start to ascend the curve, unexpected competitors from "other" industries start to attract their customers.

The media start taking notice as companies move still higher on the curve. Companies begin to realize that the climb presents both problems and new profit opportunities, in equal measure.

Toward the top of the curve, a company finds itself in a completely different game. It might well have been the leader in its own industry, but now it must compete with quite impressive and aggressive leaders from other industries, brought onto the field by the convergence process.

Usually, a radically new business design is the key to success in the postconvergence landscape.

Convergence rivalries are always intense and never evenly matched. Consider the increasing competition among computing, television, and telecommunication. Digital television development is funded by $50 billion per year of corporate advertising and cable subscriptions. Computing development is funded by $300 billion per year of corporate IT budget. The telecommunications resource engine falls somewhere in the middle.

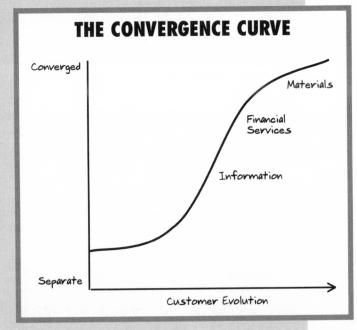

nonconvergence world. By not acting early, a company runs the risk of having an unattractive choice set as convergence becomes more obvious.

The second principle is to put the "high-end" partner in charge of significant parts of the new business. Otherwise, the key talent will never be energized to perform, much less stay with the company the minute their golden handcuffs are unlocked.

Great examples of this occur in the pharmaceutical field, where large chemistry-based companies have by and large done a good job of acquiring and managing relationships with biotechnology partners. Less inspiring outcomes have occurred in consulting and financial services, where most high-end/low-end convergence efforts have led to a rapid mass exodus of talent that had been acquired at a high price.

CONVERGENCE AND ORGANIZATIONAL DYNAMICS

We have discussed three situation-specific competitive approaches relating to the convergence pattern. There are several important organizational perspectives that apply across multiple convergence situations.

First, if your company is culturally committed to one core competence *and* to operating as a stand-alone entity, be prepared to sacrifice one of those two commitments to compete in a convergence market. Only a few, dominant, stand-alone specialists thrive during convergence. The odds are against your company's being one of them.

Second, the time to manage the convergence pattern is when it is just beginning. That's when the choice-set is the broadest. You can preempt, react, change your basic business design, select another set of customers, or, in the worst case, look to other places to invest. With every passing year, the options narrow. There comes a point when the cumulative "decisions-not-made" narrow the future to one option: a spiraling decline, stopped only by a bargain sale or bankruptcy. One of the most common causes of value collapse is that the company didn't recognize the full impact of the convergence pattern until it was too late.

Third, be brutally honest as to whether the activity your company has traditionally carried out is a "high-ground" activity or a "low-value," "low-ground" activity in tomorrow's convergence market. Many traditional leaders may be at risk of self-deception on this issue.

Fourth, when considering acquisition options to deal with convergence, do not overstate your company's go-it-alone base case. Many companies have walked away from acquisitions they should have made because they were reluctant to admit how bleak the future would be without new customer-relevant capabilities. They believed their own internal budgets or stock market stories, rather than acknowledging that convergence had already subtracted value from their base case. AT&T was accused of overpaying for Teleport and TCI. IBM was accused of overpaying for Lotus Notes. Nortel was accused of overpaying for Bay Networks.

But look at their stock prices 6–12 months after the convergence-related mergers occurred, and see if the criticisms are valid. Perhaps most telling, compare movements in their stock price against that of companies who have frozen in their tracks rather than respond to the exigencies of the convergence pattern.

The good and bad news about convergence is that it spells opportunity as well as threat. Those who quickly adapt to new competitive rules—guaranteed to be different from the rules that have driven their past success—will squeeze through the tight door of the future, and live to compete in the next round of larger, more complex convergence markets.

HOW TO PROFIT?

Identify the new rules of competition. Define your best opportunity space. Become its leader. Seal it off from other options by consistently improving the deal you deliver to your chosen customers. Motivate your new rivals to look elsewhere.

- Is the convergence pattern occurring in your industry?
  - What type of convergence is it?
- How high is your industry on the convergence curve?
- How would customers define your industry based on the needs they seek to fulfill?

- As you expand your competitive field of vision, do you see your customers being wooed by other companies?
- Do your customers have new choices that will encourage them to take their business to someone else?
- Will they have those choices tomorrow?

• Are your neighboring industries growing faster than your industry? Are they siphoning customers or profit away from you?

• Are you growing at a much more rapid rate than your neighboring industries?

• Will they want a piece of your profitability?

• Can you take advantage of your position or are you vulnerable? With what competitive advantage are you attacking the convergence market? Your traditional competitive tactics or those tailored for convergence?

• Look ahead five years, with the convergence curve in mind. What can you anticipate already? How can you use that knowledge to create new sources of profitability for your company?

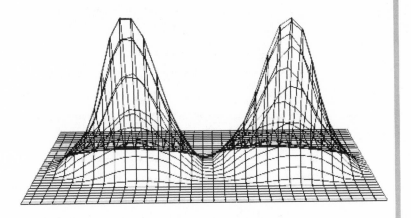

. . . towards the extremes

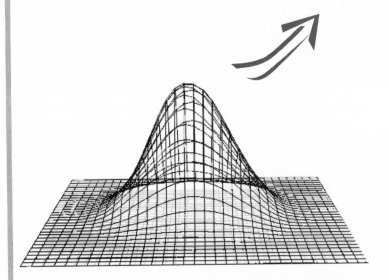

Value migrates away from the middle. . .

Collapse of the Middle

*Move from the average to the extremes,
in both your product and information offers.*

COLLAPSE OF THE MIDDLE: A PRODUCT PERSPECTIVE

Until recent years, most business designs were rooted in product manufacturing economics. Within the limits of these economics, manufacturers and distributors offered customers one of three types of value propositions:

- Acceptable quality products at the lowest price. The low cost position was achieved through efficient-scale factories, high relative market share, broad product lines, heavy asset investment and reinvestment.

- Differentiated performance products at a premium price. Unique customer utility was delivered through product benefits, design, and brand image.

- Superior focused products at an equal or premium price. Companies won by customizing the product and providing the best value proposition for a very specific segment or "niche" of the market.

These three winning propositions were a staple of strategic decision making in the 1980s. Even at that time, however, there was a danger of being caught in "the middle" (i.e., achieving neither superior cost, nor superior benefit, nor superior focus).

Being caught in "the middle" is a lousy place to be, strategically. The increasing sophistication of the global business community has, in most markets, punished "the middle" unmercifully.

For an example, consider the shifts in shareholder value in retailing formats over the past 10 years. The winners, who together created $163 billion in shareholder value, were the price discounters (low cost position), the superstores (focus and low cost combined), and the high-end specialists (differentiation with a price premium). The losers? Department stores (all things to all people, stuck in the high-cost, moderate-benefit middle).

COLLAPSE OF THE MIDDLE: AN INFORMATION PERSPECTIVE

For those who like strategic continuity, the good news is that these three positions continue to work, provided that the competitive game being played is purely a product-centric one.

The bad news is that fewer and fewer games are product-centric. The relentless development of the microprocessor and the growth of information as a decision factor have modified the rules of the game, making all three of the classic strategic positions less valuable than they had been in the past. Why? Because as precise as classic strategy ideas are about manufacturing-driven economics and customer utility, they have nothing to say about information-driven economics and customer utility. And the role of information management in the customer offer is exploding.

We tend to identify manufacturing businesses with the physical manipulation of materials: metal bending, plastic molding, electrical wiring, chip shrinking, integration and assembly. Yet, in reality, manufacturing businesses involve the transfer of mountains of information—supply-chain information, work-flow information, factory-floor information, customer value and choice information.

With computer power to track and manage this information, new dimensions of competitive advantage are emerging. And two unmistakable trends are occurring:

- Product performance-based differentiation is shrinking
- Information performance-based differentiation is growing

In today's information-intensive economy, we submit that there are at least two major winning propositions:

- Superior customer-level customization (customer priorities information management)
- Superior solutions (customer process information management)

Because of the rising importance of information-based performance, managers who think of value propositions only in product-centric, price/performance terms do so at their peril. They are in danger of being blindsided by competitors that are exploiting new value propositions made possible by information economics and utility.

The companies who are most vulnerable to this threat are those that have historically taken a middle-of-the-road approach to information transfers between their companies and their customers. This middle-of-the-road approach is called the product sales force. The sales force is to information transfer what department stores are to retailing: all things to all customers, operating in the high-cost, moderate-benefit middle.

Regardless of whether a company's sales force has been technically composed of sales representatives on payroll, commissioned brokers, distributors, or sales agents, the underlying economics and utility of any sales force as an information transfer vehicle are the same: Relatively well paid individuals play a relatively low value-added information transfer role. They explain new product features. They compare their products' performance to that of the competition (usually in a biased fashion). They give advice on when their products are appropriate to use (again in a biased fashion). They take orders.

Many manufacturers now compete in markets where product differences are no longer mysterious to customers or significant among competitors. In such a climate, information performance and economics start to overwhelm product performance and economics, and the sales force as an information transfer vehicle becomes an unaffordable luxury.

The product-centric business design, no matter how soundly positioned in product terms, is soundly beaten by low-cost, high-customization business designs on the one hand, and superior solutions on the other. The information extremes beat the information middle.

In computing, the value of original equipment manufacturers (OEMs) has shifted to Dell (low cost, high customization), to PC manufacturers who have become solutions providers (IBM, HP) and to solutions outsourcers (EDS, Andersen). Compaq, the clear winner in low-cost product manufacturing terms, has just joined the ranks of the solutions providers through its acquisition of DEC.

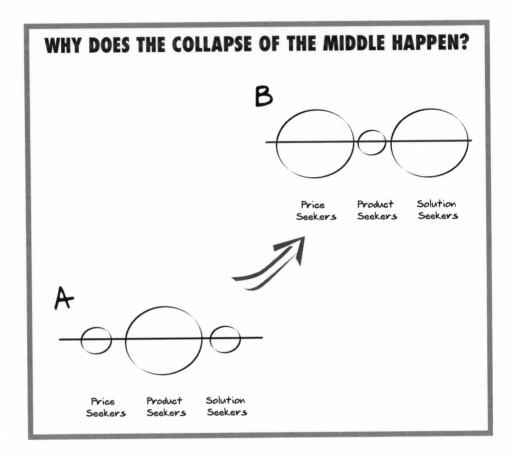

WHY DOES THE COLLAPSE OF THE MIDDLE HAPPEN?

B

Price Seekers   Product Seekers   Solution Seekers

A

Price Seekers   Product Seekers   Solution Seekers

In business forms, value has shifted from the worldwide leader, Moore Corporation (owner of the largest forms sales force), to Wallace, which offers customer-managed form design and order entry systems (low cost, high performance), and to Jet Forms, which offers electronic form enterprise software and work flow systems (solutions).

In industrial weighing systems, value has shifted from the product R&D leaders to those who offer low-cost, indirectly distributed commodity products, and to those who build turnkey factories as a solution (with weighing systems inside the factory).

CHALLENGES POSED BY THE COLLAPSE OF THE MIDDLE

It is tempting to categorize the collapse of the middle solely as a distribution channel problem to fix through some straightforward tactics (e.g., the sales rep is replaced by a low-cost channel and by the solutions consultant). However, the collapse of the middle requires organizing a company's entire business design around a new information-based value proposition. It often requires new product designs, a new product line, new competencies (such as solutions development and delivery), new profit models, new information systems, new incentive systems, and, perhaps most importantly, new corporate cultures.

The collapse of the middle forces cultural and strategic change by the company that experiences it, because the profit that used to be in one traditional business design now splits into three:

Business Design Type	Traditional Profit Mix	Collapse of the Middle
Product Centric	100%	?%
Solutions	0	?
Low Cost, High Customization	0	?

As a result, the product-centric company that experiences the collapse of the middle has to ask two tough questions:

- In how many different directions will we move to follow value? How many different business designs does that imply?
- What should be our market share per new, collapse of the middle, market segment?

IMPLEMENTATION CHALLENGES

If a company tries to capture value in each of the three value spaces, it will have to create and manage three separate cultures. If a company chooses to play in one value space alone, it will need to be much more dominant in that space than it had been in the market as a whole.

The cultural challenge can be even more daunting, because of institutional memory and the difficulties of recruiting the right new talent. Company cultures that have, for decades, taken pride in their product-driven performance are often populated with product engineers who find it hard to treat an information-based success factor as a worthy replacement. In the labor markets, the collapse of the middle is creating an imbalanced global demand for individuals who can manage projects and deliver solutions. A company that has been product-centric in its approach will find it very difficult to recruit and retain top solutions talent.

Dell has learned how to support only one culture but exploit more than one value space. Dell occupies only one value space in the collapse of the middle landscape: the low-cost, high-customization position. However, Dell also sells its computers to partners such as Price Waterhouse, Arthur Andersen, and KPMG, which are trying to create virtual IT solutions that compete with the likes of IBM's Computing Solutions division. The net result is that Dell benefits from the economics of both value spaces, but only has to manage a single corporate culture.

WHAT'S MY NEXT MOVE?

Whichever choices make most sense for your company, the value shifts that are driving the collapse of the middle—the commoditization of product positions, and the rising importance of information based differentiation—are here to stay. In the product-plus-information environment, choosing among the classic three product-centric strategic options is not possible. It is like choosing among furniture arrangements on the *Titanic*. The task facing management is not to refine its product-centric strategy position; it is to choose a non-middle position on both product and information, creating a new business design with which it can successfully compete for future value in its industry.

HOW TO PROFIT?

Be the first to go to the extremes.

- Is the collapse of the middle occurring in your industry? Is it about to occur? At the product level, the information level, or both?
- Which has better odds of success for your organization: low cost or solutions?
- Can you do both? What different organizations will it take to pull off a dual shift?

...to de facto standard.

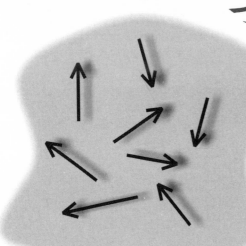

Multi-polar...

De Facto Standard

Customers crave compatibility.
Someone creates high value by providing it.

In recent years, standards battles may have generated more business headlines than any other topic. They are the business community's version of a soap opera—who is getting "married" to whom, who just double-crossed their partner for a better alternative, who is suing to break up a coalition.

The role of standards in business has changed. Standards used to be adopted to keep outsiders out (electrical sockets in Europe, apple standards in Japan, etc.). Today, they tend to serve a much more useful role for the customer:

- To assure customers of quality (Food and Drug Administration approval, ISO9000, reference products whose performance defines quality)
- To prove performance levels (refrigerator energy consumption levels, insulation warmth levels, computer processing speeds, stereo sound quality)
- To give customers product interoperability across suppliers (VHS videos, IBM clones)
- To give customers a medium that fosters usage-related productivity and communication (Microsoft Windows, America On-line subscriber communities).

In a "fair" world, suppliers who did the hard work of meeting rigorous standards would be assured of some kind of reward. In fact, however, most standards tend to do just the opposite—they tend to commoditize the suppliers that adopt them. Quality standards give customers the ability to be assured of quality at no extra cost. (Brands used to be the way that customers were assured of quality, and they paid a premium for that assurance.) Performance standards enable customers to make valid performance comparisons across products, creating transparency on which product is really a better value for the money. Interoperability standards ensure that customers can switch suppliers without fear of disruption.

In short, standards tend to organize customer thinking and information about the "performance" side of the "price/performance" equation, leaving the customer free to focus on . . . price. The widespread rise in standards over the past 20 years is a testament to rising customer power, and a widespread threat to supplier profitability.

When the de facto standard pattern comes to an industry, it becomes critical for companies who want to maximize their value growth that they own or partially own industry standards rather than simply produce products according to those standards.

Consequently, when this pattern occurs, there is a new skill required for companies who want to maximize profitability. That skill is the art of optimal coalition building. Not too few partners —you won't have enough clout to create the standard. Not too many partners— you'll move too slowly, have too many conflicting interests, and will have to split the spoils too many ways if you win.

In the de facto standard pattern, manufacturers can create profit in two ways: by 1) selling their products for profit margin, and using their differentiated performance technology to gain market share; or by 2) trying to create a standard in the part of the value chain where they have a competitive advantage. The latter option is one that did not exist two decades ago as frequently as it does today. In many industries, it is only now becoming a possibility as open system software and interoperability standards are emerging.

Two examples illustrate the trade-offs that the de facto standard pattern poses for a management team. Nellcor Puritan Bennett, a medical diagnostics company, kick-started the pulse oximetry market in the mid 1990s. (The pulse oximeter is a device which noninvasively measures blood oxygen levels through tiny electrodes on the end of a patient's finger.) When a malpractice suit was decided against a hospital that failed to use the pulse oximeter, it became clear that the whole medical industry would soon adopt the Nellcor pulse oximeter as a reference standard.

The next expected Nellcor move would be to gear up production to meet burgeoning demand. What Nellcor did in addition to that move broke the rules of the medical device industry. Nellcor licensed its proprietary algorithms to dozens of competitors, and those algorithms became the de facto monitoring standard inside the pulse oximeter.

Nellcor pulse oximeters still captured over half of the market—its intellectual property position gave it a reputational advantage. But owning the de facto standard significantly increased its level of value capture. The stock market's enthusiasm for guaranteed future Nellcor cash flows (regardless of market share position) led to market value growth and new strategic options that Nellcor otherwise would never have achieved.

The best known example of the opposite behavior was Apple computer. During much of the 1980s and early 1990s, Apple owned a graphical user interface that was far superior to Microsoft's. Apple chose to exploit its interface to sell more computers, at higher prices, rather than to build a coalition of competitors that could make its interface a standard. The rest is history—a shift of over $100 billion in shareholder value to Microsoft, which focused all of its energies on making its graphical user interface the de facto standard in the industry.

These two stories are not meant to imply that it is always right to pursue a standards position—sometimes the highest value move is to use distinctive performance capability to gain market share or to raise prices instead. But most companies are just now awakening to the possibility of standards-related strategies that have long been part of the strategic mindset in computing and consumer electronics.

Think hard about whether you could create a standards coalition around:

- Industry-level reference performance that only your product can achieve;
- Intellectual capital on how products could become interoperable across suppliers;
- Whether your standard can be shaped to facilitate cross-user productivity and communication (it is then that you start to become the most powerful kind of standard, a customer language).

If you believe that the standards strategy is a viable option, run the financial models that would result from being a standards owner (intellectual property rights profit, but potentially lower margins on

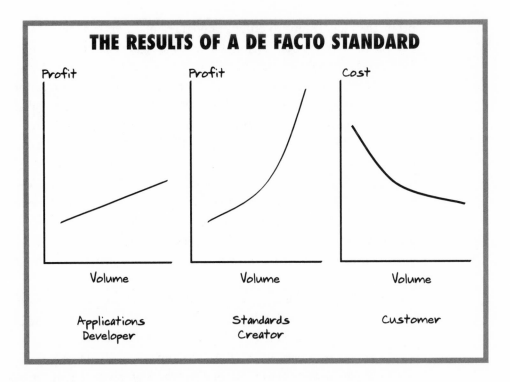

THE RESULTS OF A DE FACTO STANDARD

Profit / Volume — Applications Developer

Profit / Volume — Standards Creator

Cost / Volume — Customer

products sold), and compare those to your baseline P&L projections. Consider how a stock market analyst would view your new economics. Remember that stock prices go up when companies generate significant cash flows from a low asset base, and when the long-term sustainability of those cash flows is relatively certain. Owning the de facto standard might change both of these factors in your favor.

Finally, think creatively about how to build a standards coalition. Do you have to bring in suppliers from other geographies or neighboring industries to generate enthusiasm for your proprietary asset, or are traditional competitors interested? If you want to establish a standard, do you need to communicate to the end customer in order to brand the asset (e.g., "Intel Inside")?

Be aware that if customer dissatisfaction exists due to multipolar, incompatible suppliers, customer frustrations reach a point at which simplicity becomes the driving priority. If you don't make a standards move, someone else might.

When a company establishes its technology as the de facto standard, magic starts to happen. Customers enjoy the economic benefits of compatibility. Past investments retain future value. And, competitors start to write their business plans around the strategy of the company that owns the de facto standard. Consider how your management team can add the de facto standard pattern and related coalition building skills to its repertoire of strategic moves.

HOW TO PROFIT

Create the standard. Or, align with the emerging
standard early. Or, work on creating the next standard.

Ask yourself:

- Will the de facto standard pattern play out in my industry?
- What impact will it have on my business?
- If I could anticipate it, what would I do differently to protect my position:

   —As a customer?

   —As a competitor?

   —As an applications developer?
- Could I be the creator of the de facto standard in my industry?

Technology Shifts the Board

The chess board moves. Power changes hands.

Technological inventions happen almost daily. There are hundreds of them every year. They bring increased functionality, better costs, faster cycles, and a host of other technological benefits to producers and customers alike.

A very few new technologies lead to special outcomes. The introduction of these technologies changes the strategic landscape in a way that creates secondary, unintended consequences. These effects are not about performance improvement. They involve a large-scale redistribution of power that fundamentally reshapes the playing field. Some companies find themselves displaced or out of the game completely. Other companies discover that all of their fundamental relationships, with competitors, customers, and suppliers, have been skewed, recast, and redefined.

This "technology shifts the board" pattern results from a technological development that moves all the players in the game out of their accustomed positions. Several examples of how powerful this pattern can be are provided by the advent of television, the VCR, the automobile, and the personal computer.

When television was finally delivered into the living room, it enabled tens of millions of people to spend their evenings watching drama, entertainment, and news, at no cost. It created a fundamental change in how people spent their time. But television had other consequences that dramatically shifted value and strategic control across a number of industries.

The product itself became the technological equivalent of the gold rush. With everyone wanting a television set, there was "a fortune" to be made in production. Hundreds of companies rushed to manufacture TVs. Then they went to war with one another. The intensity of their competitive behavior created a great deal of activity but very little permanence. Dozens of the new arrivals in the television-making industry collapsed in the 1970s. In the end, a handful of major producers (Matsushita, Sony, and several others) survived and restored law and order to what had been a wild technological frontier. When the TV era began, manufacturers were counted in the hundreds. By the middle of the 1970s, the entire industry was controlled by a handful of companies.

The television drove major changes in other industries as well. In the 1950s, the power in the consumer products industry rested firmly in the hands of organizations like A&P and Sears. They, and companies like them, owned the power formula of the era: broad distribution and strong household brands. Before TV, other consumer product companies (Procter & Gamble, Kellogg's, and Philip Morris, for example) were forced to turn to newspapers and national magazines, as well as billboards and radio spots, to build national brands. But because there were few national channels for the advertising of their products, their ability to build brand loyalty in a cost-effective way was constrained.

Television changed that. It was an efficient, high-impact, nearly pervasive medium that instantly became the most powerful brand-building device ever invented.

The consumer goods manufacturers wasted no time. Television was a mini-billboard, a window into every living room in the land. The costs for communicating with tens of millions of people were extremely low. As a result, value shifted toward TV-based brand companies such as Procter & Gamble, Kellogg's, and Philip Morris. Television helped these companies build colossal successes for products like Tide detergent, Kellogg's Corn Flakes, and Marlboro cigarettes. They became billion-dollar brands that fueled the growth of billion-dollar companies.

There were other implications. As soon as it became apparent that the real money in television was in advertising, the center of the entertainment world shifted from Hollywood to New York, where the three major networks and the advertising industry made their headquarters. If you wanted to check the heartbeat of television, the place to put the stethoscope was Madison Avenue, not Tinseltown.

The next major "technology shifts the board" pattern was triggered by the videocassette recorder (VCR). The invention and wide distribution of VCRs weakened the major networks' hold over prime time, and caused power to shift from New York back to Hollywood. Japanese technology, particularly Matsushita's VHS, provided Hollywood with the perfect mechanism for capturing value. It was as though the course of a major river had suddenly been rerouted. Movie making, basically a no-profit business, found itself awash in new money provided by rapidly growing VCR rentals and sales. Hollywood could afford to continue making movies that broke even at the box office, because the films reaped huge rewards when they were subsequently distributed through video rentals and sales.

The VCR also created a vast new retailing space. In 1980, there was no such thing as a video store. By 1990, video stores were just about everywhere. Within a decade, they were generating more than $10 billion in revenue annually, a large portion of which flowed back to Hollywood. The major TV networks suffered no loss to videos in 1980. But by 1990, many families were spending several prime-time hours a week watching videocassettes instead of network programming.

Electronics retailers had a major new profit source, too. They sold VCRs, the new product that everyone wanted, and they sold lucrative service and maintenance contracts that expanded their profits.

What about the electronics firms that brought about this windfall? Their story presents a classic case of tragically flawed business design. The electronics companies created the product everyone wanted, invested the capital to produce it, but failed to design a mechanism to capture its value. They were trapped inside the mental box of the consumer electronics model. Their product was being sold at such rapidly decreasing prices that the manufacturers were not making a profit. Hollywood was counting its video receipts. Electronics stores were selling highly profitable service contracts. Even video stores were coining money. But the electronics companies found themselves in the strange position of providing the golden goose, but deriving no benefit. They put up the capital and took the risks. Everyone else captured the profits.

The TV and VCR shook the landscape. But perhaps the largest-scale technology shift of the twentieth century was triggered by the automobile.

Coal, carriage companies, and railroads ruled the transportation industry before the auto came onto the scene. But by the 1910s, the keys to the new empire were firmly in the hands of Henry Ford, the car maker, and John D. Rockefeller, the oil producer.

These industry builders were men of vision and absolute determination. They suffered defeat at the hands of very different foes. Rockefeller ran into the government trust busters, and Ford ran into Alfred Sloan, his smartest rival. As one measure of the importance of their respective roles, Ford and Rockefeller continued to grow their wealth and prosper as their predecessor technologies (carriages and coal) receded into history.

The internal combustion engine built the fortunes of Ford and Rockefeller; it also built a retailer then known as Sears, Roebuck & Company. General Woods (the CEO of Sears), whose favorite pastime was reading the U.S. Statistical Abstract, was very good at seeing patterns. He cultivated an ability to see the direction of fundamental shifts better than most of his peers. In the early part of the twentieth century, the shift was from farms to cities. Sears was there. Later, thanks to the automobile, the shift was from cities to suburbs. Sears was there again. The company bought edge-of-city real estate, built its stores there (with parking lots), and counted the cash as the customers migrated outward from the urban centers to the suburban rings. (Sam Walton used this technique four decades later. He planted Wal-Mart stores at city peripheries, then watched their value rise as population pressure pushed the demographic limits of the city outward. Sam Walton learned from Sears as diligently as Bill Gates learned from IBM.)

Television shifted power to the TV networks and their brand-building partners. The VCR infused Hollywood and its video-chain partners with newfound profit. The automobile shifted power to Rockefeller, Ford (then Sloan), and Woods. What about the personal computer (PC)?

The PC was as important (from 1975 to 1995) as the automobile was (from 1900 to 1920). Autos created fortunes for Rockefeller, Ford/Sloan, and Woods; the PC did the same for Grove, Jobs/Gates, and Dell.

In 1975, the PC space consisted of zero machines and zero dollars. In 1995, the PC space represented 100 million machines and $200 billion.

Power shifted from IBM and DEC to Intel, Microsoft, and low-cost distributors (Dell, Compaq, Gateway). A vast new infrastructure was built (primarily funded by corporate IT budgets) and created the preconditions for the Internet's emergence as a meaningful force.

What happened with autos, VCRs, and PCs is about to happen again. The current "technology shifts the board" pattern is being triggered by the Internet. The redistribution of power will be as great, if not greater, than those that happened in past occurrences of this pattern.

HOW TO PROFIT?

Go to where the power will be.

- Are there other technology shift patterns that will redistribute power in your industry?
- Who will benefit most? Who will be hurt the most?
- What can your company do to:
  –Exploit the shift, or
  –Minimize the negative impact on your organization?

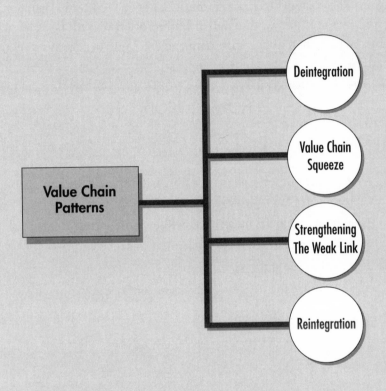

CHAPTER 5
VALUE CHAIN PATTERNS

INDUSTRY VALUE CHAINS used to be incredibly stable. Today, those value chains have been compressed, broken up, and put together again.

At the same time, profit and power have started to move along the chains more frequently and more rapidly than before.

Nor is the dynamism limited to the industry value chain itself. Previously distinct value chains are now overlapping, competing, and merging (see the discussion of Convergence, in Chapter 4). Some value chains are disappearing entirely.

Within this context, companies are using new, nontraditional criteria for value chain moves—moves driven by improving return on capital employed, achieving strategic control, creating business design innovations, and capturing the customer relationship.

Studies of how profit and value shift with respect to a company's own value chain and that of its economic neighbors have become important sources of strategic ideas.

We have tried to capture the meaning behind these moves in the four patterns that follow: *Deintegration, Value Chain Squeeze, Strengthening the Weak Link,* and *Reintegration.*

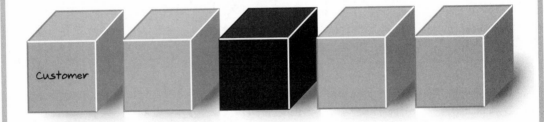

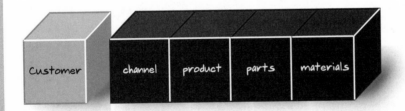

Deintegration

Focus beats integration.

For the past several decades, many major industries were dominated by the vertically integrated business model. In these industries, a handful of fully integrated players controlled the capacity and the strategic landscape. Steel, chemicals, autos, airlines, computing, textiles, plastics, aerospace, banking, consumer packaged goods, publishing, oil and gas, and pulp and paper were among the industries led by vertically integrated players.

In that past era, success was labeled "integrated oligopolist." New competitors were kept from entering via integration; customer power was managed via disciplined pricing.

Then, something happened. New competitors emerged as value chain specialists in these industries. Intel was formed in 1968. Nucor was formed in 1970. Microsoft was formed in 1975. Creative Artists Agency (CAA) was formed in 1975.

Nobody was paying much attention to these events. Back then, who could have predicted their eventual impact on their industry value chains?

One of the first steps toward deintegration was the rapid rise of outsourcing. Companies began to realize that they could become highly competent in three or four steps of the value chain, but not in twenty. Companies that tried to do too many things would do most of them poorly and would fail to provide the kind of successively better deal for the customer that was necessary to remain viable in a more competitive, faster-paced game.

The conditions for outsourcing were exacerbated when a small subset of players began to exploit the economics of specialization, making it possible for aggressive players to take full advantage of the powerful economic benefits of outsourcing.

Nike has been the leader in the U.S. athletic shoe industry for over a decade. Its success is generally attributed to marketing power and innovative designs, but something else is working behind the scenes. Nike has embraced an outsourcing strategy to such an extent that almost all of its manufacturing is completed out of house. While it keeps a firm hand on a collection of key technologies that are central to Nike's differentiation and brand image, it does not own the factories where its shoes are made; its financial and intellectual capital have been freed up for more valuable uses. Nike remains a shoe manufacturer, but it leans heavily on outside partners to perform many parts of the process.

Recognizing where the strategic control rests in the value chain; concentrating your company's operations in that step; and contracting others to perform the rest of the work—those are the key elements of outsourcing. Nike recognized the value of design and marketing, and was able to outsource almost all of its manufacturing to significantly lower-cost vendors. In contrast, if Nike had outsourced a critical activity or a strategic control point in the system, it might have missed the significant value growth it achieved in the 1990s.

Outsourcing is merely one example of deintegration. In many cases, evolving market conditions trigger not just the deintegration of one value chain step, but complete separation of the entire value chain into discrete steps. In this full deintegration, a company gives up *all* involvement in one or more steps along the value chain.

In the early 1980s, when IBM's fully integrated model made it the undisputed leader in computing, Microsoft and Intel focused on specific steps along the computing value chain. Their singular focus—concentration on creating absolute leadership in their positions in the value chain—contributed to the complete deintegration of the personal computing value chain. This triggering of the deintegration pattern unleashed an explosion of value worth $600 billion.

In the deintegration pattern, value shifts from strategic control by a few integrated producers to domination of only one or two steps along the value chain by an emerging group of specialists.

Very specific changes in market conditions can be the catalyst in this pattern. In most cases of deintegration, however, look for changing customer priorities, the emergence of new customer groups, deregulation, and changing technology. They all create openings for a significant restructuring of industry activity and for significant business model innovation.

Deregulation altered the strategic landscape and unleashed the deintegration pattern in the telecommunications industry. Not long ago, AT&T controlled all of the phone services residential customers received. AT&T made the equipment and the handsets, ran the network, and delivered local and long-distance service. However, deregulation has allowed a whole new set of companies to provide both local and long-distance services. In addition, separate carriers provide the access lines, the local loops, and the national backbone.

Rapid technological change has further accelerated deintegration in the "telecom" industry. Some companies now specialize in hardware or software, or even in different transmission standards, such as ISDN, ADSL, or others.

Qwest Communications is an example of highly focused value chain specialization. An emerging leader in the long-distance transport component of the telecom value chain, Qwest's core strategy is simple: Be the carrier's carrier. Qwest has built a national fiber-optic backbone. It resells capacity to local service providers such as GTE and U S WEST, which then deliver services to end users. This strategy has captured a great deal of value for Qwest. Formed in 1988, Qwest's value at mid-1998 was nearly $8 billion.

Deregulation is beginning to have the same impact on other industries. New and innovative business designs are now allowed to compete for market spaces that were once clearly off limits. That competition exposes the economics at every point along the value chain, often turning integrated approaches into disadvantages.

The deintegration pattern can also be triggered by other strategic market conditions and changes. Business design innovations and new technology sometimes join to create enormous value growth for companies that specialize in a limited part of the chain. Nucor, an upstart steel company, freed its business model from the costly and highly asset-intensive processes of coke making and iron making. Its business design was based on mini mills that bought their raw materials (scrap steel) on the open market. Nucor's model led to a partial, but highly profitable, breakup of the value chain. The company created a position that was closer and much more responsive to the customer, less asset-intensive, and much lower in cost.

Today, the deintegration pattern is being triggered across many industries. Thoughtfully designed and well-financed attackers are exploiting open systems, hot growth segments, technology changes, and other competitive openings so that they can focus on smaller, but highly profitable, parts of the value chain. These circumstances could fuel future deintegration in chemicals, plastics, aluminum, and countless other previously integrated activities.

HOW TO PROFIT?

Specialize in and dominate an important cell of the
new, broken-up value chain.

- Is your industry highly integrated?
- What specific economic or customer reasons originally caused it to be integrated?
- Are those reasons still valid today?
- If they are no longer valid, is there a chance to create significant new value by becoming the catalyst in a deintegration pattern?
- What steps in your industry's value chain are most valuable? How might your organization create the leadership position in those steps? What profit model will it use to benefit from that kind of change? What will be its new source of strategic control?

QWEST COMMUNICATIONS: THE NEXT-GENERATION CARRIER

What does speed-of-light communication have to do with speed-of-diesel railroading? A clear pathway to connect cities to each other via the rights-of-way for laying track. Qwest was founded in 1988 by the former owner of Southern Pacific Railroad, which, to Qwest's great advantage, owned rights-of-way all over the western half of the United States.

The new communications company used that advantage to lay fiber-optic cable all over the West. The company went public in June 1997, and raised $320 million. Today, Qwest is spending $1.4 billion to build a state-of-the-art fiber-optic cable network designed to deliver high-speed data and voice packets. To cut construction costs, the company has installed, alongside its own cable lines, fiber-optic cable for GTE, Worldcom, and Frontier—a strategy that generated $1 billion in revenue. When it is completed, Qwest's network will connect 115 U.S. cities and will represent 75 percent of the originating and terminating long-distance traffic in the nation. It has become the speed-of-light carrier of the Information Age.

Qwest's success comes from exploiting the deintegration pattern that is transforming the telecom landscape. By focusing on selling capacity on its fiber network to the RBOCs, CLECs, ISPs, and long-distance carriers, Qwest has positioned itself in the profit zone. This service is being sold even as the incumbent telco networks, built when technology aimed to deliver voice communications, struggle to meet the demand for data services. Data traffic is growing at twenty times the rate of voice traffic. Fiber-optic networks everywhere are running out of capacity. Usage rates were as low as 30 percent of capacity in the late 1980s. In 1998, they reached 90 percent of capacity.

This dysfunctionality (caused by the imbalance between traffic growth and available bandwidth) has cleared the way for Qwest to create significant value as a provider of additional network capacity for voice and data service providers. With the fourth largest fiber-optic network in the nation, Qwest has become the first choice for nearly all local, long-distance, and Internet service providers that need wholesale fiber-optic capacity. Because its technology is newer, Qwest has a strong security and reliability advantage over its competitors, which further strengthens its position as a high-speed data carrier. These benefits have allowed Qwest to wrest profits and strategic control from the traditional RBOC and telecom carriers.

Qwest has used its base position to create a potentially valuable source of new profit growth. In 1997 it won a U.S. Government contract to become the backbone for Internet2, the second-generation data network that will connect 130 universities. As funding for and usage of this high-speed data network increase, Qwest's fiber-optic network will become even more important, and potentially more valuable.

Qwest has created significantly greater value than the traditional telecom companies. In 1998, it had a value to sales ratio of 9.7 and a market value of nearly $8 billion. It is positioned to capture a significant portion of future value, because of its strategic control over the long-haul section of the telecom value chain. If the explosion in demand for data traffic capacity continues, this company, with its highly focused business design, may have a unique opportunity to capitalize further on the deintegration pattern in the telecom industry.

Nevertheless, if it is to retain its trajectory of value creation and profit growth, Qwest must continue to anticipate the patterns that are transforming the telecom sector, and to develop answers to questions such as:

- Are wireless networks and service providers a greater threat to Qwest than wireline networks?
- Are opportunities emerging for innovative players to reintegrate the value chain and offer customers integrated data, voice services, and solutions?

DEINTEGRATION, PHASE II

To better understand an industry or business that has deintegrated, and to make the next level of economic and customer detail stand out more clearly, we shift from a macro view of the whole chain and apply an economic microscope to every part of it. As value chain deintegration creates new zones of profit and value creation, the pattern exposes each step of the chain to more scrutiny. When each step is forced to compete in a "market," each activity in the system can be more clearly evaluated on its own economic terms.

Just as an electron microscope enables a scientist to look at the smallest components of an element, an economic "microscope" can give managers a tool that reveals the economic characteristics of each individual step along the value chain. Entrepreneurs depend on such a tool in their relentless search for opportunity.

One fact becomes apparent in this process: value and opportunity are not distributed evenly along the chain. A close look identifies opportunities for further deintegration, as well as the potential triggers for other patterns. Even a small step in the value chain might possibly be segmented into even smaller pieces.

Semiconductor manufacturers exemplify such second-phase deintegration. Intel's focus on chips began the deintegration of the value chain and exposed the "chip making" activity to a new level of economic scrutiny. As the complexity of chip manufacturing has risen, new specialists have entered and have taken the deintegration process one step further.

"Fabless" (short for fabricationless) chip companies began this process by focusing on design and selling, outsourcing the manufacturing. Today, some IP (intellectual property) semiconductor companies have completely deintegrated the "chip value chain." These virtual chip companies do not manufacture, ship, or sell chips. Instead, they create superior chip designs to be manufactured and sold by other companies operating downstream from the chip design process.

The economic microscope can be of great value for companies facing fully integrated value chains that are breaking up for the first time (the U.S. utility industry, for example), or for companies that are already working in a deintegrated environment (the personal computer industry comes to mind).

The challenge in the process is to identify new arenas of profit growth as the effects of changing customer priorities, technology, regulation, and information economics create new ways of serving customers.

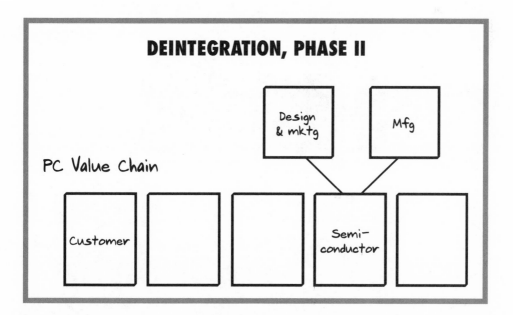

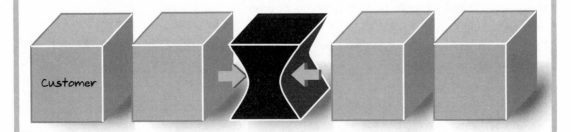

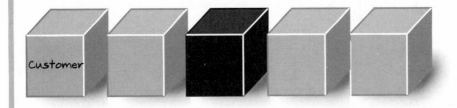

Value Chain Squeeze

Stay out of the pincers.

A century ago, a military commander's worst nightmare was to find his troops on low ground with the opposing army occupying the hills on either side. There was no way to win; there was no escape.

No commander would knowingly send his soldiers into such a trap. It could only occur due to lack of anticipation by the losing side's leaders.

In a dynamic value chain environment, a similar no-win, no-escape scenario can occur as the growing strength of neighboring suppliers and customers can effectively trigger a squeeze on the step where a company and its look-alike competitors are operating. The pressure generated by that squeeze can be so intense that it leaves no opportunity for profit growth; a whole step in the value chain may be unable to produce enough earnings to cover its cost of capital.

Why does the squeeze occur? Why does it catch its victims off guard? Three changes generally catalyze the pattern:

- Relative scarcity (of talent, for example)
- A faster rate of performance improvement by the pincers
- A consolidation at the pincer level that makes neighbors more powerful (e.g., auto suppliers)

These changes may take as long as a decade or two to occur, but the victim, usually preoccupied with other issues, misses the threat until the final few years.

A major example of the value chain squeeze is present in television broadcasting. Today's major networks, NBC, CBS, ABC, and Fox, are the "players in the middle" in this pattern. Think of the pincers that squeeze them. On one side, the networks face local TV affiliates, which have powerful local franchises and reap most of the value generated by what the networks present. On the other side are the content producers.

The National Football League (NFL), Hollywood studios, and independent programming producers are all demanding increasingly large payments from the networks, which depend on talented performers and hit shows to attract high ratings and maximum advertising dollars. The recent bidding wars over NFL telecast rights, the final round of contract negotiations for the *Seinfeld* actors, and the price paid for *ER* are indications of how vulnerable the networks are to the power of content providers. Advertising revenues continue to shift to cable networks, a situation that threatens to turn the once-powerful major networks into permanent low- or no-profit zones.

The automotive industry and professional sports present similar examples of the squeeze. In the automotive world, suppliers and mega-dealers are becoming increasingly powerful on either side of the traditional auto manufacturers. In sports, franchise owners are positioned between athletes with record salary demands and a whole host of suppliers, stadiums, and third-party providers. In each case, profit flows to the companies that control the pincers, and the industry in the middle finds itself trapped in a zone of limited returns or rapidly decreasing profitability.

Another squeeze pattern has occurred in computing. The two pincers are Microsoft and Intel. Caught in the middle are the traditional PC manufacturers. In the decade following 1987, power flowed to the pincers, away from the OEMs. In 1997, the market value of the entire PC space was about $400 billion. Microsoft and Intel owned about 70 percent of it.

Companies who want to avoid the value chain squeeze have four choices. First, they can enter an adjacent value chain step(s) early in this pattern's evolution, before the trap sets in. Second, they can take steps to encourage new entrants into adjacent value chain steps, thus weakening their value chain neighbors (Intel has regularly weakened PC makers adjacent to it by creating subassemblies that new low-cost suppliers can use to enter the OEM market). A third option is to create a business design that exploits an opportunity more than one value chain step away. A fourth and final alternative is for a company to stand and fight, hoping that superior operations and/or product innovation skills will rescue it from structural danger. This option, while sometimes the most appealing, has low odds of success.

HOW TO PROFIT?

Improve your performance faster than your neighbors (suppliers and customers) do. Preempt or limit the strength of their position by encouraging new entrants.

Put yourself in the position of the executive vice president of a major television network in the year 2005. The Internet has matured dramatically, and broadband video brings shows into the living rooms of America, without your help. Viewers have high-definition television sets that can access 500 channels. They can watch whatever they want, whenever they want. Viewers and advertising dollars are flowing away from your network. Content increasingly jumps to Web sites and specialty cable stations founded by competitors, content originators, and individual media stars. Your position is caught in a squeeze between increasingly powerful viewers and content providers.

- What can you do to make your network relevant and stem the decline of advertising revenue streams?
- How can you transform your business design to convert this declining situation into a major opportunity?

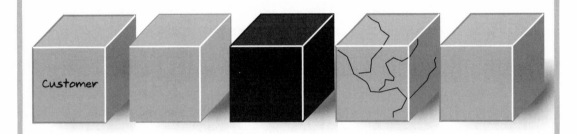

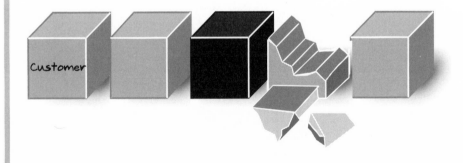

Strengthening the Weak Link

Upgrade poorly performing neighbors who block your ability to create value.

In the 1960s, McDonald's was striving to build a brand name that would be associated with absolutely consistent quality, but the food industry's supply base simply wasn't up to the task. McDonald's sought to build an empire on the predictability of perfect french fries; however, the wide variations in the processes used by American farmers compromised the quality of this key menu item. For McDonald's, that was a weak link in the value chain. The value it wanted to provide to consumers could not be delivered because of suppliers' unreliable performance. Similar issues arose with purveyors of other menu components: rolls and muffins, meat, and dairy products.

Sometimes, poor performance by a value chain neighbor limits a company's ability to increase its value to customers and to create value growth for itself. This growing dysfunctionality can trigger a new pattern: strengthening the weak link in the value chain. As this pattern plays out, smart value chain neighbors take action to improve the performance and quality of the overall system.

Over the past few decades, weak links have emerged in dozens of value chains. In extreme cases, they have triggered radical responses: stronger neighbors moved in to take control of the weak link. In less extreme cases, the response was more often a strengthening action: strong value chain neighbors shored up the weak link in response to competitive and economic pressures.

McDonald's was stymied by fragmentation and lack of storage standards in the potato industry, but it worked hard to fix the weak link by selecting the most competent and cooperative companies. It took years for McDonald's to teach its suppliers how to adhere to its system and understand its priorities and needs. Numerous techniques were involved, including consolidation of suppliers, training, consulting, and systems standardization.

McDonald's repeated this move in dramatic fashion when it decided to enter the Russian market. Ten years before it opened the landmark, three-story Moscow McDonald's, the company began creating a Russian beef and potato industry that could deliver on its customer promise of quality and consistency.

In both cases, McDonald's transformed inefficiency into competitive advantage by fixing the weak link of the value chain *in an exclusive fashion.*

The "exclusive fashion" aspect of this move is just as important as the "fix." If, after years of investment, McDonald's newly improved suppliers were free to service Burger King and Wendy's (and they are not), then McDonald's would have created a new value chain competitor rather than a new source of competitive advantage.

Toyota ran into a weak-link problem in the 1960s, when it was developing its unique Toyota Production System. It recognized, early on, that it could never realize its ambitions for lean manufacturing unless it radically upgraded its supplier base. It took years to become fully operative, but Toyota initiated a program that produced the best-trained, highest-quality, highest-response suppliers in the auto industry.

Like McDonald's, Toyota used numerous techniques to improve its weak link. Supplier consolidation, volume shifting, training, equity positions, and information sharing all played roles. Toyota's objective was to turn a major liability into a significant asset. By the 1980s, it had succeeded.

Companies are not required to buy the weak link when they seek to strengthen it. Wal-Mart faced the weak-link predicament a decade ago, but addressed the issue by forming a strategic partnership.

Low prices from its suppliers weren't enough for Wal-Mart. To deliver the value it wanted to provide to its customers, it needed to establish new goals in its relationship with suppliers: alignment of objectives, coordination, and information sharing.

In 1987, the first tentative steps were taken by Wal-Mart and its single largest supplier, Procter & Gamble (P&G). It took years for the new relationship to mature and produce the outcomes Wal-Mart needed, but the ultimate results were extraordinary for both sides. Wal-Mart realized fewer stockouts, higher inventory turns, and more informed product planning decisions by P&G.

The relationship also radically changed the economics at P&G. There were substantially higher inventory turns, fewer returns, reduced shrinkage, and a modernized production and distribution system.

That experience provided a template of competitive advantage that both the consumer goods and retail industries are trying to match. Companies that wanted to do business with Wal-Mart had to change their business models by implementing advanced systems improvements, electronic data interchange, and just-in-time delivery. The results were stronger and more efficient suppliers, and a repaired weak link for Wal-Mart.

Weak links can migrate from one part of the value chain to another very quickly. The strength in the PC value chain in the mid 1980s was IBM; the weak link was Intel. IBM decided to invest in Intel (it bought 19 percent of the company's stock) and to provide it with extensive technical support. This move was in IBM's own interest because it needed an aggressive, low-cost chip producer to meet its own strategic and financial objectives. (IBM later sold its entire position in Intel. That stake would have been worth $30 billion today, or 30 percent of IBM's value.)

Over a few years, the weak link in the value chain shifted forward—away from Intel and toward IBM and other OEM players. The OEMs were not improving the performance of their products rapidly enough to create the growth rate required by Intel's business design. Intel responded by expanding its activities to produce chipsets and motherboards. By doing so, it reduced the barriers to entry into the OEM part of the value chain, and attracted new, more aggressive players into the business.

When weak links remain damaged, they prolong dysfunctionality, block change, and create risk for their neighbors and opportunities for newcomers. The automotive industry is a classic example. Car dealers who fail to provide consistent customer service and a satisfactory shopping experience are the weak links. This problem continues to plague the manufacturers and creates opportunities for newcomers like CarMax and AutoNation, which are working hard to displace traditional dealers as the major automotive sales channel.

HOW TO PROFIT?

Fix the weak link in exclusive fashion. Tie its success to the success of *your* business design.

Think of your own situation:

- Are your attempts to create value undermined by a weak link in the value chain? Is your weak link your customers, your suppliers, or both?

- How can you address this weakness? What approaches carry the highest value and the lowest risk?

- Can you so significantly strengthen the link that it creates a breakthrough position for your company?

"When you see a good move,
search for a better one."

- Chess Maxim

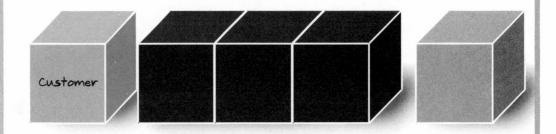

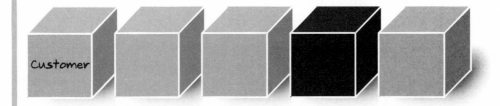

Reintegration

Reintegrate the chain to capture the profit in the system.

Over extended periods of time, small, incremental changes in economics, technology, customer relevance, investment levels, and competitive performance can lead to enormous variations in profitability along the value chain. A value chain with ten to fifteen major steps may yield variations in profit margin from 2 percent to 20 percent. Variations in return on capital tend to be even higher.

As this profit variation increases, the relative importance of different parts of the chain changes; the behavior of some customer groups becomes more important in driving the behavior of the entire system. The priorities of a lead customer group become important drivers of the future success of the other players. The key challenge for value creators requires putting an economic microscope to every part of the value chain as they search for shifting profits *and* shifting sources of power.

When value shifts occur up and down the value chain, the challenge is to expand the scope of the business model to include activities that were once viewed as upstream or downstream from your own position.

In the pharmaceutical industry, a shift in the balance of power and in the strength of customer relationships along the value chain has triggered the reintegration pattern.

Merck was the first pharmaceutical manufacturer to recognize this emerging pattern and exploit its opportunities. As Roy Vagelos, Merck's CEO, searched the value chain for new vulnerabilities and opportunities, he came to a decision that, at the time, shocked the pharmaceutical industry. Merck acquired Medco, a pharmacy benefits management (PBM) company that served employers and organized buyers. Merck's business design was transformed from drug developer/manufacturer to broader value chain manager.

It was a critical decision for Merck. The company recognized that even though it was still generating significant profits in its traditional business design, managed care was altering the dynamics of the health care industry. Changes under way in the industry had the potential to shift power away from manufacturers and toward large, organized buyers. Physicians and hospitals were yielding power to health maintenance organizations (HMOs) and managed care agencies, and there was a significant shift in drug purchasing practices. Increasingly, HMOs were negotiating large-scale contracts with PBMs to outsource the administration of prescription drugs for their clients. Merck, recognizing that the customer was changing, acquired Medco as part of its strategy to rebalance the power equation. This was part of a broader strategy to move downstream and get as close as possible to the customer, whether that customer was the physician, the group practice, the clinic, the hospital, the buying cooperative, or the managed care organization.

In the 1980s, Fresenius, a German medical equipment distribution company, faced a challenge that also triggered the reintegration pattern. The environment for medical equipment and pharmaceutical products was changing; the new area of competition was in distribution. Early in the decade, most medical equipment vendors had decided to drop Fresenius as a distributor, forcing the company to step back and take a broader look at the value chain.

As it searched for appropriate responses, Fresenius leveraged its own line of proprietary dialysis products and decided to move downstream. It began offering management services to dialysis centers. Today, the company develops its own dialysis and pharmaceutical products and technology, and distributes them to hospitals, dialysis centers, and homes. It has built, and currently owns and manages dialysis centers as well as other facilities. Increasing regulation of the German health care market stimulated the company to investigate other potential market opportunities for its highly profitable business design. Now it operates facilities in over twenty countries.

This transformation has carried Fresenius far downstream along the value chain. It has created a Product and Services group that builds hospital dialysis centers around the world, stocks them with Fresenius equipment, trains the local staff, and uses its own personnel to manage the facilities. Having found a way to reintegrate several previously distinct parts of the value chain, Fresenius is applying this same model to its transfusion business.

Another effective reintegrator is The Gap, today's leading retailer of casual clothing.

In 1969, The Gap was a single store selling only blue jeans. Over three decades, The Gap built a remarkably successful business as the leading casual specialty apparel retailer. It now has more than 2,000 stores offering attractive styles and quality clothing carried into the market under four formats: Gap (midrange), Gap Kids/Baby Gap (kids), Banana Republic (luxury), and Old Navy (value).

The Gap's rapid growth over the past decade was built on the development of a strong brand, but a key element in its strategy has been successful reintegration of the value chain. Building on its roots as a traditional retailer—buying apparel from suppliers and outside manufacturers—The Gap has vertically integrated its operations (though it still outsources the actual manufacturing). It now designs its own clothing line each year. Its in-house design team travels throughout Europe to collect fashion trends and interpret them for Gap customers.

LVMH, the French luxury goods manufacturer, has also moved to extend its activity to a neighboring part of the value chain. As a designer and manufacturer of luxury goods, LVMH always received high marks for its exclusively branded products. But because it wasn't playing much of a role in the direct relationship with the customer, it could not always control how its products were perceived or positioned against its competitors.

LVMH anticipated a shift in relative importance from product manufacturing to retail outlets, and responded by moving downstream to reintegrate the value chain. First, it accelerated its rollout of exclusive retail shops. It took more control of the relationship with customers by opening boutiques that showcased its many labels (Louis Vuitton, Christian Dior, Givenchy, Lacroix, Kenzo, Celine, Loewe, Guerlain, Fred). Then it purchased a collection of top outlets to significantly expand its role in distribution (Duty Free Shops, Sephora, Franck et Fils). Besides selling LVMH products, these outlets offer other luxury items that respond to the needs of LVMH's key customer groups. LVMH has taken advantage of the reintegration pattern to achieve sales increases of 20 percent each year for the past five years.

The reintegration pattern also surfaced in the complex world of soft drinks. In the 1970s, the value chain of the soft drinks industry included container makers (cans and bottles), syrup makers (Coke, Pepsi, 7-Up, Royal Crown, Dr. Pepper, Schweppes), and bottlers. Sometimes, the interests of these various players were closely aligned. Frequently, however, they were at odds with one another, which created dysfunctionality and inefficiency throughout the value chain.

During the 1980s, Roberto Goizueta, Coca-Cola's CEO, changed his company's business design and began to rebuild participation in and control of the value chain. But Goizueta didn't use a traditional reintegration effort. Coke didn't set out to own all of the assets in the system; in fact, it preferred not to. But it did want the entire system to be tuned toward achieving maximum availability, maximum price realization, lowest possible asset intensity, and lowest possible cost.

Coke is still working on the process, but, within the past decade, it has moved from managing 20 percent of the value chain (syrup and advertising) to managing 80 percent (from raw materials to distribution).

The reintegration pattern continues to spread to other industries, especially to asset-intensive manufacturing sectors. Manufacturers are increasingly facing situations where a partial reintegration of the value chain is necessary if they are to earn an acceptable return on their investments. As value migrates from one value chain link to another, players are being forced to reintegrate in order to maintain strategic control. This pattern is seen in industries as diverse as furniture and oil refining.

Ethan Allen, the furniture manufacturer, began rapidly expanding its retailing activity at the beginning of the 1990s. Today, it has 66 owned stores (representing 32 percent of its revenue). The company has achieved revenue growth that is twice as high as the average in its industry, and shareholder value growth of 35 percent per year (from 1993 to 1997).

Tosco, an oil refinery, saw that the profits in its industry happened downstream from its own position, and moved to capture them. In a series of acquisitions that began in 1993, the company grew its retailing position, focusing on the addition of convenience stores (the high-profit zone in the industry) to the basic gas station format. Exploiting the reintegration pattern enabled Tosco to grow shareholder value by 58 percent per year from 1993 to 1997.

Profiting from the reintegration pattern is not easy. Unocal provides a cautionary contrast to Tosco's success. Both companies attempted to exploit the reintegration pattern. Tosco executed well, and focused intensely on the high-profit zones. Unocal's strategy and execution fell short. Tosco succeeded; Unocal ultimately sold its retail assets and brand to Tosco.

Ironically, reintegration is beginning to happen in the world of computers, an industry that has just spent twenty years deintegrating. Both Microsoft and Intel triggered and profited from deintegration. Now they are both working diligently to move in the opposite direction, *toward* a reintegration of the chain.

Through its Architecture Labs, Intel is fostering a variety of initiatives that will further redefine and expand its participation in the overall system. And Microsoft has started to move downstream, closer and closer to the end user/customer. Microsoft's traditional customers were companies that put its software into their computers as part of the manufacturing process, and applications developers who could write programs that worked with Microsoft's operating system. Now, Microsoft has moved into content and transaction services, and is creating increasing levels of direct contact with the end user.

HOW TO PROFIT?

Reintegrate those parts of the value chain that matter because of profitability, customer information, or strategic control. Don't acquire unless you have to. Use contracts, relationships, or minority ownership instead.

- What conditions and triggers lead to reintegration? What opportunities for reintegration are available in my industry?
- Do I need to reintegrate to create or protect profit growth?
- What position in the value chain has the highest potential for profit growth and strategic control?
- What moves must I make to create a more valuable business design through partial or complete reintegration?
- How can I reduce the risks involved in making those moves?

REINTEGRATE THE CUSTOMER

In the past, value chain reintegration has been *backward* in nature. As a company grew in size, make vs. buy analysis often showed that it was more profitable to "make" than "buy." Reintegration naturally followed. Suppliers were acquired or supplanted. Profits rose. So did asset intensity.

Today, companies who think about strategic reintegration have turned their gaze 180° around. They are now looking *forward* in the value chain—all the way to the customer. That's because tomorrow's strategic bottleneck is less and less about product supply. It is increasingly about access to (and information about) profitable customers and profitable customer purchase occasions.

There are many compelling reasons for reintegrating the customer into your company's business design. Consider some examples already discussed in this pattern:

- Coca-Cola bought its customers to strengthen their value chain performance and to gain access to highly profitable vending machine purchase occasions
- AutoNation forward integrated to exploit a new insight about retailing automobiles— it is the best occasion to sell consumers high profit financing, insurance, and mainte- nance services
- Fresenius became vital to its hospital customers' economics by adding outsourced pa- tient care clinics to its intravenous drug line. Forward integrating into services also en- abled Fresenius to "pull through" its high-profit products as well
- Ethan Allen moved from furniture manufacturer to furniture retailer in order to control its moment-of-purchase presentation to the customer

We must add two more to this list of strategic motivations: "Internet" and "e-commerce."

How many reasons might your company have for more tightly integrating the end cus- tomer into its business? The idea deserves serious consideration, free from the objection that "We haven't traditionally played in that part of the value chain."

For if in the future you capture the customer relationship, you will likely be able to source the products required to meet their needs. But if in the future you own just the prod- uct, it is not yet clear that you will be able to reach the most profitable customers that you most want to serve.

More precisely, it is not clear that you will be able to wrest the customer away from competitors who have integrated the customer more closely into their business designs.

THE GREAT VALUE CHAIN SPLIT

Those who have read the value chain patterns closely will notice a trend cutting across many of the patterns. Companies at the forefront of deintegration are jettisoning steps *backward* in the value chain; companies pioneering in reintegration are adding steps *forward*. New start-ups are equally split between those who specialize *far back* in the value chain and those who specialize *far forward*. What's going on?

We are witnessing a division of economic activities along a new fault line: the *management of intangibles* versus the *management of physical assets.* Today, most companies manage both. Tomorrow, most companies will specialize in one or the other. The two resulting clusters of value chain activities that companies will choose to perform—the *intangibles cluster* and the *asset cluster*—will define "The Great Value Chain Split."

Many companies are focusing for the first time on Return on Capital Employed (ROCE) in order to think and act as investors would want. These companies each own a mixture of knowledge-based intangibles plus brick-and-mortar assets. As each company analyzes its Return on Capital Employed in every step in the value chain, it comes to the same conclusion: the ROCE of knowledge-based intangibles is much higher than the ROCE of physical assets. The company's current stock price is a muddled average of the two.

Companies who are dedicated to shareholder value will do the obvious. They will deintegrate via outsourcing those asset-intensive activities that are not core to the business. In addition, they will recognize the increasing value of customer information, the newest knowledge-based intangible, and will reintegrate forward to obtain it.

The result is a company whose value chain scope is the "intangibles cluster," composed of activities such as: product research and development, product design, product-related software, pilot factories, customer behavior/forecast data, brand management, customer purchase data, or product/service data.

Companies who lose the fight for knowledge-based leadership might have to involuntarily drop back in the value chain, but few other firms in existence today would choose to specialize in assets of their free will. It would be value destructive.

"In existence today" is the key phrase here. The Great Value Chain Split is likely to create entrepreneurial opportunities for new types of companies who are devoted to manufacturing and nothing else. Look for many more to come, and imagine the day when publicly held, multi-industry manufacturing conglomerates play a significant role in the global business community.

On which side of the split will your company land? Will it choose or be forced to a side through the initiative of competitors who are focused on intangibles management?

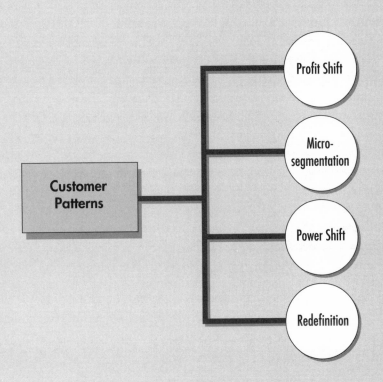

CHAPTER 6
CUSTOMER PATTERNS

CUSTOMERS ARE THE ULTIMATE arbiters of value. Every day, they vote with their time, with their word of mouth, with their dollars, and with their allegiance, for the business designs that best serve their evolving priorities. The results of their constantly shifting decisions are value creation and value destruction. Customers determine profits.

The patterns of customer-driven profit shifts are just beginning to be understood clearly. Across a variety of industries, the behavior of the customer base is changing in similar, repeatable ways. These changes have triggered numerous patterns and will continue to transform the strategic landscape in nearly every business. The opportunities (and losses) that have resulted are also beginning to repeat themselves. Customers hold more of the power in the supplier-customer equation, and they possess the information (at times unwittingly) as to what will be valuable tomorrow.

Ignorance of the complexities of customer behavior is the single greatest strategic risk facing businesses today. Indeed, changes in customer priorities, variations among customer preferences or wealth, and dysfunctionalities in customer "experience" with a product or service are perhaps the most important triggers of new patterns in every industry. As a result, customer patterns have the potential to be the most powerful and fundamental patterns of all. The customer patterns profiled here are a small subset of the customer patterns that will be characterized in the next three to five years.

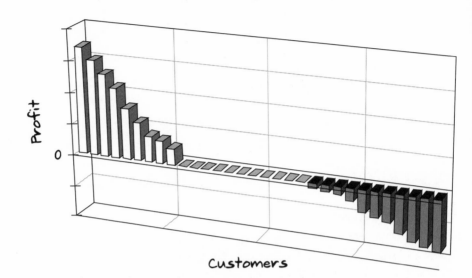

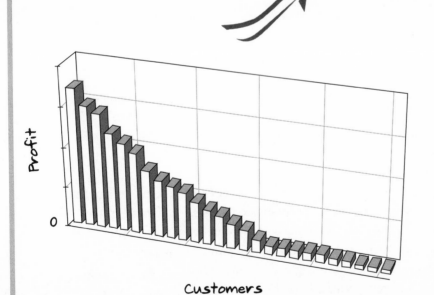

Profit Shift

All customers were profitable. Now, most aren't.

A generation ago, there was no great mystery to profitability. A seller offered a product, and a customer bought it. If the selling price was greater than the seller's cost to serve that customer, the transaction was profitable.

In today's environment, that traditional mindset constitutes very dangerous thinking. In many markets, not all customers are profitable. An intense examination of true pricing and the true costs of serving customers may reveal that a company is actually losing money on many customer accounts. In such a case, the company would be better off if it proactively channeled those customers to a competitor.

The shift from "all customers are profitable" to "many are not" has been triggered by declining gross margins and increasing variability in the cost to serve customers. Suppliers will be rewarded for being much more rigorous in (1) measuring current and potential profit customer by customer, (2) selecting the promising customers, and (3) choosing *how much* to invest in those customers.

In mutual funds, changing customer demographics and increasing variation in customer wealth have affected the profit shift pattern. In the past, the market was dominated by wealthy investors, nearly all of whom were profitable to asset management firms because their lifetime value was extremely high. Today, the market has broadened to include a wide variety of new customers. In particular, middle-class individual investors flooded the market during the bull run of the late 1990s (see the Redefinition section, later in this chapter).

Many of these new customers absorb a great deal of attention and service, invest relatively small amounts, and will not significantly increase their deposits in the future. Moreover, because their asset base is far smaller than that of wealthier customers, these new customers do not generate sufficient management fees (based on percentage of invested assets) to make them profitable to serve. As a result, many mutual fund companies' profit margins have declined, even as their assets under management have increased exponentially.

When the profit shift pattern occurs, the arithmetic of customer profitability can become quite dramatic. For Kanthal, a Swedish electrical equipment company, 40 percent of its customer base generated 150 percent of the firm's profit. Another 20 percent of the customers broke even. The last 40 percent generated losses equaling 50 percent of the firm's profitability.

WHY DOES THE PROFIT SHIFT HAPPEN?

Gross margins decline...

50%

Gross
Margin

0%

Time

...and cost to serve variability goes up

In banking, the arithmetic is almost as dramatic. For some banks, 30 percent of the customer base generates 130 percent of the profit. Another 30 percent breaks even. The bottom 40 percent generates losses equal to 30 percent of the bank's operating profit.

Several banks have recognized this profit shift and are exploiting it to their advantage. They have taken early, tentative steps to discourage unprofitable customers whom they may have acquired in their "market-share-driven" quest to grow their customer base. Early in the marketing activity chain, some banks now use software systems to sort and analyze customer data; in effect, they perform profitability analyses on customers' accounts. This methodology integrates advances in technology and information management systems into the marketing function. Based on the data generated through these systems, banks have developed product packages that charge unprofitable customers for services ranging from savings accounts to check writing. There are two results for unprofitable customers: (1) they are charged for allowing their accounts to fall below certain balances, and (2) they are tacitly "encouraged" to take their banking business elsewhere. For a given account, unprofitability may be a passing problem. To motivate customers to increase their profitability, banks provide tiered programs that feature incentives (for example, lower fees and greater number of 'free' ATM transactions) for higher balances.

The customer profit shift pattern is proliferating rapidly. It is working its way into industries as diverse as chemicals, consumer goods, telecommunications, paper, utilities, and automobiles, among others. However, it is often slow to develop and always hard to recognize. For example, one printing company was shocked to learn that fully 60 percent of its customers were unprofitable. Why the surprise? Because the profit shift pattern does not occur suddenly. Shifting customer behavior and increasing variability of the customer base (or changing industry economics) alter the profitability landscape gradually. For the printer, myths from the past regarding customer profitability reigned until someone stopped to look. The reality was immediately evident.

A steady decline in margins is a key symptom of this pattern. Think of these situations as receding tides that expose the shoals beneath the water's surface. As overall margins decline, certain unprofitable customers are exposed. There was once enough margin to cover the full cost of services for *all* customers. Now, many customers generate costs far in excess of the revenues they provide.

Unmanaged customer behavior tends to drive *variations* in service costs. When customers can receive a differential service without being charged for it, they will ask for it. Bit by bit, the profit on the account evaporates.

Customer profitability is a relative concept. When a firm's capacity utilization is low, even a "bad" customer is valued because the incremental volume helps to cover fixed costs—in the short term. For the long term, however, the fundamental issue remains: either replace the "bad" customers with good ones, or reduce capacity—or do both.

Many companies never escape the short-term perspective. They become caught in the painful trap of a perpetual catch-22: short-term decisions (keep the unprofitable customer) lead to long-term financial mediocrity (profit is eroded by subsidies to the firm's population of unprofitable accounts).

The key to reversing this downward spiral into unprofitability is an ability to continuously resegment the customer base and to analyze each customer's true profitability. A customer profitability system can reverse the process and enable a company to exploit profit shifts to its advantage. By developing an accurate and dynamic model of how profitability varies at the individual customer level, a company can select and develop strategic customers who yield the greatest long-term value. It is also a tool for managing unprofitable customers. As terms and conditions are changed, as pricing levels are adjusted, and as investment is reallocated, a company's ability to manage earnings increases. The pattern reversal happens incrementally as well. At the margin, unprofitable customers are shifted, and quarterly earnings per share get a lift.

Rate your customers by their profitability (adjusted for stage of development, future profit growth potential, and so on) every six to twelve months. Take action that allows the bottom decile to become profitable (changed terms and conditions, different pricing, different service levels). If they become profitable—great. If not, continue changing terms until they are encouraged to defect to your competitors. Otherwise, you will be asking good customers to continue subsidizing your bad ones—an outcome neither group deserves.

HOW TO PROFIT?

Invest the time and effort to build a customer profitability system. Update it quarterly. Change pricing, service levels, and investment levels accordingly.

- What factors (behavior, demographics, economics, product line characteristics) determine customer profitability and trigger profit shifts in our industry?
- Does my organization understand the model of customer profitability in our business?
- What tactics will enable my organization to secure and develop the most profitable customer relationships?
- How can we change break-even/unprofitable accounts to profitable ones through changes in terms and conditions, investment levels, or other dimensions of the relationship? If we fail to do so, how can we channel existing unprofitable customers to our competitors?
- With our new understanding of the model of customer profitability in our business, how can we acquire the right *next* set of profitable customers?

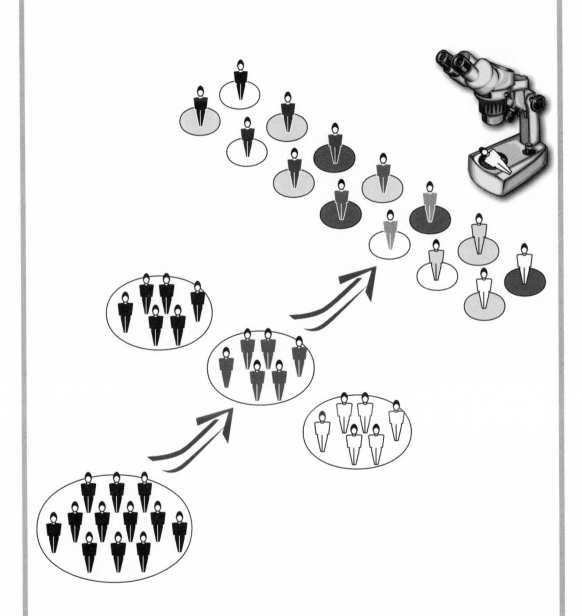

Microsegmentation

From same, to different, to unique.

As an industry matures, growing customer heterogeneity and increasing customer sophistication change the fundamental nature of the market. Early in an industry's evolution, most customers are well served by a standard product. As these customers become more familiar with the product and apply it to different needs, their requirements begin to move in many different directions. Suppliers may then begin to modify the product to better serve different customer groups.

One outcome of good segmentation is a larger market. Customers will pay more for a product or service that is well suited to their needs. In this new environment, the company that segments best, that delivers a message that best addresses customers' needs, wins.

We are now witnessing the emergence of a new customer pattern—microsegmentation. As suppliers identify even more characteristics that distinguish the preferences and needs of different customer groups, customers move from being served in segments to being served in microsegments—segments that may be as small as a single customer. This opportunity is triggered by the increasing variability in the customer base and by changes in technology that support highly targeted marketing, offer development, communication, and service.

The insurance industry illustrates the evolution of the microsegmentation pattern. In the past, its major players depended on a one-size-fits-all offering. Over time, customers' needs changed and became more particularized. More often than not, this increasing variation created a mismatch between customer priorities and existing product offerings, which were tailored to the "average" customer. Eventually, some insurance companies realized that, by segmenting insurance buyers, they could create specific options and thereby create and capture more value from specific customer groups. Different premiums were charged depending on age, sex, income level, or a number of other variables.

With time, customer segments evolved into microsegments. Today, companies can be even more precise in servicing and managing very specific customer types. USAA was one of the first insurance companies to anticipate the growing variation of customer types, and it has exploited the microsegmentation pattern accordingly. Rather than target all customers with plain vanilla offerings, USAA taps only certain microsegments with highly tailored offerings. By closely matching offers to customers' priorities, it gains revenues, reduces costs, creates allegiance, and realizes significant profit growth.

Awareness of a microsegmentation pattern allows managers to anticipate, search for, and take advantage of *emerging* microsegments. By focusing resources and innovation on the most profitable microsegments within their industry, suppliers can create significant value growth for their companies.

One of the most powerful examples of microsegmentation comes from Levi Strauss. In 1994, the company initiated its Personal Pair program, to serve women who were frustrated by the hassles associated with the conventional jeans-buying process (the need to try on fifteen to twenty pairs before finding a pair that fit). The company learned that women would be willing to pay a premium and wait a few weeks to get a pair of jeans that fit properly. By 1997, Personal Pair accounted for 25 percent of Levi's women's jeans sales at Original Levis stores.

In 1998, Levi's replaced its Personal Pair program with Original Spin, a program that builds off the Personal Pair program and includes men's jeans as well. With a sales associate, customers select features like color, model, and even a name. These feature choices, along with the customer's waist, hip, and inseam measurements, are entered into a Web-based terminal linked to the stitching machines in a Levi's factory. When the jeans arrive at the sales center two to three weeks later, a bar-code tag is attached to the lining. To reorder jeans that duplicate the same measurements, the bar-code is scanned.

Levi's programs have multiplied the choices for any given customer. The brick-and-mortar stores carry about 130 ready-to-wear pairs of jeans for any given waist and inseam. With Personal Pair, that number increased to 430 choices; with Original Spin it will increase to 750 choices. Many retailers have taken notice of Levi's program and are waiting to assess its long-term viability. But a future can be imagined in which stores do not sell apparel (clothes are ordered custom-made from the manufacturer), but act as "clothing advisers," displaying the newest styles and trends.

Three important market conditions must exist before the microsegmentation pattern can succeed. First, there must be an increase in customer heterogeneity. Second, customer sophistication must escalate; as customers' expectations for greater functionality or personalization of a product or service increase, they will demand more offerings and more choices. When these two conditions are present, a third market condition—technological change through systems infrastructure—will allow a company to service multiple segments efficiently.

The technology is already at hand to allow companies to take advantage of the third market condition. The Internet and advanced database technology, particularly with the targeting capabilities of intelligent agents, represent tremendous potential for all companies.

The challenge lies in detecting the first two factors, in being aware of the emerging microsegment and its needs. As similar opportunities become more apparent, there will be a rapid proliferation of this pattern, and a major new source of profit growth will develop for organizations that are geared to respond to it.

HOW TO PROFIT?

Cut the deck finer and finer. Identify the most profitable "slivers," and offer them perfectly tailor-made options.
Then build a fence around them, so that your competitors find them prohibitively expensive to acquire.

- Is the microsegmentation pattern occurring in my industry, or are the needs and preferences of customers still fairly uniform?
- What are the early signals that the pattern is about to start?
- If the pattern is occurring, or is about to, is my organization equipped with the mindset and the technology to exploit it?

Power Shift

The upper hand shifts back and forth.

There is always a level of tension between customers and suppliers. The distribution of power between sellers and buyers influences every negotiation or transaction, and profoundly influences the allocation of profits and value. Where customers are powerful, they capture the value in the form of lower prices and/or higher utility. Suppliers are left with little value to show for their efforts. Conversely, when suppliers are powerful, customers have little choice but to pay premium prices that create large profits for suppliers.

Significant power imbalances can translate quickly along the value chain. Plastic bottle makers selling to companies like Coca-Cola and PepsiCo have been able to successfully leverage information about the plastics manufacturers who supply their raw materials. The bottle makers have developed near-perfect information on the economics of the plastics manufacturers. This information allows them to exert significant pricing pressure on plastics manufacturers and to restrict manufacturer returns.

Several factors can trigger the power shift pattern: customer consolidation; the formation of professional purchasing groups that bring tremendous expertise to the purchasing process; an overabundance of information on suppliers' costs and performance; and suppliers' lack of differentiation in either the products offered or the business models used to serve customers.

The pharmaceutical industry of the 1990s presents an example of the power shift pattern. Pharmaceutical companies held most of the power in the 1970s and 1980s. They sold unique, patented products that had few substitutes. On the other side of the equation, the customers (individuals, insurers, and the corporations that paid for medical benefits) were an unstructured and fragmented group. Moreover, the real "purchase" decision came from an even more fragmented customer base: physicians. The pharmaceutical companies earned outstanding profits because they held most of the power in the system.

The formation and growth of managed care organizations in the 1990s began to alter the distribution of power. Suddenly, the customer base began to concentrate. As more and more members of a previously diffuse customer group were joined under the umbrella of managed care, pharmaceutical companies were no longer dealing with individual physicians; they now had to negotiate with fewer, larger, and more powerful customers: HMOs, buying groups, or other managed care organizations. In the process, the pharmaceutical companies began to lose the pricing freedom that had translated into huge profits for so many years. Bigger buyers demanded larger discounts.

The rise of managed care transformed the power structure, and pharmaceutical companies were forced to respond. The industry as a whole has responded brilliantly to the power shift. Because of the new concentration of the customer base, many companies have completely rethought their go-to-market structures. They have worked hard to win advantaged positions with the big accounts. In some cases, they have made even more dramatic moves. Merck's purchase of Medco Containment Systems, a pharmacy benefits management company, reflected Merck's recognition that it needed to have a more powerful supply position within the value chain. (Other pharmaceutical companies have followed suit, with much less success.)

In addition, the pharmaceutical companies have focused intensely on increasing their rate of innovation. They have not only invested more aggressively in internal R&D, but have intensified their licensing activity to acquire new compounds from third-party companies. They have also begun to consolidate, partly to improve the economics of development and distribution, and partly to counterbalance the power created by the newly consolidated customers.

The result? Much stronger products and a much stronger pipeline for many of the major pharmaceutical players. The rapid growth in profitable new products more than offset the profit erosion triggered by buyers' increased bargaining power.

The fast moving consumer goods industry represents an ongoing power shift that looks like two children on a seesaw. First, one has the upper hand, then the other, then back again. In the post-World War Two economic landscape, manufacturers held the upper hand.

Demand grew more rapidly than supply, retailers were fragmented, customers treated brands with great respect.

But manufacturers across a broad spectrum of industries, from clothing to home improvement supplies to toys, have experienced a dramatic shift of power away from themselves and toward superstores such as Wal-Mart, Toys "R" Us, and Home Depot. Using their position as leading sales channels, these superstores have pressured suppliers to significantly reduce their prices over the past ten to fifteen years. In the process, they have cut their suppliers' margins in half. The superstores have also pressured suppliers to follow product development and production schedules that are more in line with their sales requirements than with optimal manufacturer economics.

In the past decade, there has been a sustained shift of power from suppliers to customers. Left unmanaged, this shift will drain profits from sellers and will distort the fundamental nature of the supplier–customer relationship.

Leading manufacturers have tried to respond via globalization, via reductions in manufacturing and advertising costs, and by utilizing tools like category management to improve their value to retailers. To avoid retailer pressure, some have gone into branded retailing. Others are investing heavily in direct consumer sales through catalogs and the Internet. The most successful have stabilized their margins and, with some accounts, regained an upper hand.

The struggle between the two sides in a power equation plays out in every market every day. Each change in business design, each economic change, each change in the flow of information can tip the balance of power and reverse the flow of profits and value. Companies that anticipate and respond quickly to these power shifts will have much better success as they meet the constant challenge of protecting their profitability.

HOW TO PROFIT?

Rebalance the power equation. If that move is
impossible, redefine the customer.

- What market conditions determine and alter power relationships in my industry?
- What change could trigger a disproportionate power shift from customers to suppliers (or vice versa) in my industry?
- What is the distribution of power between my organization and my customers?
- How has it shifted in the past three years? How will it shift in the next three years?
- If the power shift works against my organization, what are my best options for rebalancing the power equation?

  –Innovate?

  –Move from product to solution?

  –Know the customer's system economics?

  –Redefine the customer?

REBALANCE THE POWER EQUATION

What can a company do if its key customers have gained the "upper hand?" Many firms respond with product innovation strategies, hoping that the next breakthrough idea travelling through R&D will return their lost power.

Unfortunately, more often than not, such approaches fail. It is a rare product that is so unique as to rebalance an industry-level power shift that has already occurred.

In contrast, a growing number of firms have rebalanced the customer power equation through more fundamental approaches. If product innovation is not enough for your company, consider the following business design moves:

- *Out-concentrate the customer.* If key customers are more consolidated than you, then consolidate back. While only a temporary solution that often masks a strategy deficit (and a looming no-profit zone), such consolidation can at times boost supplier power. Pharmaceutical companies, facing larger managed care buyers in the United States and more demanding government buyers in Europe, are merging to ensure that customers can't do without their portfolio.

  Power-oriented consolidation often creates segment-level leadership. Chemical companies, airlines, and cable companies are swapping as many of their weak and mismatched positions as antitrust law will allow, in order to strengthen their leadership in the chemical segments, airport hubs, and metropolitan areas where they have already chosen to focus.

- *Change the offer, change the customer.* When GE Plastics finds a purchasing department at a major customer that it cannot successfully budge, it has a "Plan B." GE gears up its Solutions Engineering Group to generate systems-wide cost savings ideas in plastics, lighting, and electrical systems. Then, armed with a new and expanded value proposition, Jack Welch goes on a CEO-to-CEO sales call. Purchasing is no longer the sole decision maker.

- *Leapfrog the customer.* Companies can vault past their customers via a strong end-user brand, direct channel initiatives, and innovative strategies to minimize their current customers' response.

  Levi's has worked hard to manage strong retail chains with its direct-channel personalized pants program. On the one hand, retailers hesitate to drop Levi's—consumers want to find the brand. Even more important, Levi's personalized pants program is designed to drive its store sales. Levi's has leapfrogged without retaliation. Time is now on its side.

  The world's six major music companies also craved to initiate a direct sales approach, but each feared being punished for being first. Then they developed their own leapfrog strategy—all piloting a direct sales effort at the same time. There is safety in numbers. Tower Records and Virgin Megastores are in a poor position to prevent such a simultaneous move.

- *Become the customer.* The most radical move of all is to buy your largest customer (or buy several and integrate). To generate value, make this move just before power starts shifting to customers, not after it has progressed. Merck bought the drug distributor Medco at the right time, and has joined rather than fought the rise in customer power.

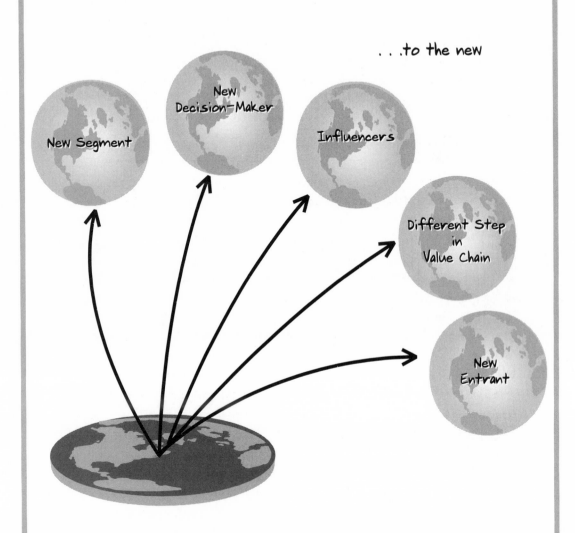

Redefinition

Who do you <u>want</u> your customer to be?

Sometimes, the only way out of a strategic cul-de-sac is to create a fundamental redefinition of the customer. Your company may be faced with an irreversible power shift to your buyers, or it may have reached a plateau in profit growth. Or, your industry may have run into a saturation problem in its customer base. You may not be serving your current customers well because another potential customer group stands in the way. When these strategic market conditions exist, the customer redefinition pattern is often triggered. Anticipating and exploiting it can create a new world of opportunity for sustained value growth.

Bang & Olufsen (B&O), a European consumer electronics manufacturer and retailer, hit one of those "profit growth" walls in the 1980s. Its traditional customers were knowledgeable audiophiles—people who knew all the ins and outs of their stereo systems and appreciated the sophisticated engineering and sleek look of B&O products. Its offerings were well matched to the priorities of this customer group, but B&O could not escape the plight of the entire consumer electronics industry—low (or no) profitability.

To counteract the deteriorating economic environment of consumer electronics, B&O had several strategic options: (1) adopt a low-cost model to compete with the rest of the mass electronics companies; (2) try to build a product pyramid to protect its high end (see the product to pyramid pattern in Chapter 8); or (3) make a major change in its business design by redefining its customer. It chose the third option.

Redefining the customer led to major changes for B&O. In the 1990s, it recognized the great potential in looking at the market through a different prism and selecting a very different customer group—one that has traditionally allowed suppliers healthy margins and high levels of sustained profitability. This customer group was the luxury-seeking segment. To achieve success with this group, engineering and product sophistication were still important. But the new driver, particularly in this redefined customer group, was elegance.

Instead of emphasizing technical quality and engineering brilliance, the company promoted its products as status symbols. That move was perfectly aligned with what was important to its redefined customer base. Brand-conscious consumers would be willing to pay more for luxury goods. The old business model had been aimed at people who thought of stereos as sophisticated pieces of highly technical equipment; the new model emphasized how the B&O product looked, and a B&O stereo's quiet, elegant message about its owner.

Redefinition paid off. B&O now commands a significant premium on its audio and video equipment, telephones, speakers, and ministereos. It has captured an important part of a major new market, even though some B&O products may cost four to five times more than competitor products. Exploiting the redefinition pattern has rebuilt B&O's shareholder value. Its ratio of stock market value to sales climbed from 0.2 in 1989 to 1.5 in 1997 (most consumer electronics companies hover in the 0.5 range).

The B&O strategy demonstrates the power of redefining the customer. These questions should be asked constantly by decision makers: What customer set is most important? What customer set is most valuable? What customer set is most underserved? What customer set can unlock a variety of new opportunities?

Like many reinventor companies, B&O was highly creative in asking these questions about its chosen segments. It is also important to ask these questions about new segments, and to apply the redefinition question more broadly. Redefinition can be achieved along a number of dimensions.

DIFFERENT SEGMENTS

B&O found profit growth by choosing new customers. Sometimes, the remedy is even simpler: look at the current customer base and rethink segment potentials. Professional sports teams have begun to do that in the past decade, as their customer base has become increasingly varied. Corporations have been buying tickets to sporting events for a long time. However, the sports industry did little to differentiate corporate customers from average fans. In fact, most of the industry focused on the image of "the average fan."

Corporations, neglected for years, have very different needs and very different motives for purchasing tickets. They want a forum for comfortable entertainment. The game is just one part—sometimes the backdrop—of that entertainment. The opportunity for sports enterprises to exploit this segment's priorities became apparent when corporations started to react enthusiastically to the opportunities to buy luxury seats and skyboxes. Today, corporate customers have become highly profitable, generating, for stadium and team owners, value many times greater than that generated by noncorporate ticket holders. The opportunity to benefit from a new emphasis on the corporate customer has become so irresistible that, in many cities, entire stadiums are being reconstructed to tap this brand-new source of profitability in a very old business.

DIFFERENT VALUE CHAIN PARTICIPANTS

The traditional customer may not be the most important customer in the system. DuPont went searching for advantage with Stainmaster, a product that helped to produce better carpets. DuPont realized that the strongest link in the value chain was at the end, with the consumer, so it developed programs focused on the end user. The magnetic pull of the end users ultimately influenced the decisions of the carpet manufacturers, who are the direct buyers of DuPont's fiber products.

By convincing end users that Stainmaster could deliver a much more attractive product, DuPont created demand at the end of the system. Instead of painstakingly trying to create Stainmaster converts all along the value chain, the company recognized the greater power in going through consumers to create demand pressure on the people who actually produced the end product.

Similarly, Intel redefined its customer by looking further along the value chain. It would have been natural for Intel to continue to view OEMs as the key customers. But Intel did not limit itself to the conventional view of who its customers were; instead, it worked to improve its position by defining/creating new customers. Intel's first step was to start making chipsets and motherboards. Intel was producing not just standalone chips, but the guts of computer systems. By ensuring high quality and dependability, the company was able to encourage new manufacturers to enter the game.

However, the redefinition didn't stop there. Intel correctly anticipated that its most important customers were the end users, not the PC manufacturers. In response, it altered its marketing and branding strategy to appeal to consumers rather than direct customers. "Intel Inside," a message to the broader marketplace, was intended to capture mindshare among the end users of computers. It carried the company far beyond the factories where computers are assembled. Intel's message went right into the homes and offices of the people who actually paid for computers at the end of the chain.

Coca-Cola's late CEO, Roberto Goizueta, made one of the most visionary moves in his company's long history by redefining bottlers as the key customers in the system. This was a radical change for a company that had spent most of its time and money focusing on the consumer. Goizueta's contribution was to act on the recognition that bottlers determined profits because they controlled how the product was actually placed in the market, and how much investment was made in fountain and vending sales—the high-profit zones in the business. Billions of dollars of value were created for Coke by shifting strategic emphasis to another, more important customer along the value chain.

INFLUENCERS

The most important customers are often not actually involved in the economic value chain of a product. Instead, they are advisers—sources of authority—who are key to success. The most obvious types of influencers are people who review and rate offerings for the benefit of the broader market. Reviewers, whether in creative markets such as movies and books, or in technical markets such as computers, are seen as profit gatekeepers. Walter Mossberg, the *Wall Street Journal* columnist who reviews and recommends technology products for users, has become one of the most important customers in the entire market. Technology companies assign priority responsibility to developing and maintaining relationships with major reviewers.

One of the best examples of the redefinition pattern is provided by Texas Instruments (TI) in its calculator business. TI has redefined the customer and is focusing on the teacher as the key actor in the system. TI has developed an array of programs for communicating with teachers, listening to their concerns and input, and making changes in response to their suggestions. This change in perspective has helped TI become the runaway leader in this field. The recommendations made by teachers to students and to buying groups have become the primary driver of TI's extraordinary success in this market.

Bayer, the German chemicals company, creatively focused on influencers in its battle to establish its brand Baygon as the premier insecticide in Europe against S.C. Johnson's worldwide leading brand, Raid. Rather than focus exclusively on the consumer, Bayer also marketed to the concierge (apartment manager) in urban European apartments. By creating a pro-Baygon voice of authority within apartment buildings that had products available for emergency situations, Bayer established Baygon's reputation as the most efficient product for tough bugs.

NEW DECISION MAKERS

Within a targeted customer set, redefining the decision makers can be the key to unlocking new profit. In industrial settings, this may mean moving from purchasing departments to senior management. GE has redefined its customers in this way and is able to capture superior profits based on its ability to solve senior managers' toughest problems. Or it can mean moving from the purchasing group to the users of the product. Parametric Technology Corporation rapidly penetrated the CAD/CAM market by focusing on the frustration of the user rather than the bidding specs of the purchasing group.

NEW ENTRANTS

Sometimes, the redefinition opportunity derives from the arrival of a new customer group.

Most industries have a stable set of customer groups whose needs and priorities will gradually shift over time. Corporations that remain customer-centric in their focus will be able to adapt their business designs to respond to these changes in customer priorities. In certain industries, however, following the current customer is not enough; radical shifts in value will be triggered by the introduction of completely new customer groups.

These groups emerge for many reasons—deregulation, dramatic changes in costs and prices, technological innovation, or a violent twist in the evolution of customer priorities. The new groups often have needs and priorities that are wholly different from those of the traditional customers in the market. For example, in the early 1980s, large numbers of previously "savings-oriented" consumers ventured out and became "investors." This flood of new customers created opportunities for investment companies that could capture their attention and serve their needs effectively enough to create sustained allegiance and positive word of mouth.

IBM's customer for the PC was a complete redefinition of the traditional mainframe CIO customer. This new end user completely drove the decentralized PC revolution.

The shift from old customers to new in the redefinition pattern is an opportunity that should be searched for regularly, across every strategic situation. Even the exploration of the possibility creates a new type of dialogue within a company.

HOW TO PROFIT?

Look beyond your current customer set. Search the broader system for the most important and the most profitable customers. Build your business design around them.

- What is your version of a Bang & Olufsen type of opportunity? How much value can you create by redefining your customers?

- How many of your competitors are redefining their customers and, by extension, their competitors?

- Will you face new competition as companies outside your industry redefine their customers to include your own most profitable accounts?

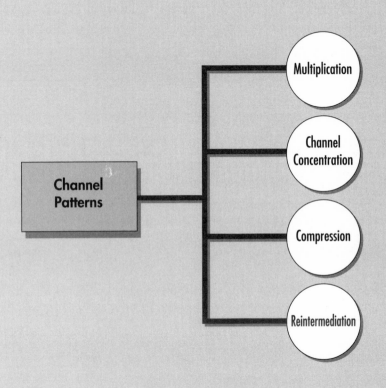

CHANNEL PATTERNS

A S POWER AND INFLUENCE shifted downstream, closer to customers, distribution channel players became more important. They had direct contact with buyers, and they could access current information on how customers' preferences were changing.

As new players created new, more specialized channels, and as traditional players expanded their repertoire to serve customers better, the available channels multiplied. The result was a rich profusion of new ways to bring products to customers.

But it was not all upside for the intermediaries. Those who added value through specialization (channel multiplication) or scale (channel concentration) grew and profited. Those whose relative value-add declined found themselves under increasing pressure. In many industries, the traditional channels underwent compression (fewer steps in the distribution process) and, ultimately, disintermediation.

No sooner had the compression process put suppliers and customers in direct contact than new creative players identified unmet needs, developed new sources of value-added, and interposed themselves between suppliers and customers in the reintermediation pattern. Their new approaches provided benefit to sellers, new value to customers, and significant profit growth opportunities for themselves.

Channels have seen their power rise, fall, and rise again. The turbulence characterizing this arena will continue into the next half-decade, accelerating the rate at which channel patterns play out, and stimulating the emergence of completely new types of channel patterns.

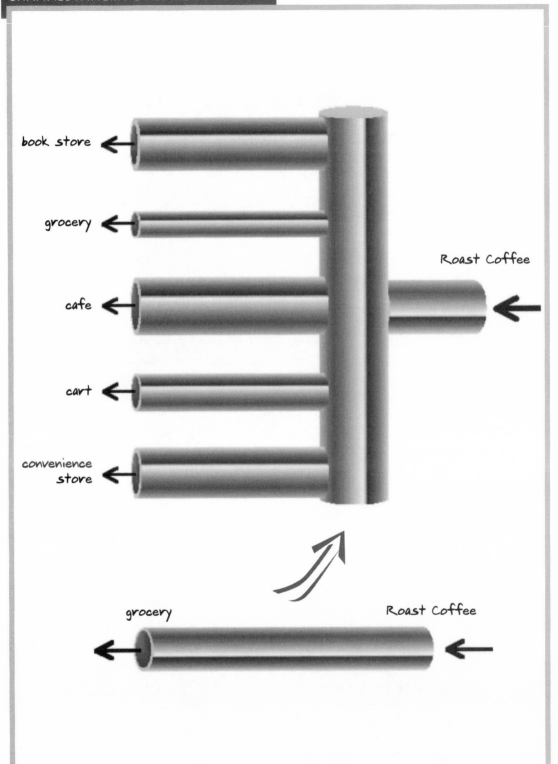

Multiplication

From few to many.

Where did you buy coffee a decade ago? Had the thought of an *espresso macchiato, cafe americano,* or *frappucino* ever entered your mind, let alone become a frequent menu item? People used to buy packaged coffee in a grocery store, or order a cup as a standard beverage in a restaurant. Today, in any big city and in many small towns, you can't walk more than a block without finding an opportunity to buy an upscale cup of coffee, a pound of arabica beans, and, at the very least, a little espresso maker to bring a touch of the European café to your very own kitchen. The former "cup of coffee" has grown into long lists of choices at kiosks, coffee shops, coffee carts, Starbucks, and restaurants.

To buy a book a decade ago, you went to a bookstore. You might have made a trip to a mall to get the latest thriller, or bestseller, or "how to" book. Today, you can purchase a book through a book club, at an airport, in a supermarket, at a newsstand, in a greeting card shop, by phone or mail, or on the Internet. The number of channels through which books are available has multiplied dramatically.

The sales world used to have a few major channels: a direct sales force, an industrial distributor, a department store, a mass merchandiser, a mom-and-pop retailer. Today, channels continue to proliferate. That multiplication didn't occur by accident or at random.

A variety of market conditions can trigger the channel multiplication pattern.

The first market condition is multiplication of customer types. In the past, most customers were comfortable purchasing products through one or two standard channels. Today, customers want to buy in different ways. They look for more buying options; they have become far more varied in their needs and preferences.

Customers who were once willing to compromise for general functionality have become much more sophisticated in ordering a particular service or product. They have very specific demands as to when they need the product and how they like to buy it. Their changing demands and priorities are revealed in dissatisfaction with existing offerings, creating an opportunity for new channels.

Significant technological change is another trigger. A sophisticated voice-mail system, or a spot on a home shopping cable channel, can now take the place of hundreds of sales representatives. The rapid evolution of the Internet has created a new channel for transactions and distribution here and abroad. Customers can purchase books, airplane tickets, clothes, cars, computers, and even large appliances, by accessing Web sites on the Internet.

Deteriorating economics due to channel dysfunctionality also encourages the multiplication pattern. If a channel is poorly matched to how the customer wants to buy, it creates inefficiencies, has high costs, and results in low profitability. A channel very closely matched to how customers want to buy can be phenomenally asset-efficient and highly profitable. Think of Dell, or Amazon.com, or CarMax. Each of these companies has designed ways to sell that are very accurately matched to current customer needs and priorities.

The retail industry presents the best examples of these market conditions and the channel multiplication pattern. Traditionally, customers would interrupt their day—frequently, for several hours—to go shopping. As customers became more and more frugal about their time, this shopping experience became more "expensive." The first response was the rapid growth of shopping malls where a family could meet many of its shopping needs in just one trip. Malls spawned the multiplication of specialty retail stores such as The Gap, Structure, Bath & Body Works, Banana Republic, and Victoria's Secret.

Today, for many purposes, shoppers don't even have to leave home. They can pick up a phone and dial an 800 number; fill out a mail-order form and fax or mail it to the seller; or click on an icon on their computer screen. L.L. Bean, Eddie Bauer, J. Crew, and a host of other retailers are thriving as catalog mail-order businesses. Even the U.S. Postal Service has begun to sell historic replicas and assorted casual clothing via a catalog. And because competition demands it, most mail-order sources have developed Internet businesses. Shoppers now have a multiplicity of channels, rather than a single, traditional, dominant outlet.

Many manufacturers are uncomfortable with channel multiplication. It disrupts their established go-to-market system and invades the comfort of their existing channel relationships. Some companies hesitate to adopt new, more customer-friendly channels for fear of angering their traditional partners. Whether real or imagined, this channel conflict holds them back.

Their fears are well justified. No one is more turf-sensitive than traditional distributors—particularly when the distributors' value added is weak. In the short term, avoiding the issue earns peace for the manufacturer and the distributor. In the long term, it undermines the competitiveness of both.

Other manufacturers see channel multiplication differently. Their view is simple: more channels lead to more sales. These manufacturers know there will be some conflict and tension in making the transition. But, then, there always is with any transition. To deal with the conflict, they follow a two-pronged strategy: (1) develop new programs that will address some of the key concerns of the existing channel, and (2) aggressively pursue the new channel opportunities.

HOW TO PROFIT?

If you're the manufacturer, use the new channels early. Be *their* first choice. If you're a traditional channel, launch new channel business designs that respond to how your customers and prospects want to buy.

- What impact will channel multiplication have on the distribution of power, profits, and value within your industry?
- What strategic control can you gain, early in the game, by exploiting the multiplication pattern in your own business?
- What specific opportunity/threat does the Internet as a distribution channel present for your business? Which of your competitors are moving to exploit this opportunity (or neutralize this threat)?

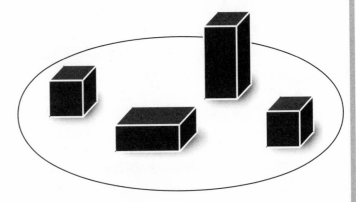

A few major sites

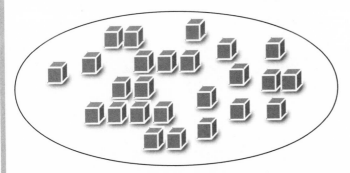

Many small locations

Channel Concentration

From many to few.

M any industries are characterized by a vast number of traditional, small-scale retail outlets. Because these outlets are easily accessible and provide local customers with personal and
individualized service, they meet many of their customers' buying criteria.

On the other hand, small operators have high overhead and administrative costs. Consequently, their customers must pay higher
prices for a limited selection of products or services, and customers
often have to visit several outlets to find everything they need. The
multiple dysfunctionalities of the fragmented system (inefficiency, in-
convenience, and time lost) are the ideal preconditions for triggering
the concentration pattern.

In the classic channel concentration pattern, value shifts when a
newcomer brings economies of scale to a fragmented, high-cost market. The innovators consolidate the small fragmented shops and service
offerings into larger units. They transform fifty outlets into five outlets. There is a trade-off in this kind of change, but customers don't
mind the reduction in the number of outlets, because they can buy
more for less and get better service.

A concentration pattern can fundamentally transform the retail
landscape. Carrefour, a French company, opened its first hypermarket in
a Paris suburb in 1963. Within three decades, Carrefour has become an
international chain of hypermarket stores generating roughly $29 billion
in annual sales with a market capitalization of about $20 billion. The key
to Carrefour's success was the extraordinary efficiency it created for customers. Before Carrefour's arrival, France had a highly fragmented system of *petits commerçants* (small shopkeepers). In each town, each
neighborhood had its own *boucherie* (butcher shop), *boulangerie* (bak-
ery), and numerous other specialty outlets. The shops were viewed as an
inseparable part of the national character, but they were a highly inefficient commercial mechanism for both customers and suppliers. For the

customer, shopping trips took hours. For distributors, shipping their goods to hundreds of small locations took considerable cost and effort. The multiple dysfunctionalities and inefficiencies of this system (lost time, high prices, limited selection) triggered the channel concentration pattern, and Carrefour exploited it to create significant shareholder value.

Carrefour recognized how all of these diverse shops could be rolled into one hypermarket, creating a radically more valuable situation for both customers and suppliers. Bread, meat, cheese, car tires, and children's clothing could be bought in one trip, all under the same roof. Suppliers were offered the advantage of consolidating delivery. The hypermarket format served customers and suppliers much more efficiently.

The concentration pattern is not limited to the superstore/hypermarket model. Instead of putting the mom-and-pop competition out of business, some companies are consolidating by buying the smaller players in order to create one large, market-leader position. Although the physical format is different, the same advantages are created: economies of scale and improved service to customers.

Sometimes, customer priorities do not allow for a "superstore" format. Can you imagine a funeral home superstore? But, Service Corporation International (SCI) has still been able to consolidate the funeral home industry in the United States. SCI, the largest publicly held owner and operator of funeral homes and cemeteries, has aggressively expanded through acquisition over the past fifteen years. It now operates 3,900 funeral homes, cemeteries, and crematoria in eighteen countries.

While SCI has kept the many small funeral homes it has acquired (the front office), back office operations have been consolidated across regions. Operational efficiencies have been central to SCI's success. By focusing aggressively on operating improvements, it has achieved 15 percent operating margins since 1980, a significant premium above the industry average. As a result of its improved use of resources, reduced operating costs, and greater revenue-generating ability, SCI's market value to sales ratio has grown sixfold, from 0.8 to 4.8.

SCI continues to expand internationally through rapid acquisition. It seeks operational efficiencies and value growth through resource sharing, cost minimization, and elimination of the industry's historically large price variations.

Republic Industries, a Florida-based retail automobile consolidator, is taking advantage of both concentration and consolidation through its dual auto superstore/dealership consolidation strategy. Republic has opened twenty-five AutoNation megastores across the nation since 1996. It has also invested $9.5 billion to acquire 268 dealerships. Republic is building regional market dominance by organizing the dealerships into dealer groups. In South Florida, for example, Republic has acquired thirty-two dealerships in addition to its three AutoNation stores. This consolidation of 7 percent of the regional market enables Republic to tap product sources more effectively, reduce floor plan expenses, cut parts inventory and delivery truck fleets by 20 percent, and lower new-car supply to 45 days for inventory. Although its market value has fluctuated since 1996, Republic has generated over $6 billion in value growth.

USA Waste Services has taken advantage of the concentration pattern in the solid waste industry. Starting in 1994, USA Waste began to acquire smaller players in the nonhazardous waste industry. With 123 locations in thirty-two states, USA Waste is now the third largest solid waste collector. It has focused on becoming the low-cost provider by cutting administrative costs, rationalizing collection routes, and creating other operational efficiencies. Its market value has grown from $25 million to $11.2 billion since 1990.

Blockbuster Video exploited the concentration pattern in the video store market. Barnes & Noble did so in bookstores. In each case, the winning company recognized the evolving strategic market conditions—customers' dissatisfaction with current offerings (and their rising expectations of low prices and large selection) and the lethargy of existing business designs—and anticipated the profit and value growth potential of the channel concentration pattern.

Concentration leads to better selection, more shopping convenience, and improved service for the customer. Small-scale operations are displaced; large-scale operations dominate the market landscape and generate superior profitability, at least until the next shift in the system (e.g., video on demand, or online selling) threatens to make the current business model obsolete.

HOW TO PROFIT?

Lead the process. Always be thinking of what the *next* generation model should be.

- Is channel concentration about to occur in your industry? Why?
- How long will this pattern last?
- What will trigger the next pattern?

FROM PRODUCT CHANNEL TO CUSTOMER OCCASION CHANNEL

In the past, retailers were traditionally organized around and known for the products they sold. The grocery store. The dry cleaner. The music store. The bank.

Over the past two decades, innovative retail formats have added new benefits of selection, speed, and low price to product-centric offers. The results have been so dramatic that retail channels are now often known by their format: The convenience store. The supermarket or superstore (super = big). The category killer (even bigger).

In this world of innovative retail formats, consumers' choice of where to shop is often based on nonproduct criteria. The customer chooses which format best matches his or her priorities—lots of selection, near to home, low price, no hassle, and so on—and then buys the product there. Of the $163 billion in new shareholder value created by U.S. retailers from 1986 to 1996, $144 billion was created by innovative channel formats.

A new pattern emerging in retail channels promises to be the Next Better Deal for time-pressed consumers and a new wave of value creation for its early exploiters. It is called the "Customer Occasion" channel format, and it is based on an understanding of the important purchasing occasions and activities consumers would like to cluster together in their daily or weekly rhythm. By clustering these activities under one roof, the channel creates a format that mirrors the combination and sequence of a consumer's activities on that shopping occasion. This pattern is still relatively young, but early examples are beginning to emerge.

- How can we define the channel that offers, under one roof, groceries, light household-improvement items, kids' clothes, rental videos, photo processing, dry cleaning, pharmacy services, ATM banking, and gasoline? The labels "grocery store" and "supermarket" do not capture the full intent. Such a format is being rolled out today by major retailers such as Carrefour (France) and Sainsburys (UK). Its Customer Occasion name might be the "Home Manager's Weekly Chores" format.

- How can we explain the airport retail stores that are looking more and more like high-end impulse buying malls and are growing three to four times faster than traditional retail stores? Customer Occasion thinking would call it the "High-Income Person's Only Moment to Shop" format.

- How does Sears, one of the world's largest retailers, think about new retail formats to launch? It carries out Customer Occasion research. Sears has found that customers prefer to decorate their home as a coordinated activity, room by room. The act of shopping for room décor was an identifiable and unique purchase occasion that called for a new type of format. Sears also determined that light home-improvement projects represented an identifiable purchase occasion. It called for close-to-home stores that carry merchandise organized around specific, common projects. Sears is now rolling out new formats specifically designed for each of these customer occasions. Each format contains a nontraditional mix of products, consulting advice, and service—exactly the mix that customers were not getting from product-centric formats in the past.

Customer Occasion channel strategies are, in short, process reengineering on behalf of consumers. They use research to understand what processes consumers would like to cluster. Then they do the clustering for them.

Customer Occasion strategies show the value of segmenting customers by identifying the intersection of identity-based and occasion-based attitudes. They don't start with the number of customers in the market; they start with the number of purchases and segment them by combinations of customers and occasions. This approach to segmentation may well lead to the next round of major channel innovation.

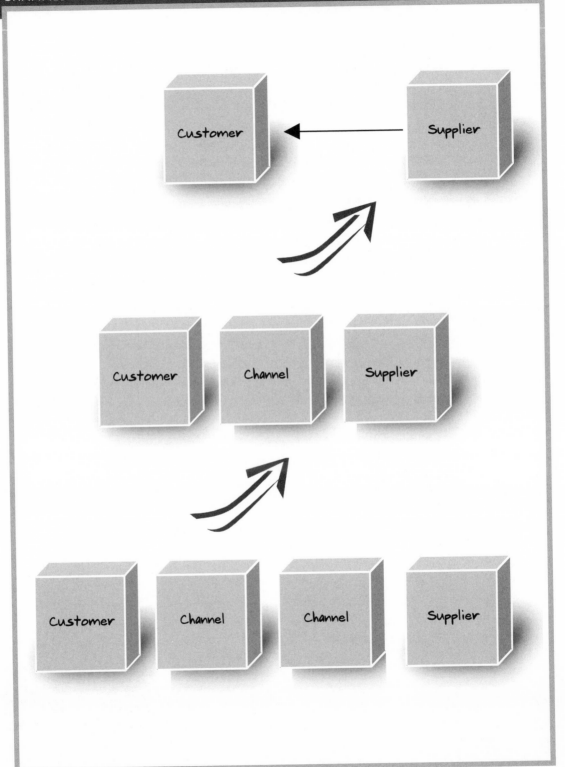

Compression/Disintermediation

Redundant steps disappear.

Multistep distribution systems (wholesaler, distributor, retailer) were a common feature of the classic business landscape. They functioned to break bulk and bring products successively closer to customers.

But their function was achieved at a price: long cycles, high costs, and low responsiveness to changing conditions. Two forces put pressure on the traditional, multistep system: (1) consumers' search for lower prices and greater convenience; and (2) manufacturers' search for greater distribution efficiency.

As the gap between these emerging priorities and existing business designs has widened, the channel compression pattern has been triggered in many industries. The result has been the compression or disintermediation of traditional distribution channels in favor of more efficient, closer, or even direct relationships between customers and suppliers.

Calyx & Corolla, the San Francisco-based direct-mail flowers company, anticipated this pattern and exploited the new market realities to its advantage (see Harvard Business School Case No. 592035).

The traditional distribution system in the flowers industry involved multiple steps: from growers to regional distributors to wholesalers (who sold to florists, pharmacies, and supermarkets). In most big cities, wholesalers' and retailers' interaction at flower markets created a sort of flower industry stock exchange. Everyone who handled the flowers along the distribution chain added some amount to the price, in order to make a profit. By the time the bouquet reached the dining room table, the consumer was paying over 800 percent more than the grower's selling price. Moreover, because the distribution process often took as much as seven to ten days, the flowers weren't fresh anymore. By the time they arrived in retail stores, the "fresh" flowers were frequently more than a little brown around the edges. In the end, customers were extremely dissatisfied with the high prices and poor quality. They expected more.

Ruth Owades, founder of Calyx & Corolla, recognized the growing dysfunctionality in the traditional flower distribution network. She envisioned Calyx & Corolla as a direct link between growers and customers. To accomplish that objective, the company needed to develop partnerships with both suppliers and distributors. Calyx & Corolla established close relationships with thirty top flower growers, convincing them to install computer hardware linking them to its own network. The company could then transmit its orders twice a day to the growers. In return, the company provided the growers with retail materials such as boxes, cards, vases, and labels. It trained them to respond rapidly to consumers' requests for packaged bouquets (instead of waiting for the traditional distributors' requests for cartons of different flowers), further shortening the order cycle.

Calyx & Corolla worked closely with the growers to identify the packing materials that would best maintain flowers' moisture, freshness, and shape. In turn, the growers kept Calyx & Corolla constantly informed about available stocks. Calyx & Corolla could then seek alternative suppliers during a shortage, or offer special products when excess flowers were available.

Calyx & Corolla also formed an alliance with Federal Express. The link to FedEx's tracking and shipping network helped Calyx & Corolla to ensure on-time, rapid delivery. FedEx's reliability and rapid response have enabled Calyx & Corolla to sell flowers through its catalogs, by phone, and on the Internet. The benefit? By compressing the system, the company is able to deliver flowers directly from grower to consumer in as little as two days from the time they are cut. Customers have the added benefit of shopping at home. The compression formula has worked so well that Calyx & Corolla has become a leading player in the $10 billion retail horticulture business.

Channel compression removes steps in the distribution system and transforms customer dissatisfaction and inefficiency into customer satisfaction and streamlined delivery. Calyx & Corolla, for example, reduced the number of delivery steps from seven to three. In its most extreme form, channel compression leads to complete disintermediation:

low-value-added distributors are eliminated, and the direct link formed between supplier and customer creates enormous benefits for both. Costs fall, assets are reduced, and the quality of mutual information flow is vastly improved.

The coming proliferation of Internet capabilities (on the part of both sellers and buyers) will accelerate the compression/disintermediation pattern. Cisco already sells nearly half of its volume to customers directly via the Internet.

Other aggressive players are racing to catch up. In the future, sellers will make electronic pathways their key distribution channels at an accelerating rate.

The value shift in the compression/disintermediation pattern will intensify as suppliers and customers become increasingly unwilling to incur transaction costs and to pay distributors to act as "go-betweens." To gain the best information and the lowest prices, customers will eagerly migrate to new channels or to direct relationships with the suppliers themselves.

HOW TO PROFIT?

As buyer and manufacturer, create direct links early. If you are still "the old channel," create new value-added offerings, or disinvest, before you are disinvested by your value chain neighbors.

You run a travel agency. Customers pay you for their travel-related transactions:

- Who are your most dangerous competitors?
- Are there "channel compressors" in your industry? Who are they? What advantages and disadvantages do you have relative to them?
- As they grow, can you ensure your own future profitability?

Reintermediation

Create a new value-added step in the system.

The channel compression/disintermediation pattern eliminates traditional distributors and creates direct relationships between a company and its customers. The benefits of the direct link are lower costs for the company and lower prices for the consumer.

In a small but growing number of cases, however, a pattern of reintermediation follows and allows the "ousted" distributors or new players to come back into the picture in another role. These distributors reintermediate because the direct relationship between the customer and the supplier, while quicker and more efficient, is often limited to transaction processing; in many cases, direct sales channels do not offer the value-added services of the "face-to-face" experience or of other types of value-added benefits that are important to customers. The customers then become increasingly dissatisfied with the new "disintermediated" system. Companies that recognize the key gaps and unmet needs can reenter the system as value-added intermediaries.

These new intermediaries return to do one of two things: (1) provide customers with new, important value-added services not provided in the new direct customer–supplier relationship; or (2) provide customers with significantly more efficient means of transacting business. With either activity, the result is a new distribution channel built on a meaningful new value proposition for the customer.

Rosenbluth International, a century-old travel agency, anticipated this pattern ten years ago and searched for ways to provide new value-added services to its customers (see *The Digital Economy,* by Don Tapscott, pp. 193–195). CEO Hal Rosenbluth transformed his business design: "We are no longer in the travel business, we are in the information business." Rather than using various airlines' reservations systems—each of which had a bias toward its own flights—Rosenbluth created his own reservation data system and incorporated information from numerous airlines. Because of his new proprietary system, Rosenbluth was able to guarantee his clients the absolute lowest price on flights. Moreover, Rosenbluth International allowed corporations to link directly to its system as strategic partners. The company's core product, Dacoda, allows 1,000 corporate clients to search the flight deals offered by airlines, and to build travel cost models based on their specific corporate needs.

Rosenbluth's clients can create their own travel management systems based on information on airfares, preferred carriers, and special deals. As an added benefit, Rosenbluth's Trip Monitor constantly tracks clients' arrangements, rebooking them as necessary when lower fares become available. Using Dacoda, Rosenbluth's clients can take 10 to 20 percent off the standard corporate discount offered through direct channels.

Rosenbluth found a way to provide new, high-value services to customers, in a classic example of the reintermediation pattern. By creating unmatched services, the company avoided the disintermediation that will plague traditional travel agencies in the new world of online reservations. Rosenbluth's business design creates a capability far beyond the processing of transactions. Rosenbluth offers its corporate clients a complete travel management system that is guaranteed to cut travel expenses and maximize convenience. Customers can easily make hotel or airline reservations by going online without Rosenbluth, but Rosenbluth can help customers consistently achieve the lowest price.

This transition succeeded because Rosenbluth recognized the channel compression pattern early, and moved aggressively to build its next business design while its old business model was still profitable.

Technology is creating new opportunities for reintermediation. Priceline is an Internet-based service that has inserted a new step between travelers and travel service providers. Priceline adds value by helping travelers to get lower prices and helping service companies to get higher utilization.

Travelers-to-be provide Priceline with information on where they want to travel, where they want to stay, and what price they want to pay. Priceline links its system to airlines, hotel chains, and car rental companies. When seats, rooms, and cars are available, the service provider will accept even very low priced offers, to avoid letting the seats, rooms, or cars remain empty.

Priceline has created a new intermediate step in the process, offering new value to both sides of the transaction.

Reintermediation is also beginning to occur in industrial distribution and in retailing. W.W. Grainger (a maintenance and repair products distributor) has understood that low-cost distribution is no longer enough. It has created programs of value-added services for large corporate buyers, while searching for even lower-cost models of distribution for small and medium size buyers.

Another form of reintermediation occurs when new players step in to provide customers with dramatically more efficient means of transacting business. In these cases, the pattern is triggered in industries where power is so diffuse that great inefficiencies or dysfunctionalities exist. Many sellers communicate with many buyers in ways that are costly for everyone involved. The greater the number of sellers, the greater the need for buyers to gather information about sellers, make decisions about which sellers to use, and find ways to contact each one at each level. On the selling side, having too many fragmented buyers means high marketing costs, high distribution hurdles, and complicated logistical issues.

In this variant of the reintermediation pattern, the fundamental shift that occurs is from a fragmented state to a highly organized switchboard that magnetizes the loyalty of buyers and achieves the grudging acceptance of sellers. In this pattern, there is an opportunity for a farsighted player to move into the inefficient void between buyers and sellers. The player becomes a high-value intermediary by creating a switchboard business design that significantly increases the efficiency of both buyers and sellers. Being that switchboard can lead to profitability and strategic control within an industry.

The formation of Creative Artists Agency (CAA) in 1975 is an early example of the pattern. CAA is a Hollywood talent agency that interposed a link between movie studios and stars, writers, and directors.

CAA's unique approach was in creating a package. Rather than negotiating one contract for one star in one movie, CAA recognized the value of combining stars, writers, and directors in an integrated package. Each individual involved gained more bargaining power because the package brought more value to the studio and increased the likelihood that its constituent stars would appear in a movie.

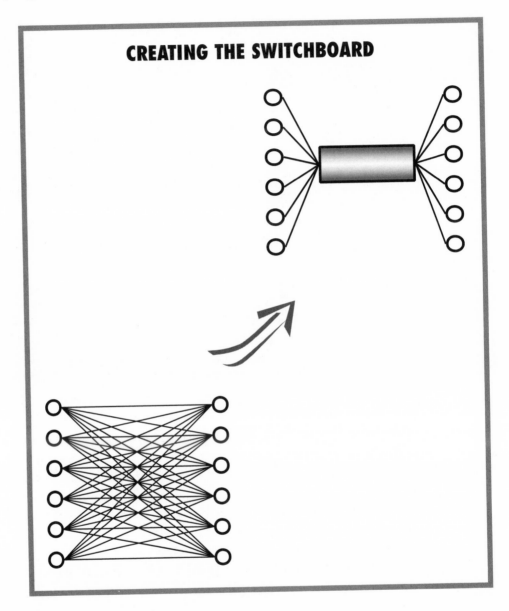

CREATING THE SWITCHBOARD

The inefficiency of traditional investment brokerages has also triggered the reintermediation pattern in financial services. Previously, individual investors dealt directly with mutual fund brokers or companies. If an investor wanted to own shares in six different mutual funds, he or she opened six different accounts and incurred the costs of dealing with six different statements. If the goal was to gain the simplicity of a single account statement, the client was left with only a handful of choices from a broker.

Charles Schwab, recognizing customers' dissatisfaction with the increasingly complex process of investing, exploited the reintermediation pattern in response. Through its innovative OneSource offering, Schwab gave its customers a new option that offered a compelling value proposition. Schwab would act as the "switchboard" connecting hundreds of asset management firms with millions of investors. One phone number, and one account, accessed thousands of mutual funds. Schwab simplified the process of investing and created significant value at the same time. (See Chapter 8 in *The Profit Zone* for a discussion of Schwab's switchboard design.)

Marschollek, Lautenschlager and Partner (MLP), a European financial services firm, has also exploited the reintermediation pattern. MLP started as an agent for financial services focused on university students and young professionals with high earning potential. It assumed these young adults would have little or no experience managing money. MLP's value proposition was to arrange insurance and financial service products from various providers for its clients. MLP operates as a switchboard between high potential earners and a multitude of financial service companies. As its customers grow in age and assets, MLP will play a key role in determining how they invest.

NECX, formed in 1980, has created a switchboard business design that links sellers and purchasers of semiconductors. By serving as a centralized nexus between these buyers and sellers, it facilitates transactions in a way that reduces the sellers' costs and the buyers' costs and hassles.

eBay has created a switchboard service in multiple categories, from antiques to equipment to general merchandise. Instead of placing ads in newspapers and experiencing the hassle of dealing with multiple buyers, sellers can list with eBay, which will run an electronic auction. eBay provides customers with better price realization, greater convenience, and lower selling cost. With the motto "We help people trade practically anything on Earth," eBay's Web site lists over one million items. The company already makes a profit—one of the few "Internet stocks" to do so—which is one reason it has attained a market capitalization of $7 billion less than three months after its IPO.

The emergence of the Internet has created multiple opportunities for reintermediation. But it is not a risk-free environment. Auto-by-Tel tried and succeeded in its first phase, thanks in part to a partnership with Microsoft. But in its second phase, the Microsoft partnership turned from asset to liability, when Microsoft decided to go into the business on its own.

When it was formed in 1995, Auto-by-Tel wanted to be the intermediary between auto buyers and dealers. It grew rapidly, handling 387,000 purchase/lease requests over twenty-one months, and enlisting 1,715 dealerships by the end of 1996. Auto-by-Tel was paid by the dealers, who (like the mutual funds joining Schwab's OneSource) didn't love it but realized they had to be a part of the switchboard. They couldn't afford not to be.

Despite (or because of) Auto-by-Tel's success, Microsoft severed its business relationship with the company in 1997. The Redmond software giant decided to create its own business, Carpoint, to serve as the nexus between auto buyers and dealers. That event was a foreshadowing of other reintermediation moves that Microsoft will try to effect.

The potential value of the shift to a switchboard model has spawned several intense competitive races. In each race, two front runners emerge and vie to be the leading switchboard in the business:

- Schwab's One Source versus Fidelity
- Auto-by-Tel versus Microsoft CarPoint
- Travelocity versus Microsoft Expedia

As the Internet presents more opportunities for buyers and sellers, more battles will emerge as companies seek to create highly valuable switchboards to facilitate electronic commerce and transactions.

> ## HOW TO PROFIT?
>
> As buyer and supplier, use the new channel early. It will save you money. As the new channel, maximize the value added and accelerate your investment program, to minimize the window available for the number-two entrant.

- Think of the intermediaries that you deal with:
  - Do they provide transaction processing or added value?
  - What new value added would you like to see from them?
- What is the likelihood that this new value added will be provided by:
  - Incumbents?
  - New players?
- Is there room for switchboard intermediaries to improve the efficiencies or economics of your industry?
- Who is best positioned to create and manage the switchboard?

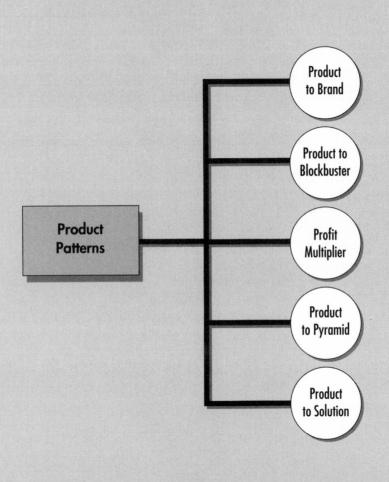

CHAPTER 8
PRODUCT PATTERNS

Prior to the mid-1980s, the product was king. Profitability was directly linked to the product because the functionality it provided was important or was unique. Television sets in the 1960s; cars or steel in the 1960s or 1970s; software programs or pharmaceuticals in the 1980s. The product was the manufacturer's source of competitive power and profit.

In recent times, however, profit and value have begun to migrate away from the product along several dimensions, via many different patterns. The common denominator across these patterns is that the value that had existed in the product itself has moved next door, economically speaking, to new scarce assets such as brands, blockbusters, and solutions.

The laws that govern these new scarce assets, however, have little in common. What a strategist must do to capitalize on the shift from "product to brand" is quite different from what must be done to exploit the pattern of "product to pyramid," or "product to solution." Each pattern has a different success logic—and each needs to be understood on its own terms.

Coca-cola is a registered trademark of The Coca-Cola Company. Evian is a registered trademark of Groupe Dannone. Swatch is a registered trademark of The Swatch Group Ltd. Intel is a registered trademark of Intel Corporation.

Product to Brand

The tangible intangible.

Products and functionality were once the key points of differentiation for a company. If consumers were offered unique products or services, the company was profitable.

However, today's consumers are exposed to countless products that are no longer differentiated by function. Among many products, there is also no discernible variation in quality or price. The more consumer advertising there is, the smaller the window of exposure per product. Time is scarce. People want to find a product that they know will satisfy their purchasing goals, and they want to find it immediately.

In this world of extreme product proliferation, a curious thing happens. The customer has too many options. The more options, especially undifferentiated options, the greater the confusion for the buyer.

This combination of too many options and absence of differentiation creates incredible levels of frustration for the buyer, and, among other factors, triggers the brand pattern.

Brands provide an answer. They provide differentiation and the promise of customer satisfaction. In many categories, customers pay less attention to the product than to the brand that has been built around it. This creation of a second economic reality around a product builds a virtual relationship with the customer, communicates the meaning of the product, and introduces an element of trust into the relationship between seller and buyer.

As the brand becomes a proxy for the product, decision time is reduced from several days or hours to a few seconds. As a result, profit and value have started to migrate away from individual products toward the brands themselves, which provide customers with a perceived "guarantee" of quality. Astute manufacturers and retailers recognize this and manage accordingly. They are selling an image, a message, and a promise rather than a product. The sale is not just a transaction, it is part of a relationship.

As a result, brands have been built in places that traditional marketing theory would find unusual. Consider the following series of products: Evian water, Starbucks coffee, Stainmaster carpets, NutraSweet aspartame, Swatch watches, Perdue chicken. Commodities all. Commodities no longer. An entrepreneur, a company, or a management team, working with a unit of basic functionality (be it water, coffee beans, floor covering, sweetener, a timepiece, or a chicken), built a set of perceptions, beliefs, and responses that actually caused customers to deflect away from typical commodity buying behavior ("What's the lowest price I can find?").

Consider the chicken industry. Poultry had become an intensely competitive business by the 1970s. To the big processors, price meant everything. Even a quarter-cent-per-pound difference would make them switch suppliers. This mindset was passed directly along to consumers, and chicken became a commodity product, like a bushel of wheat.

But not to Frank Perdue, who realized that if he wanted to create profits in the poultry business, he was going to have to develop a chicken that was and seemed special. He chose to create a brand that would focus on the quality issue, on specialness. First, he reorganized his poultry operations to make certain he would be able to deliver on the promise. Then he went on television to emphasize nonfrozen delivery and his chickens' golden yellow color as perceptible indicators of superior quality.

His ad line, "It takes a tough man to make a tender chicken," struck a responsive chord with homemakers, who were most sensitive to messages about food quality. Perdue chickens were able to command an additional ten cents per pound, a price premium unheard of previously, and sales grew rapidly for the next sixteen years. The company's products vary little relative to its competitors, but Perdue has built a reputation for quality and service far ahead of its competitors.

When the pattern of value shifts from product to brand, it is not moving from the concrete to the intangible. Quite the contrary. Real brands have an edge every bit as tangible as the product around which they are built.

In 1994, for example, you could put two personal computers side by side. Same processor, same memory, same performance features. The label on one said Compaq; the label on the other said IBM. The Compaq sold for $200 more.

In the early 1990s, two cars rolled off the assembly line at NUMMI, the GM-Toyota joint venture in Fremont, California. The two vehicles were identical in every respect. They were made by the same workers using the same processes.

The only difference was the name. One said GM; the other, Toyota. The Toyota sold for $400 more, and it sold faster.

When Nicolas Hayek was testing the market for Swatch, he found that, if confronted with exactly the same physical object (a watch), customers would pay $20 more if it said "Made in Switzerland" versus "Made in Hong Kong."

Brands can determine preference as well as price. Recently, in a test project, a new animated movie was shown to two audiences. Each audience experienced exactly the same product, in every detail. One audience was told the name of the actual studio, the other audience was told it was a Disney product (which it wasn't). The latter audience liked the film much, much more than the first.

Same product. Same type of viewer. Different brand.

Examples of the product to brand pattern are occurring in numerous industries, as companies strive to create new value for customers, to differentiate their products from competitors' offerings, and to create new value for investors. In each case, a lack of variation among products triggered the opportunity for a branded offering to capture customer mindshare and to cement strategic control.

Moët Hennessy Louis Vuitton (LVMH) has exploited customers' increasing desire for branded and luxury goods by cultivating its hard-earned image as a producer of the ultimate luxury products. Louis Vuitton is best known for its high-end luggage; Moët Hennessy is renowned for its spirits. Luxury apparel brands such as Christian Dior and Givenchy are also part of the LVMH family.

Unlike the many other design firms that center on a personality, LVMH focuses exclusively on building and expanding its brands. After finding well-performing niche brands and taking them global, LVMH will not hesitate to replace designers and executives to improve the brands' performance.

Through its aggressive program of brand acquisition, development, and expansion, LVMH has successfully captured a leading mindshare position with both the luxury customer and the long-term investor. Rather than depending on one brand, LVMH has created a portfolio of the world's most renowned and expensive luxury goods. Its name—or rather, its list of names—instantly creates an image of luxury, quality, and style in the mind of the consumer.

Other companies, recognizing the movement of profit from product to brand, are working to align themselves with the shift. Look for the pattern in many more industries as companies replace product profit with brand profit.

On the face of it, the product to brand pattern seems obvious. In reality, it isn't. Despite the migration of value away from products, countless branding opportunities remain untapped. Many companies are simply afraid to make the investment. Others believe they own a brand, based on high awareness. Awareness, however, is just the first metric. More important are: unique position, and preference that is powerful enough to drive behavior. Most important is the ability to achieve and protect a meaningful price premium. There are lots of "awareness" brands; there are few "sustained price premium" brands.

Even when branding is pursued, examples of brand acceleration (see p. 182) are extraordinarily infrequent. The biggest barrier to exploiting the shift from product to brand lies in not really understanding the customer, and therefore not being able to create a brand that has high meaning and motivational power for the buyer.

HOW TO PROFIT?

Realize that customers *want* and *need* valuable brands.
Bite the bullet. Build the brand.

- What changes, dysfunctionalities, and/or variations in customer preference could trigger the product to brand pattern in your industry?

- Which brand names will really matter in financial services, tele-communications, bookselling, retailing, and computing? In your industry?

- What could your organization accomplish with a strong brand?

- How strong is your brand's awareness? Preference? Price premium?

A NOTE ON BRAND ACCELERATION

Amazon.com is the largest bookstore on earth.

Amazon has become as widely known as its "bricks and mortar" rivals, Borders and Barnes & Noble, even though it only has one-tenth of their revenues. How did a company like Amazon achieve that kind of accelerated brand creation? Did it spend much more money than its competition? Or did it exploit the new pattern of brand acceleration?

Three rapid changes in the marketplace—the advent of new technology, the formation of networks and user groups, and new modes of buyer behavior—all triggered by the Internet, have dramatically changed the competitive landscape for the brand-building process. As a result of these conditions, it is now possible to construct a brand in ways that were unavailable just a decade ago.

Amazon anticipated the power of the Internet for branding, and it actively exploited the brand acceleration pattern to its advantage. From the outset, Amazon consciously focused on triggering brand acceleration. Amazon offered a percentage of sales to "associates" who put links on their Web sites through which customers came to Amazon to buy books.

At last count, Amazon had 25,000 associates in the program, which means there are more than 25,000 Web sites with Amazon banners. Amazon recognized the value of this kind of extended exposure long before anyone else, and was able to move aggressively to establish its identity all over the World Wide Web.

Amazon also anticipated the importance of mindshare (both consumer and media), and it has been assiduous in cultivating the press. Amazon represents an interesting story, and the company has made the most of the retelling. Hundreds of articles have carried the Amazon story, or referred to it, creating awareness, recognition, and customer trial.

Once a trial is triggered, Amazon's system does the rest. It treats customers as customers. It bends over backward to

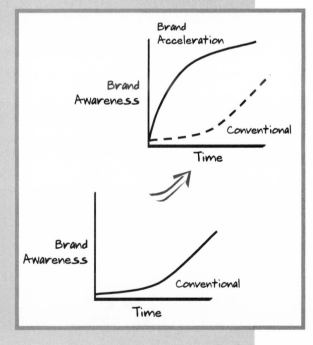

provide great service, great information, and great convenience. That combination is almost perfectly designed to trigger and maximize the word-of-mouth effect. Delighted customers can't stop talking about Amazon to potential prospects. (For more information on Amazon's customer acquisition and management successes, see Chapter 11.)

Amazon is now moving into a more traditional branding battle with its rivals. Each side will bring out its ad budgets. But to reach this point, Amazon took advantage of a brand acceleration strategy that put it on the same awareness and recognition level as its competitors, at a fraction of the cost.

It's not only how much you spend that counts; it's the whole system you build around whatever amount you spend. The system can discount, multiply, or be neutral. Amazon's system multiplies.

NEW BRANDING

If you said the word *brand* in 1975, your listener was likely to think about soap, soda, or cigarettes. In that year, manufacturers of traditional packaged goods and processed food accounted for over 60 percent of all advertising. Today, they account for less than 30 percent. The second association with *brand* in 1975 was probably "television." Television was the medium that brought the highest degree of product awareness to consumers. The sixty-second advertisement was synonymous with brand building. Today, TV advertising is only one of many tools at the disposal of the brand builder—and, for many products, it is not the most important one.

Value is shifting from companies that build brands "the old-fashioned way" to those that use new approaches. This distinction is strategic because a brand that can summon *strong emotion* and *potent meaning* at the point of the customers' purchasing decisions can bring its owner:

- Three to six points of additional operating profit.
- The potential for strategic control.
- A cornerstone from which to pursue new opportunities.

Great brands help convert a customer's product-oriented, price/performance comparison into a brand-oriented, emotion-filled decision. Consequently, brands' power can be enhanced with the ability to recall memory and emotion. Some of the best "new branding" in the world today takes place in extended, experiential environments. Customers experience the luxury of Häagen Dazs ice cream in the half hour that they spend in its European-style cafés. Shoppers internalize the style of The Gap as they repeatedly see strong poster-based advertising while they shop. Visitors to Sony Wonder stores don't leave with tomorrow's electronics alone. They leave impressed with what it means to own a Sony.

Branded retailing is just one example of extended, experiential brand building. Others include:

- Intermingling of advertising messages and emotional content (James Bond escaping the world's latest villain in a ten-minute BMW chase scene).

- High-stakes customer interaction and service (airline brands are distinguished more by what they do when a business traveler misses a plane than by what they do when a traveler departs without incident).

- Creation of social groups that share their experiences involving the brand (in all the world, is there a stronger brand for its customers than Harley-Davidson?).

- Personification of the brand, which is very different from celebrity sponsorship or endorsement (Michael Jordan was a sixty-minute flying example of Nike, not a sixty-second talking head for it).

Several decades ago, brand superiority used to be predominantly about quality and reliability (extrinsic benefits). The emergence of government regulation, better business bureaus, global competition, and total quality control has made reliability something that customers now take for granted. In most industries, it is an obsolete and profitless boast to make about a brand.

Today, as companies take their brands global, extend them across wide product lines, and diversify from manufacturing alone into manufacturing/service hybrids, they are shifting their brand meaning emphasis to intrinsic benefits that rely less on specific product performance and offer the customer more value in terms of self-identity. Benetton is not about a better shirt; it is about a better attitude toward all of the world's shirt wearers. Nike is not about shoes that help you run a faster mile in the morning; it is about having the courage to get up and run at all.

These examples of new brand meaning do not detract from the importance of great product features. But in a world where great products are becoming commodities and where technology changes the definition of the most important product feature every twelve months, the domination of an attractive self-identity space in the customer's psyche may be much more valuable than dominating a particular extrinsic benefit position.

In addition to strong emotion and potent meaning, the third and final ingredient in a strong "new" brand is the attention paid to the customer at the moment a purchase decision is made. When does the customer decide? Why does the customer decide at that point? What messages are being delivered to the customer at his or her moment of decision?

Major retailers have taught consumers that it is worthwhile to wait and to inspect the choices available on the display shelf before deciding what to buy. Products are reduced to a common price-per-ounce label that naturally increases shoppers' price sensitivity. "Our own label" products, priced at 20 to 40 percent below major brands, are given the center-aisle, eye-level sweet spot that is designed to catch shoppers' attention.

Retailers' rewards to shoppers who wait to decide are highly effective. No wonder that, with regard to most fast-moving consumer goods categories, between 30 percent and 70 percent of consumers enter the door of a supermarket not knowing whether they will buy a private-label product or a major brand! Indecision rises to two to three times that level if consumers are asked which major brand they will buy!

Many buyers make their final decisions, then, in a mental space that is filled with antibrand messages. This trend accentuates the economic reward of linking brand building to the moment of purchase decision. In a future world where direct access to the customer can be created, it may be a wise investment to build direct access (so purchases can take place in a branded or brand-supportive environment) rather than to double the promotional budget.

All three of the new branding trends described in this pattern turn the spotlight back on a company's business design. What extended experiences does the customer have with that brand? What differentiated meaning does the brand communicate? What feature of the business design creates a more conducive brand environment at the moment when purchasing decisions are made?

. . . to Blockbuster

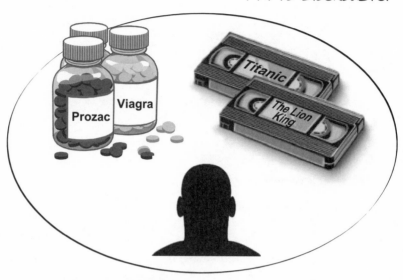

From Portfolio. . .

Product to Blockbuster

From many projects to few.

In many industries, profit migrates from a balanced portfolio of products to a few blockbusters. This usually results from dysfunctionality brought about by two conditions: (1) deteriorating economics of development and production, which make the "average" product a money loser, and/or (2) increased variability in the outcomes for any product. In these situations, the winning business design focuses on creating a consistent series of blockbusters. Filmmaking, pharmaceuticals, music, publishing, investing, real estate, sports talent, and network TV are all examples of industries in which the profit that used to be in a portfolio is now concentrated in blockbusters.

Over the years, *Cosby, Cheers,* and *Seinfeld* were blockbusters that had significant impact on the value of NBC. In the current schedule, *ER* and *Friends* are its blockbusters. The TV newsmagazine *60 Minutes* plays a similar role for CBS. For Fox, it's *Ally McBeal* and *The X-Files.* For ABC, it's *NYPD Blue.* The networks recognized the shift of value toward "hits," and they focused their resources on shows that could attain blockbuster status. These blockbusters became engines of enormous profit growth, not just for the blockbuster, but for big chunks of the primetime schedule.

The blockbuster program creates massive viewership for the surrounding programs, raising their chances of becoming successful. This effect sometimes stretches through an entire evening of primetime television. In 1996 and 1997, NBC orchestrated much of its primetime schedule around *Seinfeld,* its key weekly blockbuster. Before *Seinfeld* exited, NBC used it to nurture other shows until they could build their own loyal viewership. When audience response was steady and high enough, the shows surrounding *Seinfeld* could safely be transplanted to other time slots on other evenings. Some were used to create the same effect, if on a somewhat smaller scale, for the next generation of newcomers.

The blockbuster pattern has also occurred in filmmaking. Over the past decade, the average cost of making a movie has risen 150 percent, average marketing costs have risen over 300 percent, and the range around these averages has expanded dramatically.

As a consequence of this increasing variation in costs, most films lose money. Studios try to compensate by investing heavily in (some would say betting on) potential blockbusters, whose enormous returns will not only pay for all those losses but will create some excess profits. However, in the absence of a business design that consistently creates blockbusters, the industry winds up playing a high-risk game, and the risk level for all players goes up over time.

Most studios, with the possible exception of Disney's animation business, have not been successful at creating a *system* that consistently delivers blockbusters to the industry.

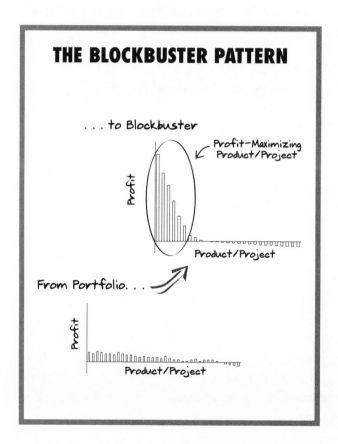

THE BLOCKBUSTER PATTERN

The best model of consistent blockbuster development comes from the pharmaceutical industry. One company, Merck, began building its blockbuster model in the 1970s. The launch of Vasotec (a blood pressure medication) in 1981 introduced the first product of the new system. Merck perfected its blockbuster development system and never looked back. Over the following decade, it created fifteen blockbuster products, more than the next five pharmaceutical companies combined. Today, the entire industry is driven by the blockbuster model. Every major company can point to a blockbuster, whether it's Claritin (Schering Plough), Prozac (Eli Lilly), or Viagra (Pfizer).

The same pattern is at work in real estate, investment banking, music, publishing, and many types of talent-related industries. The profit opportunity and value flow to the blockbuster projects, performers, or transactions, and away from the portfolio of average products or transactions.

Although the economics are similar in these other domains, no consistent player has emerged in the other fields. The opportunity is still there for a company to create the right business design and take advantage of the blockbuster pattern. The benefit to its customers and its owners could be enormous.

HOW TO PROFIT?

Work on the system. It's impossible to produce a consistent series of blockbusters without a carefully developed and nurtured system.

- What market factors/conditions would trigger the blockbuster pattern in your industry?
- Is your industry's profitability driven by a brand, a portfolio of positions, or a handful of blockbusters?
- If a handful of blockbusters is driving profitability in your industry, do you have a business design that is geared toward producing a consistent series of blockbuster products or projects?
- What would it take to create a blockbuster-focused business design?

Product to Profit Multiplier

Profit from the asset seven times.

The profit multiplier pattern is a shift in the locus of maximum profitability from a single product to a system that reuses that product many times. The pattern is triggered by businesses that successfully recognize their customers' perception of their "winning asset" (their product, their brand, or any other asset) relative to their competitors, and successfully reuse the asset to generate tremendous revenues and value. The untapped opportunity to respond to customers' preferences and affinity for the company's products or information triggers the eventual development of a profit multiplier pattern.

There are several standout examples of the profit multiplier pattern: (1) Disney, (2) Bloomberg L.P., (3) Richard Branson's Virgin Group, (4) Michael Jordan, and (5) Martha Stewart.

Disney's movie *The Lion King* illustrates the power of this pattern. Where do you look for the true value in an animated movie? Is it in box office receipts, or is it in the ideas, characters, and brands that are identified with the movie? To Disney, the answer was clearly the latter, and the company shaped its business design accordingly. *The Lion King* theme was developed across the entire Disney business system: toys, clothing, comic books, the TV show, the musical, and the ice show. Because it found ways to take a unique asset and multiply it across many businesses, Disney produced returns that dwarfed the returns generated by the motion picture alone. Even several years after its release, Disney continues to build on the value of *The Lion King* theme, most recently in the form of its new Animal Kingdom theme park and a sequel titled *Simba's Pride*. The company is the best in the world at applying a multiplier process to the content it creates.

Bloomberg L.P., a key source of daily financial information, also exploits the profit multiplier pattern aggressively. A Bloomberg reporter finds a news story in the field and produces a short video clip. The video clip moves to Bloomberg's TV shows. The audio is stripped out and used on Bloomberg radio. The transcript is sent to the Bloomberg Web site and may serve as the base for a more in-depth article in Bloomberg's professional and personal finance magazines. All of these formats may then be sent to the Bloomberg terminals that reside on the desks of tens of thousands of financial professionals. From one piece of information, Bloomberg can multiply its profit several times.

Other profit multiplier patterns are based on brands derived from the charisma and talents of individuals.

Richard Branson and his Virgin Group have succeeded in creating a brand name that represents quality, innovation, and irreverence. It has been able to win market share and profits from rivals such as British Airways and Pepsi. The profit multiplier pattern is the key to this success.

Virgin's brand is an extension of Richard Branson and his media personality. His image—that of an upstart who wins against the odds—is one of the company's valuable intangible assets. A segment of consumers like the daredevil-and-innovator image fostered by Branson. They look to Virgin as a spunky alternative to the sluggish Establishment. Just as Disney found ways to multiply *The Lion King* across many different products and offerings, Virgin multiplies the idea of Richard Branson across many different businesses.

Another example of the profit multiplier pattern is Michael Jordan, whose persona and skill as a player and communicator have been multiplied across basketball, endorsements, merchandise, filmmaking, athletic shoes, and other profit-creating activities. His multiplication economics reflect those of Disney; he has earned a relatively modest portion of his income from his core "asset" (his basketball career), but has earned handsomely by parlaying that asset into other arenas.

Similarly, Martha Stewart has parlayed her skill as a home economist and arbiter of style into a branded product, and has multiplied its value through a multimedia operation called Martha Stewart Living Omnimedia (MSLO). Through publishing, online access, and television, Martha Stewart distributes advice on various home care issues and sells Martha Stewart brand products through a Martha-By-Mail catalog and partnerships with Kmart and Sherwin-Williams. MSLO revenues are projected to increase from $125 million in 1996 to $500 million in 2001.

The recent acquisition of sports teams by big media companies indicates that more multiplier strategies can be expected. A hockey team was just a hockey team until Disney turned *The Mighty Ducks* into a profit engine. It is unlikely that Rupert Murdoch views the Los Angeles Dodgers, for which he paid a record $311 million, as just a baseball team. His profit multiplier plans will extend far beyond Dodger Stadium.

Examine your own company's assets from a profit-multiplier perspective. You are likely to find several unexpected opportunities for your assets, tangible or intangible, to do more for your customers and your company.

One manager articulated the spirit of the profit multiplier mind-set as "making the company's assets sweat" from exertion. Are your assets "sweating"? Or are they resting comfortably while a competitor works more creatively to capture your industry's value?

HOW TO PROFIT?

Challenge your organization to identify *all* the possible vehicles through which your product, brand, or skill can be sold. Pick the best seven. Build a system that puts them to work.

- Is it possible to multiply every type of product this way? Or are the odds greater with a blockbuster like *The Lion King* or Michael Jordan?
- Are your assets being leveraged to the maximum extent possible?
- What organizational systems or methods are in place for doing so?
- What is the magnitude of incremental value growth that could be created by a profit multiplier model in your business?

PLATFORM POWER

A profit multiplier strategy is, in its essence, a *platform* strategy. Platforms are assets that have been created or designed specifically for multiple uses.

The platform multiplier is complementary to the blockbuster. Each has the same goal in mind—to amortize the increasingly high cost of developing proprietary assets. They just approach the problem differently:

- The blockbuster aims to amortize fixed costs all at once through a giant commercial success.
- The platform aims to reuse an asset several times to generate multiple, moderate commercial victories. It is a blockbuster on an installment plan.

In some cases, a company can exploit both the blockbuster and profit multiplier patterns (Disney, Michael Jordan). In most cases, a company will focus on one or the other to maximize its returns.

If a company succeeds at either approach, its financial results will be vastly improved compared to a traditional product approach. The advantage of platforms over blockbusters is that mere mortals can more easily produce them; consistent blockbuster success is reserved for the most talented few.

How can a company utilize the power of platforms to its advantage? The starting point is to recognize that there are several kinds of platforms, each with its own success factors.

Image and Information Platforms are revenue generators. *The Lion King* (image), a Reuters news spot (information), and the Windows icon (a hybrid) are multiplied in front of the customer's eyes through various formats. If the customer approves of the multiplication, the reward will be multiple purchases and platform loyalty.

The key success factor for an image or information platform is to marry a world-class stand-alone product (be it a plush doll, a news broadcast, or a spreadsheet) with real value added from the platform. Customers are offered a value combination that they could not have found elsewhere, and they remain receptive to the next multiplier offer.

Product hardware platforms, by contrast, operate out of the spotlight, unknown to the customer. Yet they can also be very effective. They are the cost savers.

One of the best examples of a hardware platform comes from the automotive industry, where the next generation automobile platform costs several billion dollars to develop.

Because of the major investment involved, Volkswagen will re-use the same auto platform on VW, Audi, and Seat cars throughout Europe and the world.

Product platforms are everywhere these days, not just in cars. They have been developed in television, semiconductors, furniture, and clothing design. They are also critical to software development strategies. Whole blocks of code are re-used in chunks to save valuable programmer time.

The key success factor behind product hardware and software platform strategies is to create a "no excuses" culture within the company. Every product manager always has a good business story—why "just this time" his or her product should have unique features that are incompatible with the platform. Most often, this platform nonconformity is positioned as being sensitive to customer needs.

The irony is that customers are served better once a "no excuses" platform culture is achieved. A company that accepts "just this time" platform non-compliance will, over time, fall behind in the customers' eyes.

This is true for two reasons. First, well-designed platforms eliminate many of the trade-offs between cost efficiency and customer choice. The number of car models (different "skins") being offered to customers today is increasing at the same time that the number of platforms is decreasing. A nonplatform company must ask customers to pay higher prices for choice due to its higher cost of customization.

Second, through platforms, the customer also receives better service. Semi-finished platforms can more quickly and flexibly be converted into a finished product. After-sales parts are more available and affordable.

How well is your company exploiting platforms? Platform strategies will continue to proliferate because the rising cost of innovation will force out of the market those companies who don't reuse their assets. Platforms have the power to create win-win opportunities on both cost and customer dimensions. If your company is not exploiting the power of platforms fully, it will be vulnerable to the first competitor who does.

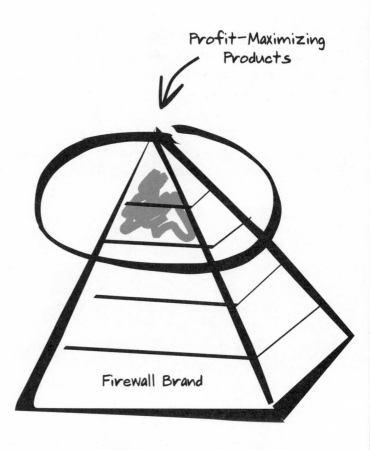

Product to Pyramid

Create a multilevel system.

Sometimes, profit opportunity shifts from focusing on excellence in a single product to creating and managing an entire product pyramid. A product pyramid consists of multiple product levels with different price points, brands, styles, designs, functionality, and performance attributes. All of these levels are managed as a system, to maximize and protect profitability.

Think of a Barbie doll as part of a pyramid. Mattel constructed a product pyramid aimed at covering a very wide price range with its Barbie dolls. The low-end Barbie dolls are priced aggressively and are available to everyone. Their purpose is to keep the competition out. The highest priced Barbie dolls, sold to collectors, carry price tags of $200 or more. Their purpose is to bring the profit in.

The product pyramid pattern can be triggered when markets experience increasing customer sophistication and income stratification. The goal of the pyramid is to have a company use its knowledge and experience to serve both the low end and the high end of its customer spectrum in very different ways. Channel relationships, operations experience, component volumes, and brand names can sometimes be leveraged to compete in both segments. On the high end, the pyramid provides profits. On the low end, it serves as a firewall to build strategic control and keep the competition away.

This same pyramid approach was taken by American Express when it identified increasing variability in customer sophistication and income levels. By introducing the Gold Card for $100 and the Platinum Card for $300, Amex was able to reap great returns at the top of the pyramid. Benefits to these card members include access to invitation-only events (for platinum members) and tickets to events in advance of public sale. At the same time, Amex's standard cards serve as a barrier to minimize the rate at which competitors might steal market share and mindshare of the other wealthy customers in the system.

Some pyramids take the form of product-line extensions at different levels (e.g., Barbie and the Amex card). Others are constructed of different brands that work together to give a company a system that protects its profits.

Nicolas Hayek, creator of the Swatch/SMH product pyramid, took a page from Alfred Sloan's playbook, and then added a step of his own. Hayek built a firewall brand (Swatch) at the base of the pyramid to keep the competition from working its way from the bottom to the top.

The Swatch firewall is a sturdy business in its own right, but its real power is in the protection and leverage that it gives the upper levels of the pyramid. At those levels, SMH earns superior returns with brands such as Rado, Longines, and Blancpain.

Much of Gillette's value growth in the past decade has been the direct result of building a highly lucrative set of upper layers onto what had been an underdeveloped product pyramid. Gillette had always managed a pyramid with a broad price spectrum. Its products ranged from paper-wrapped razors sold at kiosks up to the Trac II, which was the company's flagship product until the mid 1980s. There was, however, plenty of room above the Trac II, and this is the space that Gillette began to develop in the late 1980s. Recognizing that its customer base was separating into multiple layers, Gillette anticipated the value of the product pyramid pattern and took advantage of its potential.

The first higher layer was the Sensor, a breakthrough product launched in breakthrough fashion. Millions of units were sold, and the high price point enabled it to generate revenues and profits far out of proportion to the unit volume of sales. On the next layer up was the Sensor Excel—fewer units, more profits. The most recent layer is the Mach 3—fewer units, even greater profits.

And that's just in the United States. Most of the rest of the world has yet to experience the full force of the top of Gillette's razor pyramid.

Does the variability of customer preferences and incomes allow the construction of a product pyramid in your industry? An opportunity may be right in front of you today. Or should you anticipate that the preconditions for this pattern will make the opportunity available tomorrow?

Intel may have recently learned a similar lesson in the semiconductor industry. In the past, all customers voted for the newest, fastest computer. The market was homogeneous in its demand for greater processing power. Intel was there to provide the high-performance chip for them. Because it maintained a two-year lead in chip innovation, Intel could capture the greatest share of value in the industry.

But, as is always the case, the market has moved. Customer preferences have become more varied. A new segment has emerged, demanding cheaper computers and indicating a willingness to sacrifice maximum performance for lower prices. For Intel, this represents a radical restructuring of the market. Suddenly, new strata have emerged at the bottom of the market. Intel has the layers near the top of the pyramid, but competitors such as AMD and National Semiconductor are establishing themselves at the bottom. If Intel can develop an effective response, it can build a profitable business at the base and protect the profit of its high-end chips. If not, new competitors will beat Intel to the punch and wrest a hefty portion of its strategic control and its profits.

HOW TO PROFIT?

Build a firewall at the bottom. Build the profit maximizers
at the top. If necessary, create the key layers in between.

- Are your customers beginning to separate themselves into an income or preference hierarchy? Are there new customers that have different (higher or lower) expectations for your products?
- How vulnerable are you to attacks on the low end? How strong is your firewall?
- Are there cracks in the firewall of the market leader in your industry? How could you attack that firewall?

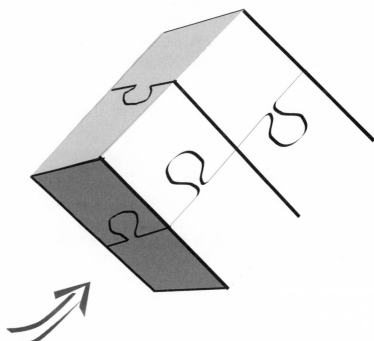

Product to Solution

Improve the economics of the system.

The pattern in which value shifts from the product to the solution will become significantly more important in the next decade. The pattern is triggered as customers begin to understand their systems economics, and as suppliers struggle to differentiate themselves. Great product functionality is no longer enough to solve customers' problems. In response to this dysfunctionality, innovative providers develop bundled offerings of products, services, and financing which create more value for customers (and suppliers) than merely selling "boxes." This shift to solutions demands a new language, a new set of metrics, and a new way of thinking.

A Swedish manufacturing company, Tetra Laval (formerly known as Tetra Pak), possessed this new mindset when it invented the block package for milk, aseptic beverages, and other fluid food. Tetra Laval created its design in response to the introduction of the euro pallet, a crate on which items are stacked for shipping and storage.

Low-cost supermarkets place the euro pallet, stacked with product, directly in the sales area. This change in method caused retailers to alter their operations to use space more efficiently. Tetra Laval's new block package further increased that efficiency. In addition, its aseptic technology made it possible for beverages to be distributed without preservatives and with no refrigeration. Together, these benefits significantly reduced costs for the supermarkets without reducing the price of the packaging itself. The new system was a dramatic improvement in the economics of taking beverages to market.

Solutions are often extremely difficult to develop. They require learning customers' economics, and going beyond the product, to create services and systems that add value far beyond the functionality of the object itself. Value is measured not only in functionality terms ("This calculates percentages automatically," or "This slices bread," or "This machine stamps out widgets at the rate of twenty per minute") but in economic terms ("This saves me three hours," or "This improves my yield by 7 percent," or "This reduces my total systems cost by 15 percent"). By anticipating the evolving systems economics of its customers, a company can exploit the solutions pattern, create a unique offering, and achieve strategic control in the marketplace.

The aerospace industry provides an additional illustration of the pattern at work. In the late 1980s, Boeing faced a situation of high development costs and stunted profitability. Boeing's response was to remove costs from the system by squeezing parts and components suppliers.

Honeywell, a major Boeing supplier, confronted the problem of Boeing's cost pressures, and saw the opportunity hidden behind them. Honeywell approached Boeing about forming a completely new customer-supplier relationship for the construction of the new 777 airliner. Rather than assembling Boeing-designed subsystems, Honeywell offered to take responsibility for the design and delivery of the entire avionics system. By concentrating on improving the entire system, Honeywell would reduce Boeing's risk, cost, and development time.

How did this new relationship benefit Honeywell? Besides gaining a long-term contract and a closer relationship with the industry's leader, Honeywell was now in a position to become the leading player in avionics systems, and to significantly enhance its share of "airplane value."

Like Honeywell, General Electric anticipated its customers' changing systems economics and developed solutions in its jet engine and hospital equipment businesses. In the early 1990s, General Electric recognized that value was migrating away from products, but the customer economic pressures that were the root cause of that movement signaled an opportunity. GE turned to its customers with an expanded offering (maintenance, service, and financing) that created more value for the customers and allowed GE to capture value for itself. This yielded GE tremendous downstream profits that were simply unavailable through a "product seller" business model.

As more companies understand the power of solutions, they will begin to reinvent their businesses to exploit this pattern. As its clients' distribution costs soared, Ryder Systems recognized an opportunity to provide solutions that could lower these costs. Ryder reinvented its

PRODUCT TO SOLUTION

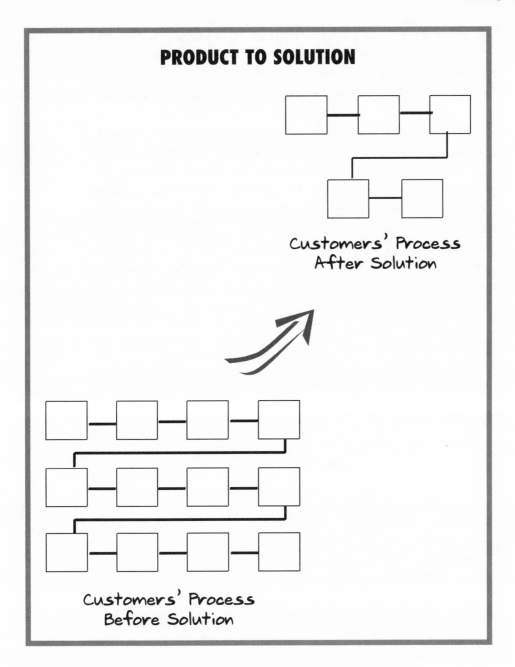

Customers' Process
After Solution

Customers' Process
Before Solution

business; the former truck lessor emerged as a complete transportation/logistical solutions company. Its logistics revenues grew at a compound rate of 30 percent from 1993 to 1997.

Deregulation prompted Enron to move from gas transportation to gas trading, helping to create the market for natural gas. To move closer to its larger and more profitable customers, Enron has begun to offer "energy management" services. Through the linkage of its competencies in equipment maintenance, operations, and strengths in commodity trading, Enron provides its customers with unique offerings that align with their business objectives. For example, by charging for energy as a percentage of customer revenues, rather than at a fixed price per kilowatt, Enron transfers financial risk to itself and then uses its commodity trading expertise to reduce that risk as much as possible. Customers pay a premium for Enron's services.

Despite their value to customers, solutions are not "forever." Like products, they will commoditize. Moreover, customer needs will continue to evolve, rendering today's solutions incomplete in tomorrow's market. The dysfunctionality of an incomplete response to the customer's problem will emerge once again, so suppliers will have to be alert for the next pattern, the next opportunity, the next stage in the evolution of the supplier-customer relationship.

HOW TO PROFIT?

Study your customers' systems. Know their systems
economics better than they do. Create unique
solutions to improve their systems.

- Is your product becoming a commodity? Is that commoditization accelerating?
- How much does your customer spend in total systems cost around your product?
  - Twice the product cost?
  - Five times the product cost?
  - Ten times the product cost?

- How much friction, frustration, and/or inefficiency is there in your customer's system?

- What services, systems, and other offerings could you provide that would reduce your customer's total systems cost by more than 15 percent?

- Which customers, if any, would share some of those solution-generated savings with you?

- When your solution becomes a commodity, what will be the next pattern of change that your company can profit from?

THE SOLUTIONS MINDSET

The list of solution pattern examples was not nearly as long as was expected by 1998. Why? The single most powerful factor is mindset. We were all trained to be product-centric thinkers. The magic was in the product. We built entire systems to manufacture the product efficiently and distribute it effectively.

The magnitude of the abyss between the product world and the solutions world is well illustrated in the arena of desktop software.

In 1991, if you could look into the mindset of an executive at Lotus, or WordPerfect, or Borland, here's what you'd find:

"We sell shrink-wrap software. We sell it by the pallet-load. High, high volumes. We sell it through distribution. Our direct salesforce is there just to stimulate demand, but all of our sales go through distribution.

Our entire manufacturing, storage, fulfillment and accounting system is optimized around selling pallet-loads of shrink-wrap software through distribution channels. Period."

Now imagine stepping into this mental world and suggesting that this same company should offer customers a solution (not a product) sold by the salesforce (not through indirect channels), with pricing per site (not per unit of shrink-wrap), with consulting services sold per day, and with the solution made available through numerous external VARs (value-added resellers) who possess significant industry-specific experience that is important to the customer.

The response? Immediate and complete immune system rejection.

That's why it was so hard for Lotus to make the transition from shrink-wrap software to communications products and solutions. That's why Borland, WordPerfect, and others never made the transition at all.

A second example comes from the world of automotive plastics. Car makers in the 1990s were increasingly interested in suppliers who could provide services and solutions, not just products, so that the carmakers' total systems cost could be reduced.

A senior executive at a major plastics producer worked for months to develop a value-added relationship with a major carmaker, and to persuade the customer that his company's technical and engineering professionals could add significant value to the carmaker. But, he couldn't give that resource away for free. He needed at least a service contract that would compensate his company for its effort.

After much negotiation, posturing, and positioning, the two sides came to an agreement: a two-year, $20 million service contract that both sides strongly felt would be of significant mutual benefit.

The executive was delighted. This was a breakthrough—the first step, and a critically important one, in decommoditizing the relationship between the plastics supplier and the automaker.

The executive returned to his company, joyfully waving the signed contract before his boss. The boss was delighted as well. This was very good news indeed. All of this "solutions" talk had finally resulted in *real* new revenues for the company.

A happy ending—right? Wrong. The executive and his boss learned that there was no way their company's accounting system—optimized around accounting for sales of millions of pounds of plastics—could deal with a $20 million, two-year service contract! Months passed before the accounting issue was resolved.

If the supplier's mindset is the most powerful barrier to creating solutions, the customer's mindset is a close second. Numerous suppliers, when seeking to make the transition from product to solution, have been terminally frustrated by customers who:

- Have an almost religious belief that suppliers should not make money.
- Talk about solutions and value sharing, but continue to demonstrate purchasing agent "beat-the-price-down" behavior.
- Agree to a fair price or a value-sharing structure, but then seek to renegotiate after a year, before the supplier can recover the costs incurred in developing the solution for the customer.

Just as suppliers have been trained to be product-centric on the supply side, customers have been trained to be product-centric on the demand side. The mindset on both sides of the equation seems to have conspired to do what was least valuable for seller and buyer alike.

The force field generated by powerfully held beliefs can be incredibly difficult to alter; the transition can absorb a tremendous amount of energy, with little guarantee of success. The mindshift required is as extreme as the shift from the worldview held by pre-relativity physicists, to that held in the post-relativity world.

Mindset obstacles notwithstanding, the product to solutions pattern will be triggered repeatedly in the next few years because: (1) its economic effects are so powerful, (2) customers need to become increasingly focused on the few things they do best, and (3) a critical mass of precedents provides the evidence that it can be done. More importantly, these precedents provide a rapidly expanding training ground where the skills required to build a solutions business (and the skills to move an organization from a product to solutions mindset) can be learned.

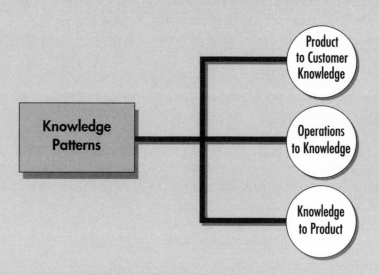

CHAPTER 9
KNOWLEDGE PATTERNS

KNOWLEDGE IS A FORM of energy. It is quiet, clean, and effective. In the new value chain, which starts with the customer on the left and ends with the organization on the right, knowledge is becoming the primary raw material that fuels the system.

Knowledge can be disorganized, dissipated, and squandered. Or, it can be organized, focused like a laser, and profited from—immensely—by both supplier and customer.

A great deal depends on how we think about knowledge, and on the choices we make when we are creating and using it.

Knowledge patterns and their variants will proliferate in the next few years, as the focus of the economy shifts from the manufacture of goods to the application of useful ideas. Several major knowledge patterns have already emerged, but because they were not anticipated or planned for (or because they don't fit the traditional strategy model), these patterns are still unexploited by many companies that are in a position to take advantage of them.

This chapter explores three of the major knowledge patterns that have emerged to date: (1) product to customer knowledge, (2) operations to knowledge, and (3) knowledge to product. The key to profiting from knowledge patterns is to develop a deep understanding of the patterns we already know, and to be the first to anticipate the plethora of new knowledge patterns that will emerge in the next several years.

Product

Product to Customer Knowledge

My product business teaches me about my customer.

In the product to customer knowledge pattern, profit-oriented suppliers convert a flow of product transactions into profound and systematized knowledge of customers' preferences, price sensitivity, and buying behavior. This knowledge can produce new profit streams in many different ways: category management, precision merchandising, or dramatic increases in the innovation success rate.

CATEGORY MANAGEMENT

In the grocery store shelf wars, there is no shortage of products. The excess is made worse by the multitude of new products introduced to the market each year. In many categories, knowledge about customer behavior, not the product itself, is becoming the true source of profitability. Product expertise enables manufacturers to create and capture that knowledge. The most profit-focused manufacturers convert their product expertise to a new, knowledge-based offering for retailers: category management.

Category management addresses a major problem for merchandisers. Most grocers and retailers stock more product lines and stock-keeping units (SKUs) than they can really master. Each category of products (be it packaging materials, diapers, or soap) is its own little universe of buying behavior and market dynamics. The mismatch between what's on the shelves and what customers want leads to lost sales and customer frustration. In each product category, the manufacturers know (or could know) more about customer preferences, price sensitivity, and buying behavior than the retailers do, and can work to correct any mismatch.

The manufacturer offers to manage the entire category (not just its own product) for the retailer. Superior knowledge of customer behavior enables the manufacturer to generate significantly higher gross margin per square foot, through skillful manipulation of the combination of manufacturers' brands, house brands, generics, and quantities of stock that will produce the greatest return on shelf space. The value is not in the products that the manufacturer makes; it is in the unique customer knowledge that enables the manufacturer to create the maximum returns for the grocer.

PRECISION MERCHANDISING

Category management addresses a chronic dysfunctionality that bedevils all retailing activity—the imbalance between demand and availability at a given moment in time. Excess inventory means excess carrying cost. Insufficient inventory means stockouts and lost gross margin.

The product to customer knowledge pattern enables companies to attack this dysfunctionality on several levels—not just by store, but also by region. Wal-Mart's huge flow of transactions by region has enabled it to develop predictive algorithms that help model demand patterns with previously unimagined accuracy. This customer knowledge at a macro level helps reduce the dysfunctionality of stockouts and excess inventory on a region-by-region basis. Precision merchandising replaces "educated guesswork" merchandising.

A micro example (location by location) of precision merchandising is being developed by Coca-Cola. Coke is exploring the application of telemetry technology that will enable bottlers to monitor the "in-stock" status of each individual vending machine. New profitability will be generated because both stockouts and service calls will be reduced, based on actual knowledge of customer purchasing behavior. If its new programs are successful, Coke will have moved to a new source of profitability well before the prior source of profits (gross margin on soda sold) has been eroded.

INNOVATION SUCCESS RATE

The product to customer knowledge pattern also plays out in industrial settings. There are two triggers: the product becomes a commodity, and the supplier learns deeply about the customer's usage system, deeply enough to create an accurate model of the customer's true economics. GE, for example, has developed highly sophisticated models of the technical and economic performance of its products (locomotives, jet engines) in the context of the customers' usage systems. This information is used to define and drive those product and service innovations that matter most to each customer. The magic that used to be in the product now resides in the proprietary model of how the product works for the customer.

One specialty chemical company has taken the idea of modeling the customer one step further. Like GE, it has developed proprietary models of its products' economic and technical value added to the customer. But it has also developed a model of the customers' political hierarchy and decision-making process. The company (whose financial success hinges on selling innovative materials and fabrication methods into an automotive manufacturing environment) knows that, more than the economic value added, it's the political value added that matters. A wonderful economic innovation will go nowhere if it means significant career risk for the decision makers.

The company's "politics *and* economics decision-making" model (developed on a plant-by-plant basis) enables it to introduce its innovations into settings where there is a high probability of acceptance, given the political milieu prevailing at the moment. Although its competitors have the technical skills to create economic value added, they lack the political knowledge of the customer that would convert those skills into a high success rate on new product introductions.

HOW TO PROFIT?

Listen to what your transactions are telling you about the customer. Hear and capture the message. Apply it to (1) create new offerings, (2) develop new systems, and (3) improve the customer's economics and your own.

Operations to Knowledge

Assets to essence.

There used to be a great deal of profitability in owning fixed assets and in running operations based on those assets. This was true for airlines, hotels, bookstores, steel mills, computer manufacturers, and many others.

Some of these operations are still profitable. Many, however, have become profitless or do not return the cost of capital. Overcapacity, customer power, and competitive intensity have driven profits away from these operations. When profit begins to disappear from basic asset-intensive operations, there are numerous opportunities to create profit in new ways: build a unique knowledge position, fill a niche that has room for just one player, or create services built on knowledge so scarce that it makes these services valuable to buyers and sellers alike.

A minority of players have had the foresight (or the luck) to develop these new profit-making activities, based on the knowledge and experience they acquired in the course of running their operations.

In other cases, outsiders capitalized on the operations-to-knowledge pattern. The airlines and the television networks have a hard time making money. The *Official Airlines Guide* and *TV Guide,* however, are extremely profitable. They often generate more profit than the industries from which their information is derived. Both are provided by players from outside the base industry.

One of the most pervasive forms of the operations to knowledge pattern is the selling of contract services. After divesting itself of ownership of its hotels, Marriott concentrated on providing management services, both in its formerly owned hotels and in new situations where hotel asset owners sought out Marriott to run their operations for them. Disney's expertise in theme park operations enabled it to structure Euro Disney so that others own the assets while Disney owns the management contract. Barnes & Noble's expertise in running bookstores enabled it to compete successfully for contracts to run college bookstores. The institutions retain the assets, and Barnes & Noble profits from the ownership of the management contracts.

Each of these companies moved while its original business models were still profitable. In other cases, the operations to knowledge pattern was exploited in the face of collapsing profitability in the core operations. A case in point is the Japanese steel industry. Japanese steelmakers siphoned value away from U.S. steel mills in the 1970s. Then they saw their own value decline in the 1980s. Value was shifting from ownership of capacity to knowledge-based value.

Unlike their U.S. predecessors, the Japanese steelmakers did capitalize on this shift from operations to knowledge. They sold proprietary processes and process expertise to steelmakers around the world. They also sold plant design and engineering services to new steel installations in Latin America, Korea, and other markets. They generated enormous profit margins from these knowledge-based services, while steelmaking margins were dropping to zero. By doing so, they extended the returns on their economic activity by a decade longer than would have been possible in a pure asset-ownership-and-operations business model.

The classic example of the operations to knowledge pattern is the American Airlines SABRE system, developed in the early 1960s as part of the company's process of upgrading its reservation system. For more than a decade, American Airlines used SABRE in-house. In 1976, it decided to roll the system out to travel agents. After launching SABRE, American continued to add customer-relevant enhancements to the system. From the late 1970s to the mid 1980s, American expanded SABRE to include hotel reservations, car rentals, tours, and cruises. Then SABRE launched an information technology business to service outside companies. American exploited new technology by adapting SABRE to provide electronic ticketing. It also developed the first PC-based SABRE system. SABRE further expanded its Internet capability when it created the Travelocity system in 1996.

American Airlines was able to capitalize on its operational knowledge by offering a service that provided great value for the customer. The best measure of its profit-creating success is the fact that, from 1991 to 1995, SABRE captured almost one-fifth of the airline industry's operating profit. Most of the time, the value of the American

Airlines SABRE system is greater than that of its airline business, even though the airline business creates revenues many times greater than the revenues created by SABRE.

In several operations to knowledge patterns, there is a type of knowledge-to-profit arbitrage going on. *Potential* profitability often lies trapped inside the complex structure of asset-intensive organizations. Profit-oriented suppliers create new, knowledge-based vehicles (management contracts, information systems, or financing services) to unlock that *potential* profitability and turn it into a major new source of profit growth for the company.

This pattern remains largely unexploited by many asset-intensive businesses, even though they have enormous potential to profit from the knowledge content of their activities. Many chemical companies today are in exactly the same position as the steel mills in the 1980s. Few have exploited the Japanese steel example of how to create new profits from process controls, management contracts, and other knowledge-intensive services.

Hospitals represent another example of highly asset-intensive knowledge creation factories. Few, if any, hospital systems have converted their privileged knowledge flow into a new source of profit growth.

The biggest obstacle to exploiting the operations-to-knowledge pattern is not financial or physical, but intellectual. A mental block causes organizations to think, "We're a manufacturer," or "We're a hospital," as opposed to thinking: "We're a business organization whose job is to create customer benefits and wealth through the constant search for new sources of profitability."

HOW TO PROFIT?

Translate operations experience into unique knowledge. Create a form (a contract or a database) for selling it. Shed the assets, sell the knowledge.

- Is there significant knowledge value hidden inside your business?
- Where? In what form?
- How can you profit from it?
- Will someone else profit from that knowledge before you do?

Knowledge to Product

Expertise—crystallized.

The shift from value based on tangibles (product, operations, bricks and mortar) to value based on knowledge is beginning to permeate the economy. But there is an important movement in the other direction, as experience, expertise, and knowledge are transformed into products.

In many business situations, knowledge is valuable but inaccessible. Trapped in the labor-intensive economics of professional service firms, or in fragmented databases, it is hard to access and hard to apply. An embryonic but increasingly frequent pattern is one in which knowledge is converted into a product in a way that creates benefits for customers (convenient, cost-effective access) and suppliers (the opportunity for much higher rates of value growth).

Incyte, an information firm based in Palo Alto, California, organized a set of genomic databases, and created a set of software tools for easier and more orderly access. It converted scientific knowledge into a subscription product (database access plus access tools) for which major pharmaceutical firms pay Incyte $5 million per year.

Cambridge Technology Partners (CTP), founded in 1991 in Cambridge, Massachusetts, has grown at an annual rate of approximately 80 percent in recent years and recorded over $400 million in sales in 1997. That extraordinary performance resulted from CTP's conversion of its experience in information technology (IT) project development and execution into a product called RAD (Rapid Application Deployment).

Most IT consulting services are billed as "time and materials," a variable cost model in which the risk and the costs of a project are borne by the client. This arrangement is common in technology-related industries because consultants are dealing with rapidly evolving technologies and with the challenge of getting the right people to execute against clients' demands. They need as much flexibility within a project as possible. On the client side, IT departments are under constant pressure to maintain their current systems and upgrade to new technologies, a situation that leads to rapidly changing needs within these organizations.

In contrast to the norms in its industry, CTP delivers to customers a fixed-time, fixed-price contract. This shifts a significant amount of risk away from the client. The consulting company carries the burden of any over-budget costs caused by a late project.

The arrangement creates a powerful incentive for CTP to systematize its knowledge so that it can complete its projects early and under budget. It benefits significantly from jobs done before deadline. The value of the fixed-time, fixed-price product to the customer is very high. It eliminates the open-ended nature of more traditional IT contracts, with their potential for cost overruns. The client can plan its business with a clear understanding of when the new IT structure will be up and running.

More leveraged examples of the knowledge to product pattern are provided by SAP, SDRC, and PeopleSoft.

- SAP (the German software company) develops an array of software systems designed to help companies link their internal business processes. Previously, companies had to develop internal systems, often by purchasing large quantities of systems integration services, to achieve this result. SAP converted knowledge of these internal processes and challenges into a product that enabled companies to address these "business process linkage" issues more effectively and at a lower cost.

- SDRC (Structural Dynamics Research Corporation) was originally an engineering consulting firm. It converted its engineering expertise into a CAD/CAM program (for finite element analysis) that enabled customers to do nondestructive testing of new product designs, which shortened their time to market. The "productization" of SDRC's knowledge brought dramatic value growth to the firm.

- PeopleSoft converted its in-depth knowledge of human resource (HR) processes and procedures into a software product and platform for HR applications. The product enabled customers to make their HR processes more efficient, and it enabled PeopleSoft to create dramatic value growth.

IMPACT ON SUPPLIERS

How fast can a large professional service firm grow? Not very fast. Some of the best-managed large firms grow at an annual rate of 15 to 23 percent. How fast can a product-based firm grow? Very fast. CTP grew revenue at 84 percent per year (from 1992 to 1997). PeopleSoft grew at 91 percent per year (from 1991 to 1997). SAP grew at 48 percent per year (from 1995 to 1998e).

In the knowledge to product pattern, the achievable growth rate is completely redefined. In many cases, it more than doubles.

Reuters, the European financial services and information provider, represents a different type of the knowledge to product pattern. The company has always been known for providing access to information, whether in the form of news, international events, stock prices, or currency exchange rates. Over the past three decades, Reuters has successfully productized and branded its information. It has crafted news stories and events into Reuters Service Subscriptions and Reuters Online. Stock prices and equities dealing have been productized as Stockmaster, Videomaster, Equities 2000, Equities 3000, and Instinet. Monitor Money Rates, Mini-Reuters Monitor, and Monitor Dealing 2000 were all developed by Reuters from foreign exchange prices and dealing.

Competition in providing information products to financial services companies is intensifying (with Bloomberg, Dialog, and EBS gaining market share). Consequently, Reuters is looking for new arenas where it can apply its ability to productize information. It is searching for other customer groups that need accurate and objective information on a timely basis to support critical decisions. It has found several new markets for its productization skills; it is providing ad prices to media buyers, medical information to health care companies, and insurance rates to insurance and risk management companies.

In the next decade, the knowledge to product pattern will grow dramatically. As knowledge becomes increasingly valuable, more companies will find new ways to turn their embedded knowledge into products, so that they can profit from making that knowledge more accessible and more cost-effective for their current and future customers.

HOW TO PROFIT?

Identify the most valuable knowledge your organization has created. Crystallize your expertise into a highly replicable structure that is easy to sell, easy to train, and easy to improve. Advertise it. Sell it. Improve it.

- Is a knowledge to product pattern occurring in your industry?
- Do you depend on several individuals within your firm to create value for the customer? Is there a way to systematize and leverage their knowledge?
- Are there opportunities to trigger the knowledge to product pattern in your industry?
- How valuable would it be? What resources would be needed?

KNOWLEDGE AND STRATEGY

"Imagination is more important than knowledge..."

- Albert Einstein

"...assuming you have the knowledge."

- the rest of us

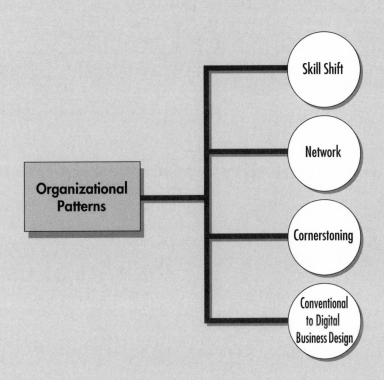

CHAPTER 10
ORGANIZATIONAL PATTERNS

THE DOMINANT PARADIGM in business used to be asset efficiency in the value chain. Today, it is targeted value creation for the customer. Tomorrow, it will be a simultaneous focus on the customer and the supplier's organizational system.

The organizational system links external customers (the buyers) with internal customers (the talent) in a flow of interactions that create (or destroy) value for buyers, employees, and owners.

In the past decade, the customer has become more important than the product. A similar shift has made talent more important than assets.

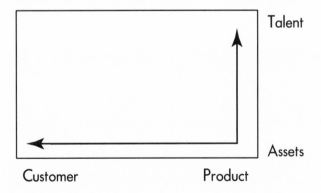

The shift from product to customer explains why, in so many product patterns, value migrates away from the product to something else, and why changes related to customers are key triggers to those patterns. Because of the shift from assets to talent, organizational patterns will be among the most important patterns in the next half-decade.

Just as the most inventive managers devised new ideas and methods for dealing with value migration, they are now developing new ideas and methods for managing the key *organizational* challenges in an economy characterized by extreme dynamism and complexity.

The organizational system can have a huge impact on the company's profit. The organizational system can add value to, or subtract value from, the company's product franchise and business design. The outcome depends on how well the organizational system creates (1) alignment behind the company's business strategy, and (2) an energy level that is sufficient to enable brilliant execution of that strategy.

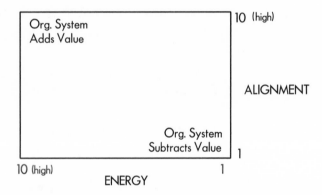

The reinventor companies profiled in *The Profit Zone* inhabit the upper left-hand corner of the accompanying diagram. They have created not only great business designs, but also great organizational systems. They have applied the best principles of advertising (right message, simple message, repeated message) to the internal customer (the talent). Their organizations add value and profit to the business because of the alignment and energy they create.

This "alignment-and-energy" factor is intangible, but its presence is very real. Go to Redmond, Atlanta, or Crotonville. It won't be hard to sense the degree of alignment, or the energy level, within any of those organizations.

The alignment created is not just alignment with the company's strategy; it is also alignment with the customers' top priorities. That's what makes the pyramid to network pattern (see pp. 239–245) so important. By increasing exposure to the customer, it raises the odds that the organizational alignment created is both internally and externally on target.

Even though great organizational systems create organizational energy, there's never enough of it to go around. The importance of the cornerstoning pattern lies in its ability to conserve and make maximum use of the energy created by the organization. The digital business design pattern goes even further in conserving organizational energy and providing phenomenal leverage to the talent operating within the organizational system.

Many of the patterns we've discussed are triggered by serious dysfunctionalities. This is equally true for organizational patterns. Being remote from customers and being adept at the wrong skill set are two dysfunctionalities that hinder many companies and trigger the pyramid to network and skill shift patterns.

Other patterns are triggered by the changing nature of opportunities. Cornerstoning and digital business design fall into this category.

In all of these patterns, there is a mix of exogenous factors and company initiative. Some are more exogenously driven (skill shift, for example). Others are more driven by initiative (e.g., cornerstoning). Even the patterns that are driven by initiative, however, respond to exogenous conditions that define the best pathway to tomorrow's profitability.

Many organizational patterns have played out in the past decade (functional to business unit structure, functional to matrix, vertical to horizontal, and others). There will be an incredible profusion of new organizational patterns in the next several years, as creative companies invent new ways to solve the organizational part of the value creation equation.

However, many of these solutions will have one factor in common: the redefinition of the relationship between the talent and the customer. Just as today's economy requires that we "reverse" the value chain and begin our strategic thought process with the buyer (see *The Profit Zone,* pp. 20–23), so tomorrow's economy will require that we fold over the value chain and create the maximum possible direct linkage between the customer and the talent in our organization.

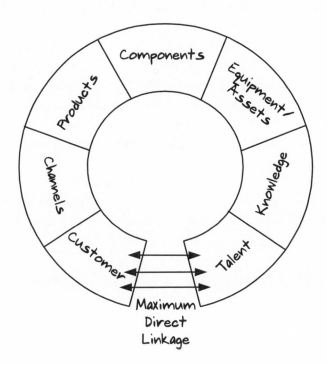

This direct contact will expose skill gaps early and will trigger the skill shift pattern accordingly. It will also define the most efficient pathway for cornerstoning in the numerous cases where the customer franchise, rather than the product, will define the optimal profit growth path for the company.

Finally, the foldover of the value chain will bring to light the full importance of the shift from conventional to digital business design. The ultimate value of this shift will be the creation, between external customers and internal talent, of the kinds of bridges that will maximize the economic performance of both groups.

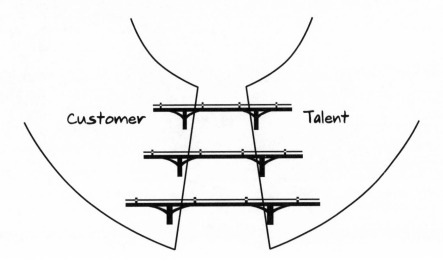

Skill Shift

Yesterday's source of advantage becomes today's cost burden.

When companies lose touch with changing customer priorities and market conditions, they get out of sync with the kinds of skills that are most important to customers and that produce the greatest profitability. The external environment changes; the skill mix inside the company doesn't. A gap develops. The dysfunctionality of this mismatch grows more acute over time.

It also produces a major management headache. Functions and skills that were once critical to customers become less important, or even irrelevant. However, these functions retain their cost base and their intense pride. They build defenses. The situation becomes almost impossible to manage. Organizational effectiveness declines as the threatened go to extremes to protect their turf. Ultimately, the skill shift pattern is triggered when a company recognizes this dysfunctionality and responds to it effectively.

Therein lies the profit opportunity for the few players who see the gap and move first to close it. These organizations exploit the skill shift pattern by engineering radical changes in their skill mix to match the market—well before their competitors do.

The skill shift pattern can work along several dimensions:

- *Functional* (e.g., value shifting from manufacturing, sales, and R&D, to channel or account management, or licensing)
- *Technical skill* (e.g., hardware to software engineers, organic chemistry to biotechnology, and so on)
- *Managerial skills and values* (e.g., from focus on cost to focus on service, or from performance to performance *plus* people values such as communication, people development, and coaching)

FUNCTIONAL SHIFT

In many situations, the key to unlocking new profits is a shift of emphasis and resources from one major function within a company to another.

An example is found in biotechnology. Numerous efforts are under way to map the sequence of human DNA. Labs full of biologists are cataloging portions of the complex human genome, building mountains of information. The government-sponsored Human Genome Project makes the raw data available for free. Why, then, would a company called Incyte Pharmaceuticals ask $5 million a year for access to its genome database?

Incyte understood that the real value was not in producing vast collections of data, but in manipulating and analyzing the data. The key skill had shifted from biology to programming, and the employment rolls at Incyte reflect that change. In 1998, it had only 125 biologists, but 175 programmers. Its database is so valuable to other pharmaceutical companies that it generates $100 million in revenue a year. Recognizing the skill shift paid off. Incyte has a market value that is over eight times its revenues.

Functional shifts have been key patterns in the success of many notable companies:

- In the early 1990s, Hewlett-Packard was built on the functions of engineering, manufacturing, and technical selling. It maintained those skills but also made a highly successful shift to marketing, channel management, and account management.

- Merck and Pfizer, in their preclinical R&D work, made a successful shift from discovery to discovery *plus* strategic licensing. The new function enabled them to detect high-promise compounds (invented by others around the world) early, and to supplement R&D with S&D (search and develop).

- Lotus, in the early 1990s, made the difficult transition from sales management and channel management to applications development, value-added reseller management, consulting, and account management.

TECHNICAL SKILL

New profits can also result from changing the composition of skill sets within functions.

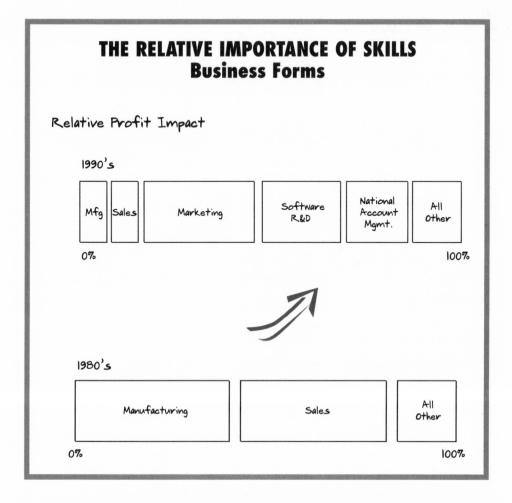

THE RELATIVE IMPORTANCE OF SKILLS
Business Forms

Relative Profit Impact

1990's

| Mfg | Sales | Marketing | Software R&D | National Account Mgmt. | All Other |

0%   100%

1980's

| Manufacturing | Sales | All Other |

0%   100%

At Boeing, for example, engineers are still important to the company's business model, but the *type* of engineer is very different. The company's success used to hinge on engineers who wanted to design planes that "flew higher and faster." Today, its success hinges on engineers who want to design planes that are dramatically more cost-effective.

Anyone who knows engineers knows how big a difference that is.

At Nokia, or at Lucent, the most important engineers used to be the hardware engineers. Today, it is the software engineer that matters most. For Monsanto's R&D division, it used to be chemists who mattered most. Today, it is geneticists, biochemists, and experts in other biotech disciplines.

MANAGERIAL SKILLS AND VALUES

Until recently, Continental was an airline focused exclusively on cost. The customer came second. That focus, and its associated skill set, robbed attention from other areas, resulting in service that was subpar and plane flights that were unpredictable.

In 1994, Gordon Bethune, the new CEO, realized that the organization's focus and skill set had to shift from cost to service. He aligned his entire organization behind this new focus. Every employee would receive a monthly bonus if Continental moved into the "top five" airlines in on-time percentage while keeping the entire system working smoothly.

This shift created a tremendous charge of organizational energy within Continental. The airline began to climb up in the rankings. Organizational energy continued to rise. Employees were proud to wear the uniforms of their company.

The managerial skill set shifted to include excellent service. The change was not only about skills, but also about managerial values. The customers became important. So too did the employees.

Continental's skill shift contributed to creating extraordinary results. The positive upward spiral (among customers, managers, and employees) triggered by the skill shift has increased Continental's market value nearly fivefold in the past four years.

An equally powerful focus on new managerial skills and values has been catalyzed at GE. In the past, great performance (turning in the numbers) was what was required to succeed.

Today, the required skill mix has become great performance *and* great values (communication, coaching, people development).

Although the values-focused skill set may seem "softer," it isn't. Peer evaluations, as well as upward and downward feedback, can pinpoint those who are subtracting from organizational capital instead of contributing to it.

In a world where success increasingly hinges on talent and on the organizational system that leverages it, this skill shift at GE is a precursor of ideas and practices that many other organizations will adopt in the next decade.

The frequency with which the skill shift pattern occurs often depends on the metabolism rate of the industry. In slow-change industries, it could be once a decade. In "hyperactive" industries, it is much more frequent.

The skills necessary for success in the world of personal computers have shifted several times. The original skill that companies were built on was engineering. The first shift was from engineering to brand management and efficient distribution; then to solutions and customer relationship management. In each case, evolving customer priorities changed the core skill set on which successful companies needed to focus. These shifts proved difficult for many of the PC companies. Few made the brand skill transition effectively. Even fewer moved on to build their organizations' capabilities in customer relationships and solutions.

One company that successfully moved in tempo with the demands of the customer was Compaq Computer. It started with great engineering. It then built a great brand.

When it was confronted with the shift to solutions skills, Compaq didn't have much of a presence in the world of solutions. It lacked the capability to deliver high-value services such as application installation, training, and information technology strategy development.

The company knew it had a skill gap, and it undertook a strategy of aggressive alliances and acquisitions to repair it. The culmination of this strategy was the acquisition of Digital Equipment Corporation. With a large installed base, a well-developed distribution network, and a service force of over 20,000 people, Digital transformed Compaq's business design. Compaq transitioned from being a "box manufacturer" to being a product and service solutions provider. Compaq's new position has the potential to set a new standard for enterprise-level service and will challenge Dell, HP, IBM, and other competitors in the corporate PC space.

Sometimes, the skill shift pattern is about big numbers. (Think about Nokia or Lucent building up an army of software engineers.)

Sometimes, it isn't. In areas such as project management, or "search and develop" (an innovative strategy based on licensing others' discoveries and developing them), or positioning a product, only a handful of new skill players are needed.

The point is not in the numbers. The point is in the changing relative importance of skill sets. The point is in making certain that the company's business model is equipped with the new skills that respond to the new requirements of the external environment.

The skill shift pattern works beyond the level of the organization. It works at a macro-level for the economy and at a micro-level for the individual.

At the macro-level, there is constant tension between the skills we have and the skills we need. To go to an extreme, blacksmiths, wheelwrights, and ironmongers probably aren't as valuable as they once were. On the other side of the equation, we continue to be plagued by acute shortages of programmers, geneticists, and really effective educators. This mismatch between what's needed and what's available is a dysfunctionality in the system and a major impediment to profitable economic growth.

The pattern also plays out on a personal level. What skills have been most important to your professional growth? What will those skills be tomorrow? Personal transitions are every bit as difficult as organizational ones.

Recognizing a skill shift pattern isn't enough. The proof is in the unambiguous redeployment of resources. Companies become so ingrained in the way things have always been done that it is almost impossible for them to change.

How does a successful company create the dramatic internal change that is required? By paying a very high price. The price is creating the discomfort needed to align the organization around key new skills, and sustaining the energy needed to keep pushing the shift until it is complete.

HOW TO PROFIT?

Look at how the customer is changing. Identify tomorrow's skill, and redeploy resources to build it today. Don't stop until your advantage ratio is three-to-one.

- What were your company's three most important skills in 1990?

  ☐ Manufacturing   ☐ New business development
  ☐ Quality management   ☐ Software engineering

       ☐ Sales   ☐ Distribution

       ☐ Account management   ☐ Brand building _____

       ☐ R&D   ☐ Other_____

       ☐ Marketing   ☐ _____

- What are they today? What will they be in 2001?
- What process will you use to manage the transition from old skill mix to new?

THE PSYCHOLOGICAL DANGER OF THE SKILL SHIFT

The skill shift pattern can be a psychological disaster area. Skills that were once critical become less important, but the costs remain. A function that was "golden" before the shift suddenly becomes neutral, and finally becomes a liability. In many companies, research and development functions move through a transition in which these former sources of competitive advantage are reduced to cost burdens. This same process can take place in the entire skill base of a company. Manufacturing, sales, marketing, finance, human resources, new business development—all can become parts of an outdated model that no longer matches the priorities of the world outside the walls of the company. Customers used to value them a lot and gladly paid for them. Now, they no longer do.

Consider a chemical company built on three core skills: research and development, manufacturing, and technical selling.

It enters the 1990s and faces a wrenching change. Four very different sets of skills become crucial: (1) account management, (2) new business development, (3) network R&D (working within networks of innovation outside the company's R&D structure), and (4) low-cost distribution.

The power and resources still reside in those privileged skills of internal research and development, manufacturing, and technical sales. Any initiatives aimed at building strengths in the new skills suffer and struggle. The weight, cumulative investment, and institutional memory of existing skills make it impossible for the new skills to take off. As a result, the stock price goes sideways for a decade.

Creating priorities for new skills in the minds of key managers is tough. Shifting resources to help build the new skills is even tougher. But staying wedded to the old hierarchy and pecking order is a formula for disaster. It is as hopeless as pledging allegiance to an obsolete product line or an obsolete business design.

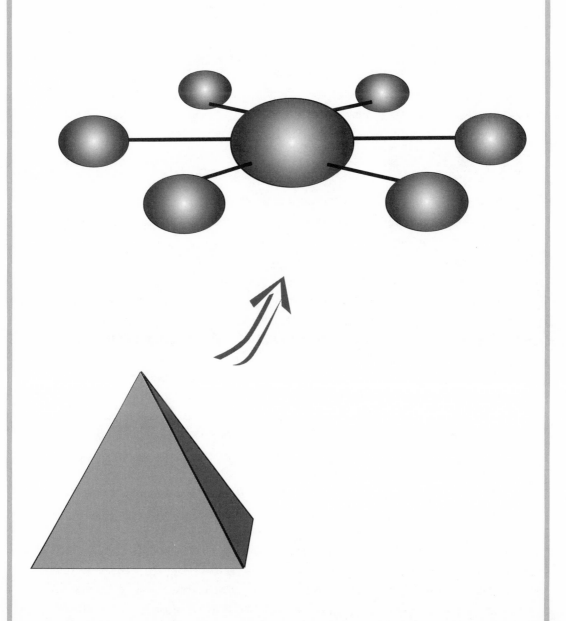

Pyramid to Network

Maximize external exposure—to customers, investors, and profit accountability.

Internal focus kills companies. The pyramid to network pattern is all about maximizing the organization's external focus—its exposure to the external environment. It's about maximizing a company's outside-to-inside ratio.

In engineering, surface area is often used to control the transfer of signals (e.g., heat) across a boundary. Arno Penzias, in his book *Harmony,* provides a wonderful example of when a low ratio of "surface-to-mass" works well, and when it doesn't.

When Hannibal was crossing the Alps to attack the Romans, his elephants survived the harsh winter for one simple reason: low surface-to-mass ratio. This low ratio conserved heat and enabled the elephants to survive in spite of the bitter cold.

What's good for elephants in winter is terrible for organizations in highly dynamic environments. In business, exposure to external factors is critical to survival and success. Customer priorities, channel shifts, infrastructure changes, competitive pressures, and valuable strategic signals transmitted by customers and investors are the keys to identifying emerging patterns in your industry. However, a low surface-to-mass ratio (found in many traditional pyramid-shaped organizations) *minimizes* the organization's exposure and sensitivity to these external signals and decreases its ability to adapt its business design profitably.

Although large organizations can overcome the "internal focus" syndrome, many do not. Recognizing the conditions for and exploiting the pyramid to network pattern can help organizations overcome the dysfunctionalities that result from success and growth and size. As organizations grow, they become remote from customers; they lose profit accountability and take on an extreme aversion to risk. The result is an organization that misses key external shifts, fails to respond to unfolding patterns, and ultimately destroys shareholder value.

The traditional structure of large organizations makes these problems worse. Most organizations are arranged along the lines of a pyramidal hierarchy. Decisions are made at the top and transmitted down to the bottom (often with a great deal of distortion as the message travels through five or six managerial layers). Information is gathered at the bottom and works its way up to the top (often losing a great deal of candor and accuracy along the way as it is subjected to successive "positive spins" on its travels upward). Diagramming how information actually flows in the organization can reveal how dysfunctional the system can be. (See Exhibit "Information Flow in Organizations.") This situation leads to an organization that is large, ill-informed, and slow moving. One strategic response to the mismatch between external market conditions and the characteristics of large organizations is the shift from a pyramid to a network organizational structure.

An example of this response is the Virgin Group, which consists of 200 or so firms privately owned by Richard Branson, the CEO. They accounted for two-thirds of 1997 revenues (the other one-third of the company's revenue comes from the rest of Virgin's holdings, a series of companies in which it owns less than 50 percent). Virgin exploits the network pattern to maximize each unit's exposure to external information and external pressures, to maintain the company's entrepreneurial spirit, and to protect its capability to respond quickly and accurately to customer changes across all of its varied operations.

Branson cites Virgin's former record company as a perfect example of the "small is beautiful" philosophy. Recognizing the lethargy and inefficiency of business designs burdened by cumbersome organizational structure, Branson exploited the pyramid to network pattern to perfection. When a unit of Virgin Records reached a certain size (about fifty people), Branson spun out a new company. The deputy managers became the directors of a new autonomous unit and could focus completely on making their new business successful. "The benefit was that each managing director ran his own destiny with fifty staff," says Branson. "He was the managing director instead of deputy to the deputy to the deputy. If you are a managing director, you will do whatever you can to excel." This organizational strategy created twenty-five to thirty small, loosely connected companies that, in the

INFORMATION FLOW IN ORGANIZATIONS

Network
(Horizontal Flows)

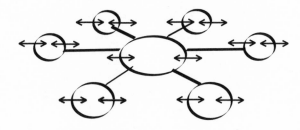

Pyramid
(Vertical Flows)

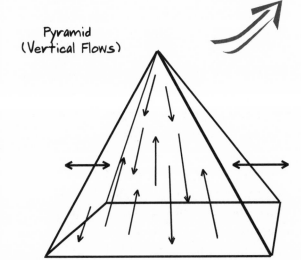

aggregate, were one of the biggest independent record companies in the world.

Overall, the Virgin network represents a system of companies that operate separately but own stakes in each other, and share a brand, a philosophy, and a powerful spirit of entrepreneurship. Lateral communication and creativity are critical features in this model, offsetting their old counterparts in the hierarchical system: vertical reporting and obedience. Order and coherence are maintained through sophisticated information systems. Common values, instilled through a strong and pervasive company culture, provide fuel for success and profit growth.

The shift from a pyramid structure to a network organization has dramatically increased Virgin's ability to detect and respond quickly to market changes. Because more employees are exposed to developments in the market, they are able to rapidly pick up and process external signals. Employees also have a clearer sense of their direct role in the company's fortunes, to which their compensation is closely tied. They strive to reach a high level of performance because they understand why that is important to Virgin and how it will affect their own personal return on the time and energy they invest in the enterprise. Because there is considerable autonomy within the organization, employees are empowered to gather information and make decisions at all levels. The result is a dramatically more efficient and effective internal process.

ABB and Thermo Electron are two other examples of how the network model achieves these desired outcomes. They are different businesses that face very different challenges, but each reflects a strong drive to break up or preempt bureaucracy, maximize exposure to customers, decentralize decision making, and push profit accountability down to very small units within a very large organization.

ABB, a global manufacturer of industrial, energy, and transportation systems, has exploited the network pattern to maintain close relationships with its customers in each market. To fully exploit this pattern, ABB is organized as a network of specialist companies. It has thousands of profit centers. As a corporation, ABB can add significant value to these units because it can purchase from its suppliers at a discount, leverage its brand name, and centralize its administrative and research and development costs. Each specialist member of the network provides best-of-breed products, fast and reliable help, and a local contact for customers. The combination of central and local strengths allows ABB to respond better to customer priorities than ABB's purely local or purely global rivals can.

Thermo Electron has used the network structure to dramatically increase its value. In 1982, CEO George Hatsopoulos restructured his company and created a "spin-out" business design. In the spin-out model, most companies in the system are minority-owned by public shareholders. Managers are directly accountable to outside investors. This new structure dramatically increases Thermo Electron's shareholder focus and customer focus; improves management incentives (managers own stock in their own spin-outs); and provides Thermo Electron with a more accurate and significantly higher stock market valuation.

Recently, Thermo Electron has run into problems that illustrate the difficulty of implementing a network structure. The dangers of taking immature businesses public, of creating businesses that lack strategic purpose, or of creating spin-outs without the necessary infrastructure to support them, are issues that confront any company that plans to exploit the network pattern. But Thermo Electron executives stand by the network model and plan to make the investments necessary to work out the bugs in the system.

(For more information on the Thermo Electron and ABB business designs, see Chapters 11 and 12 in *The Profit Zone*.)

The ABB and Thermo Electron prototypes have attracted the interest of many other companies. Most recently, IdeaLab!, an Internet startup, has used the network model as the basis for its organizational structure. IdeaLab! has one central group responsible for administrative functions and for brainstorming new companies. Every month, CEO Bill Gross and his team develop a business idea and then spin out a company to turn that idea into a business. Idealab! provides the seed money and maintains a minority stake, but each business runs itself and is responsible for its own profits and losses. The companies share talent, systems, and key learnings. The overall company objective is to keep creating new ideas and businesses; each individual business focuses on its own specific goals and markets.

The network model is still the exception in business today, but the rationale for this structure will intensify over time, as the mismatch between external forces and internal characteristics becomes more acute. These are the key elements of that mismatch:

External Forces	Internal Characteristics
More demanding customers	Remoteness from customers
Harder to create profitability	Remoteness from profit accountability
Faster moving markets	Slow communication
Investment analysts who insist on understanding the characteristics of the businesses inside a company's portfolio	Slow decision making
	Politics
	Extreme risk aversion (and, therefore, massive waves of nondecision-making)

The network pattern, with its high external exposure (high surface-to-mass ratio), applies to individuals as well as organizations. Ask yourself: What is your own level of *personal* exposure to:

- Customer pressures and signals?
- Investor pressures and signals?
- Profit accountability?

To the degree that high-talent individuals shield themselves from these external forces, their contribution to the organization goes down and their personal strategic risk level goes up.

HOW TO PROFIT?

Maximize your external exposure. Use whatever organizational change it takes. Watch your profit grow.

- In our organization, the external exposure ratio is:
  - ☐ Very high
  - ☐ High
  - ☐ Low
  - ☐ Very low

- Our organization's external exposure is:
  - ☐ Increasing
  - ☐ Unchanged
  - ☐ Declining
- In our organization, how widespread is profit accountability? How intense is it? How closely tied are the returns experienced by individuals to the returns created by the company?

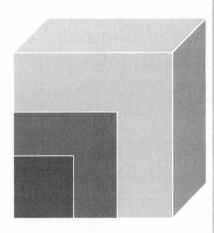

Cornerstoning

Build from strength . . . to strength . . . to strength.

What's the single best *next* opportunity for the organization to pursue? The cornerstoning pattern provides several extraordinarily effective answers to that question from companies that have answered it well not once, but several times.

Cornerstoning is a way of conserving energy, *organizational* energy. No organization has all the resources and energy it needs to achieve its ambition. The cornerstoning pattern provides examples of companies that overcame the constraint of limited resources and created maximum value growth through the discipline of a carefully sequenced progression of opportunities.

A cornerstoning pattern has three elements: (1) a terrific, A+ initial strategic position, typically with significant strategic control (you can't cornerstone up from a weak base); (2) an economically logical next opportunity for the organization (one that provides the greatest profit growth for the least incremental effort); and (3) an adjacent opportunity space that is significantly larger than the prior one.

One of the most successful, twenty-year-long cornerstoning patterns was built by Microsoft, which spent its first half-decade (1975 to 1980) building a terrific strategic position in BASIC. It leveraged that position into the much larger opportunity space that was opened up by DOS. It built out from DOS to Windows, and from Windows to winning the office applications suite.

In the next few years, Microsoft will cornerstone up from the desktop to the enterprise with Windows NT. It will use its current positions to expand into multiple adjacent opportunity spaces: the enterprise, the home, travel, automotive, and several others.

Microsoft will *have* to do this successfully in order to sustain its record of value growth. Its past record of a highly efficient progression has created an enormous reservoir of financial and organizational energy, which is available for these next moves. There is a good reason

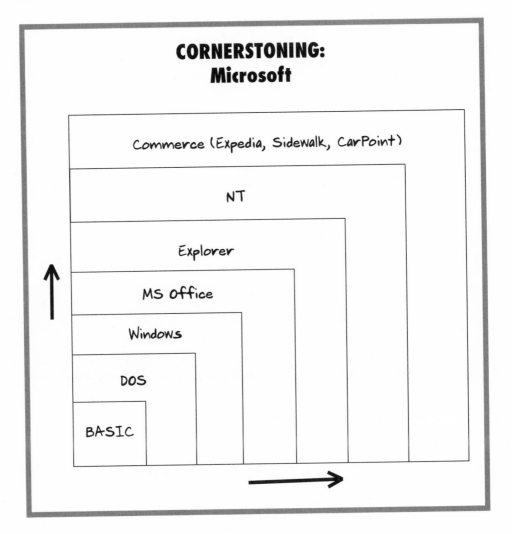

CORNERSTONING:
Microsoft

Commerce (Expedia, Sidewalk, CarPoint)

NT

Explorer

MS Office

Windows

DOS

BASIC

why so many companies have Microsoft at the edge of their competitive radar screens.

A European firm, Rentokil, provides another illustration of a sustained cornerstoning pattern. Rentokil originally operated in the pest control sector. It built a powerful strategic position in that domain, then built out from there into directly adjacent opportunity spaces.

Over a period of several decades, the company has consistently moved to enter higher growth and higher value-added sectors. It has made itself the leading business-to-business services provider of an entire array of offerings: hygiene services, health care services, office and retail cleaning, office machine maintenance, facilities maintenance, security services, temporary personnel services, parcel delivery, catering, education, and training.

This progression has generated revenue and profit growth of over 20 percent annually for the past decade and a half. It has created $13 billion of market value growth in the past decade.

Cornerstoning is becoming a more broadly available opportunity because of convergence (see pp. 67–75). As competitive boundaries disintegrate, more "adjacent opportunity spaces" are available for the organization to consider.

In financial services, the competitive boundaries among banks, insurers, brokers, and mutual funds have been eroding for some time. This erosion has expanded the number of potential cornerstoning opportunities for high-initiative companies like Charles Schwab.

Schwab was one of the first companies to exploit the cornerstoning pattern in financial services. The company built its initial position and customer base through outstanding performance in discount brokerage. This position also created a capability for extraordinary efficiency in transaction processing, which attracted investment advisers into partnership with Schwab and created the next larger cornerstoning opportunity.

That move in turn prepared the way for OneSource (serving mutual funds). A few years later, OneSource was significantly expanded, to provide services to regional banks and brokers.

Excellence and extreme profitability in each prior stage created the financial and organizational energy Schwab needed to fund the next larger cornerstone. Choosing the *right next move* was critical. In the cornerstoning pattern, the organization does not skip over the *best next* opportunity. It focuses on the single best next option, the one with the lowest incremental investment and the highest next stage of profit growth.

Cornerstoning always looks neat in retrospect. Prospectively, it doesn't look neat at all. Quite the opposite: it looks very messy. A great deal of strategic experimentation is involved. The organization casts about for the right next opportunity space, but doesn't get it right the first time. Or the second, or the third.

This was true for Microsoft, for Rentokil, and for Schwab. It will be true for all successful cornerstone patterns.

However, the strategic experimentation is driven by that one tough question: What's the single *best* next opportunity? Getting that answer right is so valuable that it's worth the two to three years of experimentation, missteps, and wrong turns required to get there.

The cornerstoning pattern is difficult but far from mature. Amazon.com may be on the verge of exploiting this pattern. It has built an A+ strategic position in its initial space of online bookselling. The single best next move is to convert its profound knowledge of customers into a platform for the next adjacent layer of entertainment/education sales: music, videos, and software. This is the space in which Amazon can create the greatest value growth with the least incremental effort. The magnitude of this cluster of new opportunities far exceeds the dimensions of Amazon's initial domain.

The first step, however, continues to be the most critical one in the sequence: creating an untouchably powerful strategic position in the initial domain. Without that base, it is impossible to exploit the rest of the pattern.

The cornerstoning pattern raises three questions for every organization:

1. How strong is the strategic position we have built in our initial domain?
2. What is the single best *next* opportunity space for us to build into?
3. What opportunities do other companies have to leverage their products and services into *our* customer base? (The dark side of convergence.)

HOW TO PROFIT?

Be A+ at something. Search for the *best* next space. Experiment to find it. Go there first—don't skip over it. Then find the *best* next space.

THE CONSERVATION OF ORGANIZATIONAL ENERGY

The Microsoft cornerstoning progression reflects a second powerful principle about the law of conservation of organizational energy:

> Never invent, when you can imitate, embrace, and extend.

This is a variation of the cornerstoning pattern. You use someone else's invention as the cornerstone of your own system. Microsoft didn't originate its major technologies. BASIC came from the minicomputer world. MSDOS was built from QDOS. Windows came from Macintosh. NT came from technologies derived from Digital's VMS operating system. Microsoft focused its energies less on innovation and more on development and value creation.

Like Bill Gates, the Japanese industrialists of the 1960s abhorred the "frivolous" cost of innovation. A famous exchange in the 1960s, between Peter Drucker and the Japanese, illustrates this point.

DRUCKER: To succeed, you must innovate.

INDUSTRIALISTS: No, Drucker-san. Not at all. True innovation is very, very expensive. We cannot afford it. And besides, it would be silly to throw away our meager resources on innovation when technology is so ridiculously abundant. What we need to do is learn it, improve it, and implement it. We must invite technologists here, we must send our students there, and, in a few years, we will have what we need.

Many years later, Drucker asserted that the Japanese were absolutely right. They had defined a strategy that saved enormous quantities of resources, created significant profit growth, and fueled three decades of economic growth for Japan.

In essence, the Japanese industrialists of the 1950s and 1960s and the Bill Gateses of the 1990s are playing the same pattern. At Microsoft, the perfect sequence was determined by customer readiness. In Japan, it was determined by relative economic leverage.

Never invent when you can embrace and develop . . . .

Create the perfectly rational economic sequence.

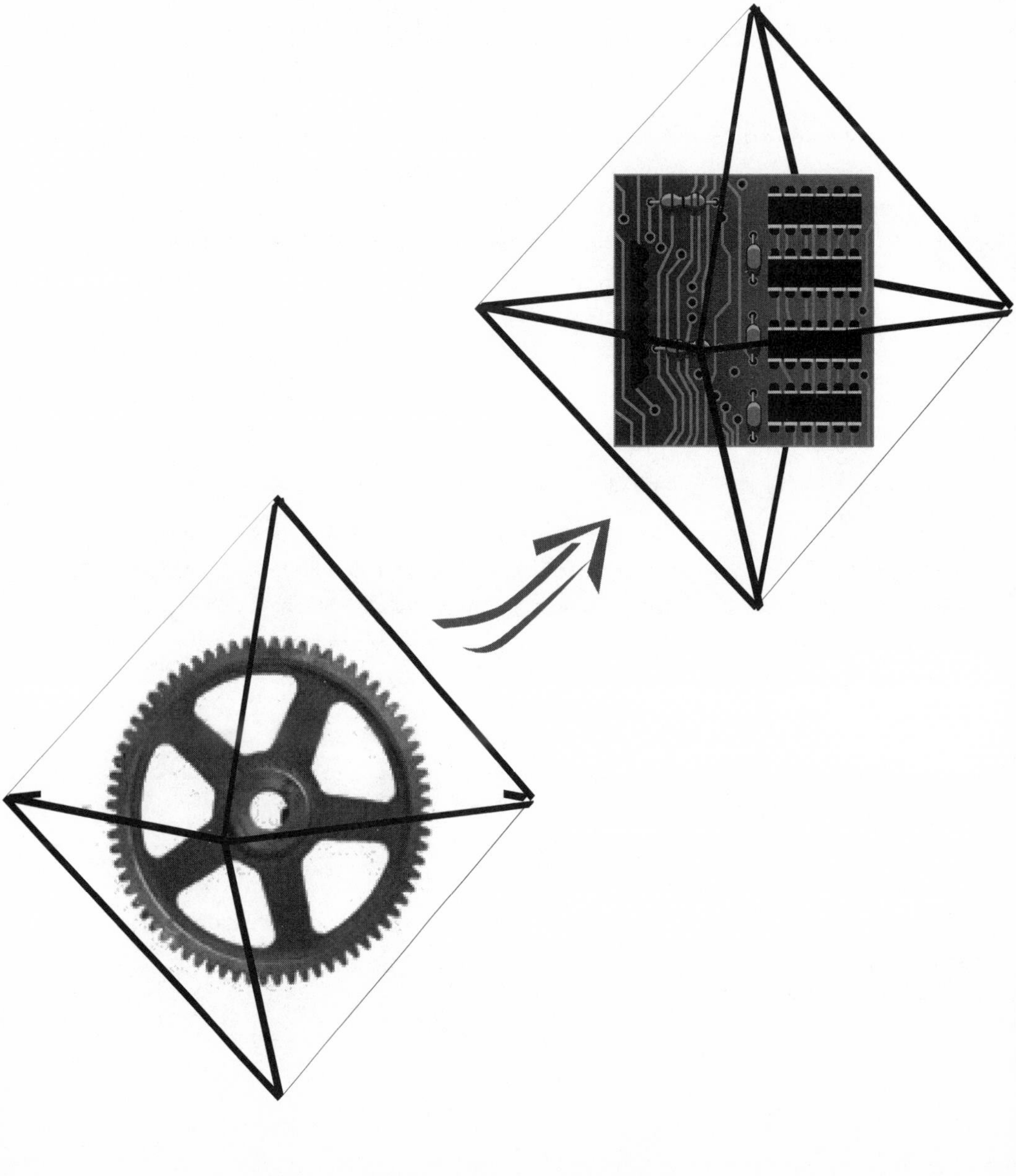

Conventional to Digital Business Design

The order of magnitude pattern.

In the early 1990s, Nicholas Negroponte talked of dividing the world into "atoms" (materials) and "bits" (information). Bits were different from atoms because they could be managed electronically.

Rapid technological advances have triggered a pattern in which companies move from a conventional to a digital business design (i.e., a conversion of the entire "non-atom" part of their business to electronic form). These companies make this shift in a careful sequence that is driven by the critical business issues they face. Some issues (productivity, response time, asset intensity) are common across all businesses. Others are specific to particular industries and companies (e.g., R&D for Boeing, recruiting for Cisco).

By moving all the non-atom aspects of the business (information, communication, knowledge, and so on) to electronic management, companies can achieve *order of magnitude* performance improvements. Productivity levels are multiplied, response times can be reduced from weeks to days, and asset intensity levels can be decreased by 90 percent or more.

The true power of digital business design lies, however, in the creation of benefits that go far beyond order-of-magnitude improvements in operating performance:

1. A digital business design can reverse the traditional customer segmentation process (companies spend millions of dollars creating approximate segmentation schemes) by allowing customers to segment themselves. Whether it's Dell's online configurator, Schwab's mutual fund evaluator, or Cisco's recruiting profiler, customers and employees interact with the supplier's Web-based system when they make choices, and they array themselves into certain highly segmented patterns of buying behavior—at no cost to the supplier.

2. Digital business design enables customers to finance business operations. Amazon and Dell have operated with *negative* working capital; Microsoft operates with negative asset intensity.

3. Digital business design enables not just customer self-segmentation but also customer self-reporting. The model shifts the nature of the supplier–customer interaction from an episodic encounter to a continuous flow of customer information, through a combination of transactions, customer service, and customer communication. As a consequence, suppliers can now see not only accurate segments, but also the direction and rate of movements in customer behavior. This allows them to anticipate where the customer is heading, and to develop new offerings, new services, and new marketing messages in an accurate response to those movements.

Digital business design can certainly work within the framework of a traditional, pyramidal organizational structure. But the power of digital business design can be magnified dramatically when it works in combination with a network organizational structure. In the flatter network structure, there are fewer reviewers and fewer decision "gatekeepers" (people who need to "sign off" on decisions made at lower managerial levels). Final decisions and actions are pushed down to those best equipped to deal with them.

The combination of network structure and digital business design can lead to extraordinary changes in performance. At a recent conference, one participant described the contrast in outcomes that can be achieved, and the impact on the number of actors, number of steps, and number of person-hours consumed.

The conventional process to get to a decision took seventeen days of elapsed time, involved four players, and consumed twelve person-hours. The digital business design process took one player, two days (of elapsed time), and less than two person-hours.

These results are simply unobtainable under conventional approaches. Consider the effect on an organization's value growth potential when this example is multiplied by the thousands of decisions that an organization makes each year.

The truly hard part of digital business design is *thinking differently*—starting with business issues ("What the business needs is . . .") rather than technology ("What the technology can do is . . .").

It also means thinking differently about what the potential benefits really are. A major retailer made the move from conventional to digital business design (it built a rich Web site to parallel its experience-rich physical locations). The retailer's initial and exclusive points of focus were: "selling more product" and "generating more gross margin from stock in inventory." It was hard to break away from a mode of thought that had dominated the business for decades.

The real point of the transition to digital business design for the retailer was quite different, however. There certainly was an opportunity for more product sales. Far more important, however, were multiple new profit opportunities from advertising, subscription fees, referral fees, and an unbroken stream of information about customer behavior.

Perhaps the most difficult reversal of perspective for the organization concerns the customer. Digital business design enables a complete redefinition of the supplier–customer relationship. The company can move away from ad-hoc, episodic interactions and information flow. It can stop constantly trying to guess what the customer really wants and can enjoy, instead, a continuous, accurate, information-rich relationship in which guesswork and frustration are reduced.

Successful digital business design requires several remarkably fundamental changes in organizational mindset and behavior. It is a little like building a greenfield site in the mind of the organization. The mindset shift in behavior is binary, not incremental. It's either on or off.

Many organizations deceive themselves into thinking that they can move to this new model incrementally. They can't. Incrementalism takes years—and that's just too long, because the goal is *not* to get to a digital business design *eventually* (by that time everyone else will have gotten there as well). The goal is to make a profit from it. That requires getting there well before your rivals do and locking in the performance differential.

Most organizations cling stubbornly to the conventional paper/personal meeting-based business design, not only because organizational habits are so strong, but because they are affordable. Full-scale implementation of a digital business design is rare, even among technology firms. Microsoft's totally paperless world is still the exception.

But the pattern is quickening. The availability of order-of-magnitude improvement is too powerful a magnet for smart companies to resist. Today, those moving to digital business design experience significant increases in profitability. Tomorrow, those who don't move to digital business design will experience increasing profit pressure and greater strategic risk.

In summary, the digital business design pattern is not about technology. It is about focusing on the key business issues facing the company. Rather than ten percent improvements, the goal is *tenfold* improvements. It is not just about operating improvements, but about a fundamental redefinition of the relationship with the customer.

The purpose of digital business design is not just to charm more profit out of the old model. The pattern generates entirely new types of profit streams from its completely new ways of interacting with customers.

HOW TO PROFIT?

Challenge your organization's "paper" and "personal meeting" mindset. Identify your most important business issues and the "bits" related to them. Manage all those bits electronically.

- What are the three to five top business issues your company faces? Which elements of a digital infrastructure can have the greatest positive impact in addressing those issues?
- What could your company accomplish if it performed twice as well on the four metrics of: (1) response time, (2) productivity, (3) asset efficiency, and (4) customer information?
- What kind of digital infrastructure investments would be required to perform at this level?
- How can your company use digital business design to redefine your relationship with your customers and prospects?

MOVING TO A DIGITAL BUSINESS DESIGN

The movement to digital business design is most often discussed with respect to technology companies, but it is an equally powerful pattern for smokestack, manufacturing-intensive, traditional industries.

Cemex is a Mexican cement manufacturer. Imagine, for a moment, what this company looks like in comparison to a company in Silicon Valley. What images come to mind for each of these companies? How do the two companies differ?

If you could take a visitor's tour of Cemex, you might be surprised. A sophisticated computer center is at the heart of the company. Every truck in its fleet has a computer on the dashboard. The company uses a global satellite system for communications. Its ability to schedule efficiently, and to respond flexibly to customers' conditions, far exceeds that of its rivals. Cemex's flexibility and rapid response are key capabilities for attacking the critical issues most important to its customers: on-time delivery and flexibility of delivery time.

This network system allows Cemex to promise deliveries of ready-mix concrete within twenty minutes of the agreed-upon time, versus a three-hour margin three years ago—a degree of reliability for which many customers gladly pay. Cemex's sophisticated use of digital technology has driven similar productivity increases in other areas, such as purchasing and production. The transition from conventional to digital business design has made Cemex the most profitable of Mexico's major cement producers. With a cash flow of 31 percent of sales, Cemex beats its major rivals by over ten percentage points.

A conventional infrastructure is typified by moderate levels of productivity, response time measured in months, high asset intensity, and a low ratio of informed decision making. A digital infrastructure radically changes the old framework and improves the performance along all these metrics, not just by a few percentage points, but by multiples.

Several major companies are exploiting the digital business design pattern. When Boeing recognized that it could no longer afford to build planes "the old way," it undertook a fundamental change in the way it did business internally, with its suppliers, and with its customers. It used a 100 percent digital process to develop the 777. Multiple groups of engineers could simultaneously use workstations to view and work on the entire plane and its three million parts. Positive impact occurred on three critical performance metrics: a 60 to 90 percent reduction in errors, elimination of huge metal-and-wood mockups, and the ability to reconfigure the plane within hours instead of weeks.

Implementing digital design is not about "wiring the entire company." It is not about IT; it is business-issue-driven. It is not about e-mail, CAD/CAM, and other tools, but about productivity, response time, asset efficiency, and, most importantly, customer information. The business design and the key business issues facing the company should dictate the nature of its digital infrastructure. The goal is to focus on areas that are most important and most improvable from a customer and business perspective, not from an information technology perspective.

As a network equipment provider, Cisco faced a critical business issue: it had to find star talent to support its strategy for growth. Part of the solution: Cisco recruits almost exclusively through the Internet. Prospective employees are attracted to Cisco's Web site, where they submit personal data and are matched against hundreds of job postings. By tapping the technology-based behavior of prospective employees, Cisco uniquely identifies and attracts many of the top engineers in Silicon Valley.

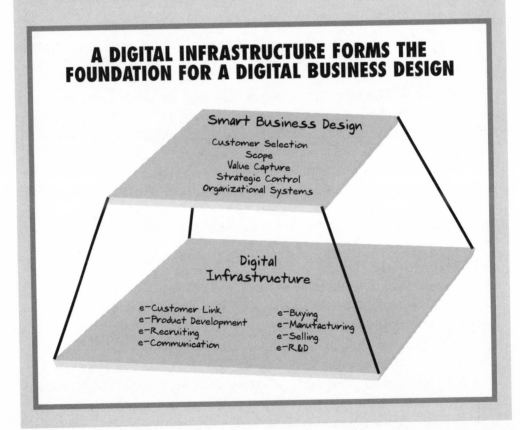

A DIGITAL INFRASTRUCTURE FORMS THE FOUNDATION FOR A DIGITAL BUSINESS DESIGN

Smart Business Design

Customer Selection
Scope
Value Capture
Strategic Control
Organizational Systems

Digital
Infrastructure

e–Customer Link
e–Product Development
e–Recruiting
e–Communication

e–Buying
e–Manufacturing
e–Selling
e–R&D

A company has several possible pathways for implementing a digital business design. The best pathway is defined by answers to questions such as: Is the greatest business leverage achieved through electronic product development, electronic recruiting, electronic buying, or the digitization of other functions?

At Microsoft, the emphasis has been on electronic communication. You can send a paper fax to a Microsoft employee, but he or she will never see it. The company has transitioned to a completely paperless model. Communication is by e-mail and voice mail. When an external fax reaches Redmond, it is scanned and electronically routed to the correct e-mail address. The addressee opens the document from an electronic inbox.

Suppliers must invoice Microsoft electronically. Paper invoices will not be paid.

In the future, when it begins to affect an increasing number of industries, digital business design will most likely be reclassified as a mega pattern. Incumbents will face major challenges, and rich opportunities, as this transition takes place. They have a vast amount of assets in place—assets that are difficult to walk away from. An even bigger obstacle was suggested by an information systems executive at Boeing. Commenting on the introduction of digital ways of doing business, he said: "We thought that all of those technical issues were going to be big, but the biggest challenge is the mindset change and culture change." Once those changes are achieved, an incumbent's ability to leverage its installed base with an entire array of dramatic performance improvements becomes a force to be reckoned with.

PART III
PUTTING PATTERNS TO WORK

CHAPTER 11

PUTTING PATTERNS INTO ACTION

Understand the Past, Anticipate the Future

WAYNE GRETZKY, the greatest player and most prolific scorer ever to play professional hockey, has achieved his success through his ability to "see" the patterns unfolding on the ice a split-second before his opponents do. Gretzky describes this unique capability very simply: "I go where the puck will be." By anticipating where the puck, his teammates, and the opposing defense-men *will* move, Gretzky is able to exploit the opportunity with a perfectly timed pass or a pinpoint shot.

In business, as in hockey, the greatest "players" are those who can anticipate and exploit patterns. When properly utilized, patterns thinking allows us to move "where the value will be." By learning and applying the methods of Strategic Anticipation, we can maximize value—for our company's customers and shareholders, our investments, and our career.

Patterns are the language of strategy. They hint at the future strategic story of a company or industry, explain the past, and describe the present. In some cases, a single pattern sufficiently describes the strategic story of a company or industry. However, these simple stories—where the rules of the game have not changed for years or decades—are a disappearing species. Today, the strategic stories of most companies or industries are characterized by several patterns—unfolding sequentially or simultaneously—that together transform the strategic landscape.

An excellent example of an industry being reshaped by several simultaneous patterns is communications. In the past decade, it has seen:

- Deintegration of the value chain
- Collapse of the middle
- Convergence
- A shift from products to solutions
- Channel multiplication
- Digital business design

As you study the story of a company or industry using patterns, something will change. You will begin to think differently. You will replace the mental "still camera" often used in thinking about strategy with a "videocamera" that plays multiple frames instead. The mental momentum you develop will carry you from the past to the present, then from the present to the future. New perspectives and insights about the future will challenge your thinking, open your eyes to new threats and opportunities, and force you to reconsider issues that you thought you had already mastered.

We have written the stories of nine companies in the remaining pages of this chapter. We have told each story through the prism of the key patterns that affected the company's strategic position. These examples highlight a set of companies that have succeeded in extremely difficult environments. They saw multiple patterns and made the right moves to take advantage of them. They were extraordinarily adept at Strategic Anticipation. They were able to "get it," to see the meaning underneath the chaos, and to go where the "puck" would be. They created enormous value growth as a result.

As you read the following nine stories, think about how the patterns described are transforming the strategic landscape in each industry. When you come to the "end" of each story, take several minutes to think about and write down which pattern(s) are most likely to play out *next* for the company being profiled. The more stories you read (and write), the more comfortable you will become with the use of patterns. In a short time, patterns will become the language of strategy for you and your team, in their role as managers, investors, or customers.

Cisco Systems

Product to solutions, de facto standard,
conventional to digital business design.

In the mid-1980s, computer networking was extremely basic and unsophisticated. The typical corporate or academic computing environment consisted of a number of discrete devices (workstations, PCs, servers, peripherals) manufactured by several different companies. Some of these machines were linked in small, local area networks (LANs), but communication and information sharing within and between departments, offices, and campuses were nearly impossible.

In 1984, Sandy Lerner and Leonard Bosack, two married professors at Stanford University, set out to find a solution to this problem. They decided that they would like to send computer messages—e-mail—to each other while at work. Each had a computer residing on a separate departmental network, so the couple created a "multiprotocol" server, a specialized computer capable of sorting and distributing data packets among several incompatible computer networks. Recognizing the potential power of local, national, and international computer networks, Lerner and Bosack founded their own company, Cisco Systems, to develop and enhance these servers, which came to be known as "routers."

PRODUCT TO SOLUTIONS

By 1992, Cisco had become a $500 million company and dominated the router market. However, as computer networking exploded, a host of new digital switching devices and technologies began to challenge routers for supremacy. By 1994, Cisco's growth slowed. Its router sales were challenged by new technologies—ATM, frame relay, LAN switches—that it did not offer to customers. New competitors (FORE Systems, Ascend Communications, Newbridge Networks) emerged to challenge Cisco's market supremacy.

As computer networks became increasingly complex, customers and value began to migrate toward providers of end-to-end technology solutions—companies that integrated these technologies into a seamless network or could offer customers a broad product line to meet all of their networking needs. In this more complex environment, customers required more functionality than Cisco's routers alone could provide. They demanded broader networking solutions that incorporated multiple technologies and devices. This shift in customer needs triggered the product to solutions pattern in the computer networking industry.

Cisco's management team anticipated this pattern, acknowledged the shift in customer priorities, and moved quickly to retain its leadership position in networking technology. To continue meeting its customers' networking requirements, the company realized it would need to offer not just routers, but rather a broader, more complete selection of products and technologies.

To capitalize on the product to solutions pattern, Cisco had two options: (1) pursue in-house development of the required technologies; or (2) obtain new products and technologies through acquisition. Recognizing that in-house development would require far too much time and R&D investment, CEO John Chambers decided to initiate an aggressive plan of strategic acquisitions.

Consequently, Cisco initiated a five-year "acquisition sprint" to build its product line and become a complete networking solutions provider. It consolidated startup firms specializing in promising technologies and in the core products it lacked. Since 1993, Cisco has acquired eighteen companies at a price of nearly $7 billion. It began this process by purchasing Crescendo Communications, a maker of hubs (devices used to link PCs in LANs), for $90 million in 1993. Cisco subsequently bought several other smaller specialists to acquire expertise in remote access, ATM, and switching. In April 1996, Cisco bought StrataCom, the largest producer of wide-area network (WAN) switches and frame-relay equipment, for $4.6 billion. Since then, Cisco has acquired ten more companies with capabilities in switching, xDSL, network management, and Internet/firewall software.

These acquisitions have enabled Cisco to develop a complete product line and to provide customers with the closest thing to an end-to-end internetworking solution that the industry has to offer. Nearly half of the company's revenues are now generated from acquired technologies and products. More importantly, Cisco's acquisition of new technologies—particularly the increasingly important LAN and WAN switches—has protected its revenue streams by replacing routers with more advanced devices.

By recognizing the need for a broad line of "solutions" before the competition caught up, Cisco expanded its market leadership across the networking value chain. The price of the acquisitions was steep—$7 billion—but the results have been extraordinary: over the same five years (1993–1998), Cisco created over $90 billion in shareholder value.

As its acquisition activity continues, Cisco has systematized the process. Scouting Silicon Valley for startups with promising technologies and talent, Cisco now assigns an entire team solely to acquisition and integration. By purchasing mostly startups and generally limiting its acquisitions to companies already in Silicon Valley, Cisco has avoided two pitfalls: (1) dislocating employees and families, and (2) destroying the "small company" startup mentality. (Indeed, although Cisco is now a very large organization, its various divisions and product sectors retain much of the feel of smaller companies. That effect is not surprising when one considers that many of Cisco's top engineers once worked for startups.) Moreover, by acquiring these companies before they launched their products and developed "brand" recognition, Cisco minimized the cost of acquisition. Today, Cisco is capable of absorbing a newly acquired startup in three weeks, and it can bring the startup's products to market very quickly.

By exploiting the product to solutions pattern, Cisco has become the largest, most convenient source of data networking equipment. Because it offers customers a multiplicity of hardware solutions, Cisco is a "one-stop shop." Rather than buying equipment from several different vendors—a process that incurs very high systems integration costs—customers can now purchase fully compatible hubs, routers, switches, frame-relay devices, and remote access equipment—all from Cisco.

The benefits of Cisco's "one-stop shop" to customers—reduced integration costs and more responsive maintenance and customer service—have increased customer satisfaction while drastically lowering the cost of systems integration.

Cisco's successful acquisition strategy has enabled it to achieve dominant or leading market share in nearly every category of network equipment. The company has nearly an 80 percent share in the router market, with $3.3 billion in sales. Although it entered the market after 3Com and other competitors, Cisco has also achieved the leading position (30 to 40 percent of the market) in LAN and WAN switches.

DE FACTO STANDARD

Cisco's market share and exploitation of the product to solutions pattern has enabled the company to take advantage of another pattern: the de facto standard. Cisco's dominance in the networking equipment market now approaches that of Microsoft in PC operating systems and Intel in microprocessors. Indeed, some industry experts have coined the term "Wintelco" to indicate that Cisco has transformed the Microsoft–Intel duopoly into a triumvirate. Like Windows and the Pentium processor, Cisco's routers and switches have become ubiquitous. Customers who seek quality products with a minimum of purchase hassle naturally migrate to Cisco's door.

In much the way that information technology (IT) managers of yesteryear lived by the mantra "No one ever got fired for choosing IBM," today's IT professionals are likely to choose Cisco's products over its competitors'. In an increasing number of cases, Cisco's products are no longer considered the best among multiple choices; rather, they *are* the choice. Cisco's increasing market leadership is creating a de facto standard.

In addition to developing equipment standards, Cisco is moving to establish the software that powers its machines as a de facto standard. Just as Microsoft has leveraged Windows' 85 percent operating system market share to drive standards for productivity software (Microsoft Office) and Internet browsers (Internet Explorer), Cisco is aggressively moving to own the de facto standard for networking software. Cisco has branded the software that controls its switches and routers IOS, or Internetwork Operating System. The company preloads IOS software into all of its products, and it has licensed the software to hardware competitors and partners, including 3Com, Nortel Networks, Hewlett-Packard, and Ericsson.

Ultimately, Cisco hopes to create the brand recognition enjoyed by Intel and Microsoft. This goal is evident in the company's latest marketing campaign, "Cisco Powered Network," which allows Cisco-built data network operators to leverage Cisco's brand name in the market. U S West, Ameritech, @Work, British Telecom, and Deutsche Telekom have all adopted this program. Just as Intel created the slogan "Intel Inside" as a seal of quality and performance for PCs, Cisco is leveraging its brand name as the stamp of reliability in data networking technology.

As owner of the de facto standard for network equipment, Cisco has become a much sought-after partner by technology firms of all types. Cisco has partnered with Hewlett-Packard to develop and sell Internet-based corporate computing systems using each other's products. Cisco, Microsoft, and Intel have jointly developed the Networked Multimedia Lab. A state-of-the art mini network housed at Cisco's headquarters, the Lab is a joint project to develop technology for delivering voice, data, and video over the Internet with the same reliability and quality as traditional voice and video networks. Cisco has also partnered with GTE to deliver comprehensive data services to the enterprise. These alliances and partnerships have further solidified Cisco's leadership position in the industry.

Cisco's ability to anticipate and exploit key patterns has allowed it to build several important competitive advantages. With a 36 percent share of the top six networking players' revenues (3Com, Bay Networks, Cabletron, Ascend Communications, and Newbridge Networks), Cisco is significantly larger than all but one of its competitors (3Com has a 32 percent share; Cabletron, the next largest player, has only an 11 percent share). This scale has enabled Cisco to achieve lower SG&A costs than its major competitors. In addition, Cisco now enjoys a cash position more than three times larger than 3Com. Along with a soaring stock price (Cisco's market capitalization is larger than its next six competitors combined), this cash advantage has enabled the company to continue its aggressive acquisition strategy. Finally, Cisco's size advantage has enabled it to greatly outspend its rivals on research and development; in 1997, Cisco spent $700 million on R&D—nearly 50 percent more than its next closest rival.

CONVENTIONAL TO DIGITAL BUSINESS DESIGN

To maintain its preeminent position, Cisco has taken advantage of the very technology its products enable—the Internet. Through its implementation of technology in all phases of its operations, Cisco illustrates one of the most important patterns of the coming years: the shift from a conventional business design to a digital business design.

Cisco's exploitation of the digital business design is most clearly apparent in its recruiting practices. Because Cisco aims to hire the top few percent of engineering and business talent in Silicon Valley, the company has had to figure out ways to attract "star" employees from other companies. First, Cisco has developed a recruiting section for its Web site. This enables the company to post hundreds of open job descriptions at low cost. To attract people to its site, Cisco advertises on popular Web sites and in newspapers. Cisco is now developing a tool called Profiler on its recruiting site. The tool will enable browsers to submit personal information online. Cisco recruiters can then use this information to match applicants with positions. By exploiting the technology-based behavior of prospective employees, Cisco has identified and attracted many of the top engineers and managers in Silicon Valley.

Cisco has also shifted other elements of its business from conventional to digital infrastructure. To facilitate employee productivity and integrate the dispersed employees of the firms it acquires, Cisco strongly encourages telecommuting. Nearly 20 percent of its employees have ISDN lines installed in their homes. In addition, the Cisco intranet consists of an astounding 40,000 Web pages' worth of product specifications, corporate information, and company news.

Cisco's digital business design has enabled it to successfully outsource 80 percent of its manufacturing operations; by linking into its contractors' computer networks, Cisco controls scheduling, engineering tests, and production. Most importantly, however, Cisco has taken its entire catalog of products online. In 1996, the company sold $100 million worth of products via the World Wide Web; in 1997, Cisco generated $3.2 billion, or nearly 50 percent of its total revenue, from its online sales. Cisco estimates its annual savings from migration to digital business design at $550 million.

Through its innovative application of technology, Cisco has improved its operations and moved ahead of its competitors in adapting to the digital future.

From its founding as a Stanford-based startup, Cisco has grown into one of the largest and most successful companies in the world. At nearly $125 billion, Cisco's market capitalization is one of the fifteen largest in the world. Its products and solutions have enabled enterprises, universities, and governments to link their computing resources into large-scale networks of shared information and real-time communications. Today, Cisco sells nearly one million routers per year, and its software and hardware products are the "plumbing" that enables 75 percent of the Internet to function. Cisco's technology has laid the foundation for today's enterprise data networks and the explosion of the Internet.

Having achieved unquestioned leadership in the enterprise data networking market, Cisco is now setting its sights on competing with Lucent, Nortel, and Ericsson, the leading makers of networking infrastructure for telecommunications service providers (cable MSOs, ISPs, telcos). Having successfully exploited the aforementioned patterns, Cisco is now attempting to capitalize on the accelerating convergence of voice and data technologies.

Despite its success in data networking, future value growth is far from a certainty. Indeed, the stakes of the new "convergence" game are far bigger. In this new world, Cisco is no longer the 800-pound gorilla; while its market value dwarfs that of 3Com, Bay Networks, and its traditional data networking competitors, Cisco is now coming face-to-face with competitors (Lucent, Nortel, Ericsson) whose market capitalization and financial resources are equal to or greater than its own. At the same time, Cisco lacks these competitors' expertise in designing the ultra-reliable networks required by telecommunications service providers. As Bill O'Shea, data networking chief at Lucent, Cisco's most important new competitor, argues: "The real challenge is to build networks that are as reliable, robust, and scalable as current voice networks, and that's something Cisco has never done in its history" (*Fortune*, 9/7/98).

Thus, while its expertise in data networking may give it an early lead over Lucent and Nortel, Cisco will need to recognize and exploit new patterns in order to maintain future value growth and create new sources of strategic control in the quickly converging voice-data space.

Honeywell

Value chain deintegration, product to solutions, de facto standard.

In the early 1990s, the airline and aerospace industries were under tremendous economic pressure. Deregulation turned the airline industry into a no profit zone; the major carriers struggled to earn even 1 or 2 percent return on sales; declining aircraft orders placed intense price pressure on the manufacturers. As airlines saw the cost per seat of acquiring and financing planes go up, they demanded more flexible financial terms (e.g., unlimited walk-away leases and turnback rights), which further ate into the margins of the manufacturers. At the same time, Airbus, subsidized by its European government backers, undertook an aggressive R&D campaign to buy its way into a significant market position so that it could compete with Boeing, the leading manufacturer of commercial aircraft.

These changing market conditions altered the strategic landscape of the aerospace industry, which had long been organized along lines similar to those of most other discrete manufacturing industries. Large, vertically integrated firms, such as Boeing and McDonnell-Douglas, combined design, engineering, and manufacturing under one roof, while a wide array of parts suppliers, such as Honeywell, interacted at arm's length to provide discrete parts based on detailed specifications. Boeing and its competitors chose parts suppliers based on short-term prices for each part, and they assumed responsibility for integrating and assembling the complete systems.

DEINTEGRATION

By 1996, however, the vertically integrated business model had become a no profit zone for Boeing. Falling sales and rising costs were squeezing Boeing's bottom line. Its unit volume fell by 50 percent from 1992 to 1996, and its net income decreased an average of 11 percent per year. These declines were exacerbated by the rising cost of developing a new plane: Boeing's R&D expense per plane sold doubled between 1991 and 1994.

With demand falling and development costs skyrocketing, Boeing had two choices: (1) attempt to cut costs, and hope to ride out the wave of low demand; or (2) adapt to the changing market conditions of the aerospace industry to rebuild its trajectory of profitable growth.

Cost cutting would have been the obvious first move, but Boeing's ability to recognize the true nature of change in its market enabled it to exploit the key pattern that would reshape the industry: deintegration. With costs rising, specialization along the value chain was becoming necessary to maintain profitability. Boeing realized that it could no longer afford to bear the full costs of all steps in the manufacturing process. Therefore, in order to keep aircraft production economically viable, Boeing sought to outsource significant responsibility for design and manufacturing.

Once it identified the opportunity to exploit the deintegration pattern, Boeing transformed the production process for its first new plane in a decade, the 777 jumbo jet. In contrast to its approach for previous new products, Boeing decided it would no longer handle all aspects of design and major system assembly in-house for the 777. Rather, Boeing handed responsibility for the design, development, and assembly of major plane subsystems to a select group of tier-one contractors, as part of a concept called "Working Together."

Rather than awarding each supplier price-based short-term contracts, Boeing made each of its tier-one suppliers a long-term strategic and business partner, with responsibility for designing, testing, and integrating major subsystems. They would no longer be paid on a traditional piece-part basis, but rather would take the risk of investing their own development dollars, tying their success to the success of the plane itself. Thus, while Boeing retained control of the overall architecture and assembly of the 777, it was able to disperse development and manufacturing costs among its partners and suppliers.

Boeing's exploitation of the deintegration pattern—through outsourcing of key systems development—altered its relationship with its parts and components suppliers. In the past, Boeing had viewed these players as pure suppliers of products and discrete systems for its airplanes. To fulfill this role, these companies emphasized technical performance, part cost, and quality. They provided value to Boeing by maximizing quality and performance at the most competitive price.

PRODUCT TO SOLUTIONS

However, Boeing's priority shift toward systems outsourcing triggered a new pattern that transformed the strategic landscape for the aerospace suppliers: product to solutions. In the new world of skyrocketing manufacturing costs, Boeing was more concerned with reducing the overall systems cost of its manufacturing process than it was in finding the lowest per-part price. By designing an offering that incorporated the functionalities of multiple components into a single more advanced and cost-effective integrated solution, parts suppliers could increase their strategic importance to Boeing.

Honeywell anticipated this shift in Boeing's priorities and exploited the emerging pattern by altering its own business design. To deliver on its promise of an integrated solution that could create overall cost savings, Honeywell thought in terms of systems economics improvement and capitalized on its extensive applications knowledge and systems integration expertise. Rather than designing stand alone flight management components—as it had for previous Boeing aircraft—Honeywell obtained official designation as the provider of the 777's primary core avionics system, the Aircraft Information Management System, or AIMS.

While Honeywell's AIMS was actually significantly more expensive than previous avionics systems, it provided Boeing with a solution that lowered overall systems costs. By bringing a high level of automated intelligence and redundancy to the avionics system, AIMS allowed the airlines to significantly cut repair time, and to fly more fuel-efficient flight profiles. AIMS also reduced Boeing's final assembly costs, because it automatically provides a test platform for other systems connecting to it during installation, eliminating a costly integration step.

Over time, Honeywell further refined its solutions approach. As it became more aware of its customer's changing systems economics,

Honeywell steadily integrated more functionality into its avionics systems. All previous Boeing aircraft had employed discrete components, such as the air data computer, radios, the navigation system, and the climate control system, which combined to control the plane; these individual parts were hardwired into the plane and into each other. In contrast, AIMS consisted of a proprietary digital bus, shared central processors, and 700,000 lines of software intelligence residing on redundant fault-tolerant computers.

This digital approach significantly cut weight and mechanical complexity and allowed for new levels of integrated functionality. For instance, the navigation system automatically selected the appropriate communication mechanism and channel based on the plane's current location. By focusing on the overall system's functionality, rather than the performance of discrete components, Honeywell provided more value to Boeing and lowered the overall cost of production.

After AIMS was deployed in service, Honeywell continued to invest in enhancements such as advanced navigation. This approach of building a trajectory of systems improvement did three important things. It steadily increased Honeywell's share of the plane's value-added content as well as the overall systems value delivered to Honeywell's end customers. It allowed Honeywell to stay ahead of its competitors by steadily raising the investment and sophistication required to match the AIMS offering. Finally, it enabled Honeywell to achieve greater differentiation from its competitors, whose focus was primarily on discrete products or functionality.

DE FACTO STANDARD

By recognizing and responding to Boeing's changing systems economics, Honeywell was able to exploit the product to solutions pattern. As a result of constant improvements in its systems and conquest of larger portions of the airplane's value, it has also positioned itself to exploit a second pattern: the de facto standard.

Honeywell has been able to earn exclusivity on the 777 and other future Boeing platforms with its proprietary digital approach and integrated avionics system solution. Just as Boeing found that AIMS improved its overall economic equation, other aircraft manufacturers have recognized the benefits of a solutions approach. As a result, elements of Honeywell's AIMS architecture are now being deployed by other manufacturers such as McDonnell Douglas (recently acquired by Boeing) and the U.S. Government on military aircraft. This de facto standard position is a powerful competitive advantage. It establishes Honeywell in an entrenched position with the largest volume customer, and it provides a larger unit-volume base across which to amortize AIMS' significant development cost (over $400 million).

Honeywell's exploitation of the product to solutions and the de facto standard patterns also enabled it to create new value capture mechanisms. Rather than simply pricing based on the cost of the system plus a reasonable markup (the traditional approach to value capture in the aerospace industry), Honeywell priced AIMS based on the value of the multiple subsystems it replaced. Honeywell captured additional value by being in an advantaged position to provide many of the key subcomponents integrated by AIMS, such as the air data internal reference unit and the collision avoidance system, as well as periodic system upgrades. Finally, Honeywell was able to reap enormous returns by replicating the basic AIMS system for other planes such as the 737-600, the MD-95 (now the Boeing 717), and various military transports.

Central to Honeywell's success was the close working relationship between it and Boeing throughout the process. This form of solution partnership helped translate customer requirements into differentiated functionality and superior performance, creating value for both companies.

Boeing and Honeywell achieved great success through their nimble responses to the patterns transforming the aerospace industry. For Boeing, deintegration of the value chain by relying on outside suppliers to define and deliver on critical elements of the 777 resulted in a significant reduction in the plane's development time and expense (development costs were reduced from $5 billion to $4 billion), a 20 percent reduction in production cycle time, and, perhaps most important, strong customer enthusiasm and plane orders from the airlines.

By successfully exploiting the product to solutions pattern and the de facto standard pattern, Honeywell has also benefited significantly. Since AIMS has been deployed, Honeywell's Space and Aviation Control business margins have more than doubled, and operating profit has tripled. Since successful deployment of the first 777, Honeywell shareholder value has more than doubled, from $4.5 billion in 1994, to $9.5 billion in 1997. Perhaps more importantly, there has been a fundamental shift in the perception of the quality of Honeywell's revenue streams: Honeywell's shareholder value-to-sales ratio has grown from 0.3 to 1.1 in this period.

Honeywell now faces the challenge of developing new systems and solutions for its aerospace and aviation customers. By anticipating the opportunities this pattern presents, Honeywell can capture a greater share of the value in its businesses and lock in exclusive relationships with other customers. However, in the future, solutions offerings will commoditize just as today's stand alone components have become commodities. The challenge for Honeywell will be to see the next pattern and to anticipate the next value-creating move it should make as an aerospace supplier.

Capital One

Product to customer knowledge, microsegmentation, cornerstoning.

I n 1987, Richard Fairbank and Nigel Morris, both vice presidents at Mercer Management Consulting, went on the road pitching their Information Based Strategy (IBS) for developing bank customer relationships. IBS was a way to determine high-value credit card customers and then appeal to them with relevant offerings.

At the time, this was a highly differentiated approach to credit card marketing. Traditionally, credit card companies had not utilized sophisticated knowledge-based technologies to target, acquire, and manage their customer relationships. Companies would solicit customers by sending out mass mailings, in hopes of perhaps achieving a 1 percent response rate. Credit cards were rarely, if ever, customized in any way to suit the customer's financial situation and lifestyle. In contrast, generalized card offerings were mass mailed to broad customer segments (e.g., all college students) within which existed hundreds, if not thousands, of subsegments. The result was a fundamental disconnect between customer preferences and product offerings.

This lack of customization, coupled with increasing commoditization as credit cards proliferated in the market, negatively affected credit card economics in four ways:

- It dramatically lowered customer acceptance rates. It offered no unique features that would inspire a customer to choose a particular card over dozens of others.
- The "one card fits all" offering never built card loyalty. Customers simply switched to the next card that offered a lower interest rate, a higher credit limit, or both.
- Mass mailings rarely offered card issuers an opportunity to achieve below-average industry default rates. In fact, indiscriminate mailings led to creeping default rates as credit-strapped

consumers started signing up for four, five, or six cards each. Indeed, random mailings often achieved "adverse selection," because the least desirable candidates were most excited by the offer of an additional credit card.

- The inability of banks to focus on the most profitable credit card segments led them to emphasize revenue growth instead of profit and value growth.

Consequently, mass marketing became an increasingly ineffective means of profitably growing the credit card business. Clearinghouses like Visa and MasterCard aggravated this situation by performing the clearing function for virtually any bank that wanted to issue credit cards.

This growing set of dysfunctionalities triggered two related patterns in the credit card industry: (1) product to customer knowledge and (2) microsegmentation. Most companies ran their own operations as if they did not recognize the real drivers of profitability in the credit card industry; however, one of Morris's and Fairbank's clients, Signet Bank, did "get it." By anticipating and exploiting these emerging patterns, Signet's spinoff, Capital One, has created enormous value in a very short period of time.

After making the decision to bolster its credit card operations in 1988, Signet hired Fairbank and Morris to implement IBS. The results were a radical new approach to the credit card business and significant value growth. From mid-1992 to 1995, the company's annual outstanding credit card debt grew from $1.7 billion to $7.5 billion. This represented an annual growth rate of about 60 percent in an industry that was growing at a rate of around 15 percent.

This rapid growth had a very positive impact on Signet's bottom line. However, the growth occurred at such a phenomenal rate that the credit card business began to consume a disproportionate share of the bank's total assets, personnel, and equipment. This left the bank with insufficient resources to run its other business units. Therefore, Signet's executives decided to spin off its credit card operations in 1993, leading to the creation of Capital One. After an IPO in 1994, the spinoff was finalized in 1995.

PRODUCT TO CUSTOMER KNOWLEDGE

The inefficiencies of traditional credit card marketing triggered a new pattern in the industry: product to customer knowledge. In the past, the key to a successful credit card business was ownership of a legitimate offering with competitive interest rates and credit lines. As a result, profit was concentrated in the product offering itself. As the industry evolved, however, profit shifted toward the quality and application of knowledge about the customer.

Using IBS as a basic tool, Capital One exploited this pattern by building the most robust customer database in the industry. Over time, the company has leveraged this database—the single largest application of an Oracle database in the world—to store up to ten years of attributes on all customers and prospects. Its relentless focus on capturing and managing customer information has enabled Capital One to successfully target high-value customers and sift out the unprofitable or slow-growth customer sets.

Capital One has developed proprietary actuarial models that forecast the customer's needs, preferences, and profitability by targeting and monitoring key consumer data: retention, activation, service requirements, account balance revolved, and pricing. The models include "test cells" comprising multiple combinations of customer segment features (e.g., credit risk and income), product features (e.g., pricing), and marketing channels.

Based on these customized models, Capital One can anticipate future customer profitability and evolving priorities, and can then design custom card features for individual customer sets. In addition, it can identify the fastest growing customer segments and target them with tailored offerings. Once it has acquired a customer, Capital One continuously supplements its data repository through credit card accounts, frequent flyer numbers, "loyalty" cards, phone calls, warranty accounts, and so on. These data are used as input in predictive actuarial models of customer usage and payment behavior.

Capital One also monitors individual cardholder profitability, and it may purposely cause the attrition of unprofitable customers through extreme repricing. Alternatively, Capital One may "reward" a customer who has good scores by offering more attractive product features such as lower interest rates.

By exploiting the customer knowledge pattern, Capital One has created the most customer-relevant card offerings in the market. Unlike its traditional competitors, which "mass mail" generic offerings to millions of consumers, Capital One is able to target its offerings based on demographics, purchase behavior, and customer profitability.

MICROSEGMENTATION

In addition to customer knowledge, Capital One has capitalized on a second pattern transforming the credit card industry. As customers have become more sophisticated in their usage of credit cards for rewards programs (e.g., frequent flyer miles, shopping discounts) and as "status symbols" (platinum cards, alumni cards, sports team cards), they have segmented themselves into hundreds of microsegments that are tremendously varied in their preferences, price sensitivity, and usage habits. The microsegmentation pattern has transformed the customer population from a group of large customer segments based on general demographics and behavior into a sea of unique microsegments based on highly particular characteristics.

Capital One has leveraged its massive quantity of user information to exploit the microsegmentation pattern and to successively tailor its card offerings to meet the unique needs of each of the most valuable segments. Microsegmentation enables Capital One to have a better chance than most other credit card issuers of putting the right pricing, features, and programs into the hands of the high-value customer sets. The ability to easily modify the terms and conditions of a credit card with just a few keystrokes allows Capital One significant flexibility in meeting the exact needs of even very small or unique customer sets.

At first, Capital One used its capabilities to focus on the clients they call the "low-risk revolvers"—the customers who pay the required amount on time, but do not pay the entire bill each month. These customers are a highly profitable user segment: they carry debt for long periods of time and incur ongoing interest charges, but have relatively low default rates.

Capital One was the first credit card issuer to not only specifically target low-risk revolvers, but also, in 1991, to use direct-mail offers of low introductory rates and no annual fees to get low-risk card users to transfer their balances to Capital One. In fact, Capital One introduced American households to the now familiar phrase: "You have been preapproved. . . . "

As the market for low-risk revolvers became saturated, Capital One used its extensive database to seek out more opportunities in customer segments that were neglected by other credit card issuers because they lived in rural areas or had moderate to lower incomes.

As a result of this targeting, Capital One has built a highly attractive, highly profitable customer base. The company's average balance per account is $1,263, five percent higher than the industry average. However, Capital One's total risk exposure from unused credit is lower than that of most other credit card issuers; its average account credit limit of $3,290 is nearly $3,000 lower than the industry average.

Capital One currently offers over 4,000 niche cards to market segments as varied as Mercedes-Benz owners, animal lovers, and students. As Nigel Morris claims, "We have not found the limits to this concept. Segmentation down to 'one' may absolutely be the right way to go. We drive down targeting with surgical precision until it no longer makes sense."

CORNERSTONING

As technological change has enabled richer data analysis tools and more robust databases, companies with these capabilities and skills have been able to leverage their information across multiple businesses. On the Internet, Amazon.com is now utilizing its book customer database to market music and other products. Dell Computer has moved from selling consumer and basic corporate PC systems to more advanced enterprise servers.

Similarly, Capital One has moved to exploit the cornerstoning pattern. Using its unique customer knowledge and database capabilities, the company has ventured beyond its financial services origins. CEO Richard Fairbank has stated that:

> Capital One is an Information Age company built to leverage technology and knowledge capital for rapid exploitation of market opportunities. Because our strategy is information-based, not product-based, we are in an excellent position to ride the macro trend of the information revolution and apply our strategy to other industries as they too are reshaped by information.

In 1995, Capital One launched a cellular business called America One Communications. Through America One, Capital One buys cellular phones from manufacturers such as Motorola and wholesale airtime from regional carriers such as Bell Atlantic and Nextel. It then resells these products and services to customers. Like the credit card market, the cellular business is characterized by high variation in customer profitability, easily tailored plan features, and a large quantity of user information for input into predictive modeling.

Just as it has in its credit card business, Capital One is leveraging its proprietary database in order to develop services and incentives that vary based on an individual customer's profile. This strategy allows America One to direct market cellular service based on customized, individually-tailored pricing and airtime plans, rather than through mass promotions. Although America One is not expected to turn a profit until 2001, it has already acquired approximately 600,000 customers and is offering service in at least 37 states.

Will this work? It is as of yet unclear. What is clear is that Capital One will continue searching for ways to use customer knowledge to exploit market inefficiencies and opportunities.

Capital One's impact on the market shares of the large banks has been dramatic. Since its rise to a top-ten card issuer after only a few years in the business, major banks (such as Citibank, Chase, BankAmerica, and Wells Fargo) have seen their aggregate share of total outstanding debt fall from 44 percent in 1991 to 29 percent in 1995. The effect of this strategy can also be seen in Capital One's value growth performance. Since going public in 1994, its stock has yielded an annual return of 50 percent.

However, companies in other industries have also begun to exploit the customer knowledge, microsegmentation, and cornerstoning patterns to create and capture greater customer value. The threat for Capital One—or the potential opportunity—is that new players will enter its industry just as it had moved from credit cards to telecommunications. Indeed, the playing out of the convergence pattern is likely to be a crucial element of Capital One's future strategic landscape; as customer data-managing companies from multiple industries (retail, telecommunications, financial services) leverage their assets, they are increasingly likely to come into competition with each other as they seek to enter new lines of business.

At the same time, Capital One may have an opportunity to exploit the knowledge to product pattern by leveraging its sizable customer database to enter new knowledge-intensive markets. With one-to-one personalization via the Internet becoming the preferred method of direct marketing, Capital One is strategically positioned to build on its core skills to enter these types of markets. Whether it focuses on these or other types of opportunities, it will maintain its profitable growth trajectory only if it can anticipate and exploit these and other emerging patterns transforming its strategic landscape.

SAP

Knowledge to product, outsourcing, reintegration.

In the 1970s, manufacturing companies began to recognize that automation and computerization of their operations could enable faster, more efficient processes, and improve the flexibility and timeliness of management. As computers invaded the enterprise, companies developed software programs such as Material Requirements Planning (MRP) and Master Production Scheduling (MPS), which enabled managers to arbitrate very complex ordering and inventory management. These enterprise management programs improved productivity by facilitating scheduling, tracking inventory turns, and managing throughput.

Despite the success of these tools, manufacturing remained an island of automation in the corporate ocean. Companies continued to view other business functions (finance, human resources) as standalone processes that were separate from operations. With computer technology still in its infancy, few companies recognized the profit potential of effectively sharing information across both the manufacturing and administrative functions of the enterprise.

However, the rapid acceleration of computing and networking technology increased the strategic importance of making the right technology decisions throughout the company. As more and more companies became networked, they began to view computer technology, electronic databases, and local networks as strategic management tools that could remarkably improve the efficiency of their operations. Furthermore, as reengineering swept through the business world in the early 1990s, companies became increasingly focused on streamlining operations and sharing information throughout the organization to maximize efficiency. As a result of these changes, companies demanded software that could become the backbone of all information-based activities of the enterprise—from the supplier to the internal/administrative functions to the customer.

The German firm SAP, founded in the 1970s by former programmers at IBM Germany, understood the importance of the shift from stand alone computer systems to networked operations. SAP anticipated the opportunity to leverage emerging computer and networking technology to link, monitor, and improve operations and functions across the entire enterprise.

Recognizing the potential to transform its software programming and systems integration knowledge into tangible products, SAP developed a new category of software known as enterprise resource planning software (ERP), which linked and automated business functions throughout the enterprise. By the time networking technology became a ubiquitous feature of the enterprise, SAP was already prepared to go to market with its ERP products.

KNOWLEDGE TO PRODUCT

SAP got its start in 1972, when it developed a customized manufacturing planning system for Imperial Chemical Industries (ICI), the British chemical company. ICI had originally approached IBM for a solution, but IBM declined the project. Two IBM programmers, Diettmar Hopp and Hasso Plattner, struck out on their own and agreed to do the work for ICI. They saw the potential for not just one project, but many projects for multiple companies, using the same set of programs and skills they had agreed to develop for ICI.

Hopp and Plattner recognized that many practices and functions within systems across companies could, with the right investment, be codified and executed by a computerized system. They anticipated the time when companies would move beyond manufacturing automation to improve the efficiency of *all* business processes, and they set out to preempt the traditional IT consulting firms in developing such tools.

Using their systems integration and programming skills, as well as their experience with the ICI project, Hopp and Plattner developed software products that could be a platform for more efficiently solving a broad array of coordination challenges, thus helping to wire the corporate system more efficiently. They exploited the knowledge to product pattern by leveraging their skills and experience to develop stock products that could be marketed to multiple enterprises and customized as necessary.

SAP's first product, the SAP Financial Accounting System, automated and streamlined manufacturers' internal accounting operations. The success of this product led to the development of another standard product, Materials Management System, with modules for purchasing, inventory management, and invoice verification. Given the focus of the SAP founders on providing integrated software solutions, SAP tied both systems together so that data in one system flowed seamlessly into the other.

By integrating one coherent system that simultaneously managed multiple business functions, ERP enabled significant improvements in decision-making time and management functions. Efficiencies that were once confined to manufacturing floor operations could now be brought to financial, administrative, and distribution functions as well.

Over the course of its twenty-five-year history, SAP has continued to exploit the knowledge to product pattern. Its products are a synthesis of the programming and integration expertise of the talent at ERP companies like SAP and the know-how of practitioners of internal business processes such as human resources, finance, manufacturing, and logistics. These skills and know-how are repeatedly translated into the framework of a software product.

Rather than reinventing the wheel for each customer, SAP has leveraged its learning from ICI and hundreds of other customers to develop multifunctional applications software that can be used as a standard on a cross-industry basis. Its applications have become the templates for customized software that meets the needs of individual clients. By "productizing" its expertise, SAP has built a portfolio of base products that allow it to minimize "wheel reinvention" of basic corporate functions and focus on customization for individual clients.

OUTSOURCING

By the early 1990s, SAP's successful anticipation of the emerging customer need for ERP software functionality had paid off handsomely. The company's flagship product, R/3 (a complete enterprise planning software package that integrated all business processes in an enterprise), was the market leader. As the corporate focus on reengineering intensified, more and more companies sought SAP's help in streamlining and improving their business processes.

However, SAP could not keep up with the demand for its software and systems integration knowledge. In order to meet this demand, the company had two options: 1) provide consulting services itself; 2) outsource systems integration by creating alliances with IT consulting providers. Recognizing the superior geographic footprint and scale it could achieve through alliances, SAP forged strong relationships with Andersen Consulting, EDS, and the other leading IT consulting firms and was able to rapidly accelerate R/3's distribution into the marketplace. SAP's choice of outsourcing enabled the company to move R/3 quickly by creating a massive force of salespeople and systems integrators. Worldwide, approximately 40,000 consultants are now trained on SAP (compared with 11,000 on Baan and 10,000 on PeopleSoft).

Suppose you are a business manager who is making critical decisions about IT infrastructure to support strategic initiatives. The broad availability of consultants trained on a particular platform that you are about to invest in provides a significant measure of reassurance. Recognizing this, SAP exploited the outsourcing pattern and established R/3 as the most popular ERP software package with both customers and systems integrators.

SAP's competitors at the time were plagued with a variety of problems. For example, the components of some competitors' client/server systems were poorly integrated. Given that the goal of many firms was to streamline their business processes, this was a significant barrier to customer acceptance. Other competitors were late to market because of poor execution or, more significantly, because they did not put their systems on the open platforms that were most attractive for their clients.

The systems integrators of the consulting world and the poor execution of their competitors all helped SAP achieve leadership in the ERP software industry. SAP's position is reflected in the relative size of its installed base. SAP currently has approximately 10,000 customers, compared to PeopleSoft's 2,500 and Baan's 2,400.

By capitalizing on the knowledge to product and outsourcing patterns, SAP has created tremendous shareholder value. Before the introduction of its R/3 system, SAP's market value was growing at a compounded annual rate of 13 percent. After the introduction of R/3, SAP's market value skyrocketed at a compounded annual rate of 90 percent. In its 1997 fiscal year, the company had sales of $3.5 billion, and a market-value-to-sales ratio of 9.4.

REINTEGRATION

To date, the majority of SAP's revenue has come from product sales. Consulting and systems integration revenue has been captured by the larger consulting firms, which generate enormous profits as implementors of SAP's software and have fueled the company's rise to market leadership. While these outsourcing partnerships have been an invaluable resource for SAP, they have also limited the company's ability to participate in the consulting firms' lucrative business as systems integrators of SAP's own products. Indeed, most of SAP's customers have far stronger relationships with Andersen or EDS than they do with SAP itself.

However, as SAP's installed base has grown, the company has placed a greater emphasis on its training and consulting divisions. As an increasing portion of SAP's revenue comes from its installed base (50% in 1998), the company has become increasingly concerned with managing its customer relationships and capturing recurring business. As a result, SAP has begun to exploit the reintegration pattern in order to exert greater control over consulting and installation of its products.

In particular, SAP has launched the TeamSAP initiative, wherein it serves as a coach or mentor to customers in order to facilitate implementation. Instead of allowing its third-party implementors to completely own the client relationship, SAP now allocates some of its own consultants to oversee the process. The TeamSAP initiative has enabled SAP to accelerate implementation of its products, reduce costs, and exert greater control over its consulting and systems integration partners. By offering customers its unique expertise not only as a software vendor, but also as a systems integrator, SAP is seeking to extend its successful exploitation of the knowledge-to-product pattern and to capture a greater share of the value in the ERP sector.

SAP has continuously leveraged its capabilities and experience as a premier provider of ERP software to expand both horizontally and vertically. From its initial product, SAP Financial Accounting System, SAP has successfully built new systems in human resources management and logistics to "attach" to this product, thereby increasing its product range and reducing the open spaces available for its competitors. This integration was at the request of customers, who have seen major business benefits from having these systems integrated. In addition, SAP has increased its vertical scope to include many industries: automotive, chemicals, healthcare, retail, consumer products, telecommunications, and high technology. SAP is also moving from standard business functions such as finance or logistics into the core business processes of each vertical industry, further expanding its reach within companies.

By successfully anticipating the key changing market conditions in its industry, SAP has repeatedly exploited emerging patterns to its advantage. Nevertheless, SAP is reaching a crucial inflection point. Competing ERP firms, which entered the market by "unbundling" the ERP "package" (creating best-in-class modules for individual functions such as human resources administration) or targeting alternative customer segments (small- and mid-size business), have become significant players in the marketplace. In particular, PeopleSoft continues to increase its ERP market share and has grown significantly (51% sales growth from 1997 to 1998). At the same time, J.D. Edwards has staked out a leading position in the mid-size business market.

In addition to the other leading ERP firms, SAP faces what may be an even more dangerous threat. Its current products were developed during the height of the reengineering era; as a result, they are designed primarily to streamline operations across the enterprise by sharing information. However, as companies shift their focus to new growth opportunities, new competitors are emerging which enable businesses to sell and market on the Internet, exploit customer data, and manage relationships with suppliers and consumers. These new competitors (Calico Systems, Siebel Systems, i2 Technologies, Manugistics) are focusing on creating software which enables profit-increasing decisions, not just cost-cutting decisions.

In this increasingly competitive environment, SAP must continue to evolve its business design if it is to sustain its value growth. While the company has responded to its new competitors by developing new "front office" products and incorporating supply-chain management functionality in its new V4.0 and V4.5 versions of R/3, which assist sales forces and enable customized marketing, i2, Manugistics, and others already have established best-of-breed products in the supply chain management (SCM) market. Although SAP remains the "800 pound gorilla" in the ERP market, it will need to deliver on its new products and continue to anticipate the next patterns that will be transforming its strategic landscape.

Staples

Channel concentration, channel multiplication.

In the 1980s, the retail office supplies industry was fragmented among thousands of local stationery shops and small regional chains. These stores had limited selection because they lacked shelf and inventory space. They faced high operating costs because they could not purchase inventory at wholesale bulk rates. The landscape was dominated by a business design that featured small scale, high costs, high prices, and limited selection.

With no alternative retail channels, consumers and small businesses did not have access to the prices or selection available to large businesses through contract stationers. Unless they ordered from expensive direct mail catalogs, consumers and small businesses were restricted to a fairly standard, limited selection of products.

Over time, evolving customer priorities placed these small outlets at a disadvantage. As customers became increasingly pressed for time, they sought convenient, quick one-stop shops that would enable them to maximize the number of purchases they made at each location. With time at a premium, customers wanted to be able to shop for groceries, fill their prescriptions, and pick up small items (such as office supplies) in one trip. They did not want to make additional stops at multiple small specialty stores. Their demands were becoming clear: low prices, large selection, convenient location. Customers wanted the best combination of lowest dollar cost and lowest time cost.

However, the incumbent retailers were not meeting these priorities. The widening gap between customer needs and existing offerings triggered new patterns in the retail industry.

CHANNEL CONCENTRATION

One of those patterns—the channel concentration pattern—swept through the retail industry, sector by sector. In each business, a new player "got it" (Staples in office supplies; Barnes & Noble in books; Home Depot in hardware) and reaped the value growth benefits of Strategic Anticipation.

Home Depot was one of the first companies to "get" this pattern. Since opening its doors in 1978, Home Depot has grown to be the number-one player in the home improvement industry. In the process, Home Depot has created significant shareholder value: the company's stock has grown at a compounded annual rate of approximately 44 percent since 1982. Its founders recognized and understood their customers' shifting priorities to convenience and selection and created a business design that responded perfectly.

Like Home Depot, Staples took advantage of customers' desire for lowest prices and lowest hassle. In 1986, Staples launched its first office supplies superstore in Brighton, Massachusetts. Twelve years later, it is difficult to pass a large suburban strip mall without finding Staples, or one of its superstore competitors (Office Depot and Office-Max), anchoring or coanchoring the center.

Through its superstore business design, Staples has transformed the high-cost economics of the office supplies industry. With hundreds of stores—each with nearly 20,000 square feet of space—Staples has leveraged its size to purchase products in volume at discounted prices. This cost advantage has enabled Staples to achieve higher margins while still undercutting the competition's prices. Coupled with the company's high rate of inventory turns, this cost advantage has enabled Staples to achieve significantly higher margins than traditional small-scale operations.

Staples' scale and individual store size allow it to stock a vastly superior selection, compared to its small-scale competitors. In addition to traditional file folders, pens, pencils, and stationery, Staples stocks entire product lines not available in traditional stores. Customers can now purchase office supplies, business machines, furniture, computers, and electronics under one giant roof; they can also access copying, printing, and faxing services while they shop.

Today, Staples superstores stock nearly 7,300 SKUs, ranging from paper clips to leather desk chairs. By expanding the definition of "office supplies" to include higher-margin items such as cellular phones, answering machines, fax machines, copiers, and furniture, the company has generated rapid growth and higher margins than its traditional competitors and has attracted a broader segment of the consumer population.

Location strategy also gives Staples an edge over traditional competitors. It has positioned itself strategically in easily accessible "power strip" malls located at major suburban intersections and along highways. By positioning its stores close to supermarkets, large pharmacies, and other large "category killers" (e.g., Circuit City, Bed Bath & Beyond), Staples attracts suburban shoppers seeking to minimize the number of locations they need to visit.

At the same time, the company's local scale has enabled it to buy more advertising at more advantageous rates than its competition. This has only strengthened Staples's position as the first choice of office supplies customers in its markets.

Over time, Staples has reinforced its locational strategy by saturating its markets with multiple stores in key locations within a town, or in closely adjoining towns. Because its stores are smaller than those of Office Depot and OfficeMax, Staples is more easily able to find multiple locations in close proximity. As a result, Staples has achieved local market density and positioned itself strategically to become the customer's first-to-mind choice, the "default option" for office supplies.

Staples provides the small/home office and household consumer with a triple threat that traditional small players cannot overcome: lower prices, greater selection, and convenient location. By 1993, Staples had opened over 200 stores and had emerged as the dominant retail channel throughout the Northeast. Subsequently, it began a period of rapid expansion throughout North America and Europe. Staples entered Canada in 1991, through a joint venture agreement with Business Depot. Staples acquired Business Depot's interest in the joint venture in 1994, and it now operates 103 stores throughout the country. Staples also now operates forty stores in England and seventeen in Germany.

In the market overall, value shifted from the small-scale business design to the superstore. This channel concentration pattern continued to intensify over time. Exploiting the same channel concentration pattern it had in the Northeast, Staples has opened nearly 600 more stores in its new domestic and foreign markets. Its annual expansion rate is nearly 35 percent. With each round of expansion, the company's business design is enhanced. Staples leverages its size to provide the best locations, lowest prices, and greatest product selection.

CHANNEL MULTIPLICATION

Despite the magnitude of their success, the Staples superstores are only one part of the story. The company's ability to anticipate evolving customer priorities has also enabled it to identify four new channels through which to market its products and reach new customer segments: (1) urban "convenience" stores, (2) wholesale, (3) direct mail, and (4) the Internet.

First, Staples reached out to urban customers and busy suburbanites working downtown who lacked the time to visit the larger, suburban Staples superstores. It opened sixteen "Staples Express" stores in the business districts of Boston, New York, Washington, DC, and other metropolitan centers. These smaller stores—with an average area of 9,000 square feet and a more focused selection of 5,300 SKUs—offered convenient location and discount prices to a previously unserved customer segment.

In 1994, Staples entered the corporate wholesale market through the acquisition of several contract stationers: D.A. MacIsaac, Philadelphia Stationers, and Spectrum Office Products. These acquisitions enabled the company to serve medium-to-large regional companies through its Staples Business Advantage program. The acquisition of National Office Supply provided Staples with the scale and reach to also serve large, multiregional firms through the Staples National Advantage program.

By maintaining integrated back-end operations to leverage its size and to rationalize the duplicative functions that its retail and contract divisions share, Staples has enjoyed a cost advantage over traditional contract stationers that has translated into lower prices for customers. Today, Staples is one of the top six contract stationers in the country.

Staples has also expanded successfully into the direct mail and online segments of the office supplies market. It acquired Quill Corporation, a leading direct mail supplier, in mid-1998. The company has also negotiated a wholesale sourcing agreement that enables it to offer an additional 20,000 catalog SKUs over and above its superstore inventory. Staples' online catalog Web site opened for business just recently, as the company responded to the explosion of e-commerce and the earlier online moves of its superstore competitors. Once again, Staples is leveraging its size to offer customers the lowest prices on the widest selection of products.

Staples' successful exploitation of the channel concentration and channel multiplication patterns has transformed it into the leading multichannel office supplies vendor in the country. The key to its success is clear: see the pattern evolving and exploit it fully. Staples has done the best job, among companies in its category, of anticipating evolving customer priorities and developing the capabilities to meet them.

By anticipating the emerging trend in its industry—customers' growing demands for lower prices, improved product selection, and convenience—Staples has generated significant value growth. In 1996, Staples' market value was $2.6 billion, less than half of Office Depot's $5.3 billion. Today, Staples' market capitalization is $8.9 billion, larger than the combined market value of Office Depot ($4.9 billion) and OfficeMax ($1.7 billion).

The Staples story illustrates clearly how the company anticipated and exploited two patterns—channel concentration and channel multiplication—to create an innovative business design and become the value growth leader in retail/wholesale office supplies. Staples "got it" early, adapted its business model to new economic realities, and captured strategic control in its industry.

Nevertheless, the company now faces several new challenges. The explosion of e-commerce is threatening to supplant the superstore "bricks and mortar" retailing model; customers can now match—if not beat—Staples' prices on computers, software, and office supplies by shopping on the Internet. Staples has lagged behind its traditional competitors in responding to this threat, and it is only now rolling out an online catalog. To sustain its profitable growth, Staples will need to exploit this emerging digital business design pattern to prevent the dis-intermediation of its traditional channels. Quick response to this and other emerging patterns will be needed in order for Staples to maintain its growth trajectory and market leadership.

Nokia

Product to solutions, product to brand, skill shift.

In the late 1980s and early 1990s, the wireless communications industry was dominated by the American giant, Motorola. Motorola led the world in the design and production of analog cellular phones and infrastructure. Its technology was state-of-the-art, and it enjoyed unsurpassed brand equity with network operators. Motorola faced major competition from Ericsson and several other large telecom equipment makers, but it led the pack in engineering and product design. In addition, it attracted the best engineering talent in the world, which enabled it to develop and manufacture the most advanced products of the day.

By 1997, a small Finnish company, Nokia, had surpassed both Motorola and Ericsson as the leading business innovator in the wireless communications industry. In the span of five years, this edge-of-the-radar-screen competitor transformed itself from a sluggish conglomerate (paper, chemicals, energy, electronics) into one of the most innovative and technologically advanced players in the wireless industry.

How could such drastic change occur so quickly? How did Nokia transform itself from a third-tier, European-based conglomerate into a first-rate, globally recognized telecommunications giant?

The answer: Nokia "got it" early and acted on it. While many incumbents failed to anticipate the major changes transforming the strategic landscape, Nokia aggressively exploited emerging realities to wrest customers, profits, and strategic control away from the incumbent leaders. In doing so, Nokia took advantage of three key patterns in the wireless telecommunications industry: (1) product to solutions, (2) product to brand, and (3) skill shift.

PRODUCT TO SOLUTIONS

Having shed its noncore businesses to focus exclusively on telecommunications, Nokia became a leading supplier, throughout Europe, of cellular infrastructure and handsets. However, like its competitors, Nokia limited itself to basic component manufacturing and assembly of its handsets. It thought of its phones and infrastructure much the way its customers, the network operators, did: as independent, stand-alone products rather than an integrated system.

However, the advent of a European cellular standard—the Global System for Mobile communications (GSM)—in the late 1980s sparked rapid growth in cellular subscribership. As a result, the cellular network operators' priorities began to shift. Operators wanted a differentiated service in a highly regulated market; they wanted to create value for their subscribers; and they needed to amortize significant early investments. To respond to these priorities, Nokia recognized that it had to be more than a traditional hardware seller. It anticipated that profit and value were shifting from products to solutions, and it responded to this pattern by creating and delivering economically attractive solutions to its customers:

- A focus on efficient network project management
- Rapid implementation of its networks and continued operator support after its networks were installed
- A technological link with its handsets so that it could provide end-to-end, value-added services for the network operators

By offering integrated solutions, Nokia has won long-term handset and infrastructure upgrade contracts with its customers and differentiated itself from the competition. Nokia has also exploited the product to solutions pattern by designing and developing generic platforms that could be quickly modified to a number of different solutions, based on a customer's needs. Telecom service providers are increasingly asking for an "all-in-one" package, so Nokia has bundled its handsets with infrastructure contracts. By offering phones compatible with all of the major digital technologies, Nokia has been able to bundle handsets and infrastructure together more often than Ericsson and Motorola. Thus, while it does not offer the same breadth of infrastructure products as other providers, Nokia can offer its customers a more integrated customer/network offering than its competitors.

In addition, Nokia has responded to the emerging demand for solutions by exploiting the turnkey model, in which it takes complete control of building a network (including cell planning, zoning for antenna sites, installing and managing the network, and providing customer support). In nearly all such cases, Nokia has received the follow-on orders because of the intimate knowledge and relationship it has forged with the customers. Thus, by understanding its customers' systems economics and bundling services with products, Nokia has locked in strong relationships and has built strategic control with key network operators worldwide.

PRODUCT TO BRAND

At the same time that network operators began to seek integrated solutions, cellular subscribers' priorities were also changing. Nokia recognized that handsets were becoming consumer products, rather than nifty gadgets for technophiles. An increasing number of nontechnical, nonbusiness cellular customers would value their phones more for their own personal image and status than for their instruments' technical capabilities. To exploit this shift, Nokia altered its handset strategy from a product-centric approach (selling high-end specialist electronics) to a brand focus (selling design-oriented consumer products).

Nokia led the charge in cellular phones and positioned its handsets as consumer products. Low-end customers wanted to buy a brand with which they could feel comfortable, a solid design, and excellent ergonomics, so Nokia emphasized the benefits of its phones as fashionable consumer items. Nokia was the earliest and fastest to design and market handsets in such a way. It used direct advertising and premium Scandinavian design and ergonomics, as well as multiple colors and styles.

Why was this move so powerful for Nokia? It enabled the company to cultivate an image as the "cool brand" of cellular phones and to make major gains in winning mindshare. Competitors' phones may have been more technologically advanced, but Nokia's handsets quickly became recognized by consumers as the most stylish and attractive accessories.

Nokia's brand-building strategy has been extremely successful, and the increasing competition for new customers has enhanced its image. Indeed, the economics of the industry work in such a way that operators provide handset subsidies to users to boost subscriptions. The handset's cost to the consumer is then well below its true economic price—a purchaser will often pay less than $50 for a phone with a true value of close to $200. In an attempt to lock in subscribers for a full year, network operators vie for "switchers" with low price offers, new service features, and always a new handset. Customers thus see handsets as disposable; mobile phones are possibly the only high-value consumer electronics item that users will replace on a frequent (even yearly) basis. Nokia's brand-building investment allows it top-of-mind status in this high-churn environment, and may even encourage the churn rate, which results in an increase in new subscriptions. Either way, Nokia's extensive advertising, styling, and imaging make it the first choice if and when users opt for new or multiple units.

SKILL SHIFT

Nokia's successful exploitation of the product to solutions and product to brand patterns has enabled it to become a major player in wireless communications. However, the company's anticipation of a third pattern has fueled its meteoric rise to market leadership and a $50 billion market valuation. By anticipating the industry shift from analog to digital systems ahead of Motorola, Nokia (along with Ericsson) was first to market with digital handsets and infrastructure. As a result, Nokia's phones are now the brand of choice for many digital networks worldwide.

Hardware engineering (for both handset and infrastructure equipment) had always been king in the cellular business. Like its competitors, Nokia's mindset in the 1980s was dominated by a focus on hardware engineering. However, the emerging digital technology demanded an increased emphasis on software engineering and programming in order to provide more advanced functionality.

Nokia understood the shift in required skills and drastically altered the composition of its engineering workforce. Within several years, its software engineering staff outnumbered that of some competitors by a ratio of five to one. This intensity of redeployment created a tremendous difference for Nokia's infrastructure customers, and built a momentum behind Nokia's position that has catapulted the company into a leadership position. Today, Nokia's digital phones are the most advanced and versatile handsets on the market; the company is widely considered to own the "broadest, most appealing cell-product line," which has enabled it to capture significant market share from Motorola, Ericsson, and other competitors.

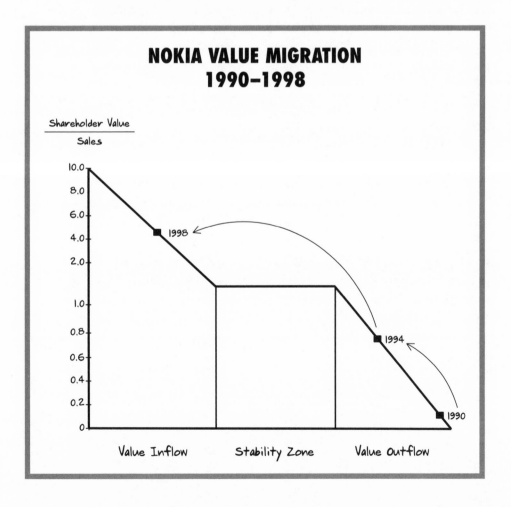

**NOKIA VALUE MIGRATION
1990–1998**

Shareholder Value
─────────────
Sales

By shifting its core skill set from hardware engineering to software engineering, Nokia built a leadership position in the European digital GSM market. When the U.S. market began to "go digital" in 1997, Nokia was far ahead of the competition in both digital infrastructure and handsets.

The results of exploiting all three patterns of change in its industry have been extremely gratifying: over the past five years, Nokia has created over $35 billion in market value. Sales have grown at a rate of 24 percent annually. Today, Nokia's operating margin on its infrastructure and handsets is 22 percent and 14 percent, respectively.

Nokia's successful pattern identification, response, and execution have enabled the company to perform significantly better than its major competitors. Nokia's return on sales has risen from 12 percent to 16 percent, compared to Ericsson at 11 percent, Lucent at 10 percent, and Motorola at 7 percent. Its assets-to-sales ratio has decreased from 0.49 to 0.32. The biggest change has been in Nokia's market-value-to-sales ratio, which moved from 0.1 in 1990 to 2.1 in 1997 and is higher than those of all of its competitors.

Despite its extraordinary success, Nokia's momentum may soon be threatened. As data, voice, and video technologies continue to converge, the boundaries between communications and computing will blur. Nokia has at least partially anticipated this convergence, and is rapidly developing the most advanced wireless data products on the market. However, it will need to continue to anticipate evolving customer priorities and emerging patterns if it is to play on the same field as Intel, Microsoft, IBM, Cisco, and the other major players of the computing industry.

Dell Computer

Collapse of the middle, channel compression, value chain deintegration.

Ten years ago, computer shoppers had few choices. While deintegration of the value chain had loosened the mainframe manufacturer's hold on the computing market, personal computing options remained severely limited. A handful of computer dealers, such as Computerland, sold a limited selection of machines from IBM, Apple, Tandy, and Commodore. Each PC system came with a package of preset options—memory, floppy disk drive, software—which were designed, assembled, configured, and delivered to retail channels by the manufacturer.

In this early stage, the vast majority of customers were ignorant of the available products. To make an educated purchase, they required a high degree of "handholding" by sales representatives, who could explain the mysterious world of RAM, ROM, and 5¼-inch floppy disks. Dealers like Computerland provided a valuable service to these hesitant and anxious first-time buyers.

Today, the PC market is completely different. Over the past decade, an increasing percentage of the population has become not just "computer literate," but "computer savvy." The world of computing is no longer limited to mainframe programmers and corporate IT professionals; today, nearly half the population uses personal computers on a regular basis. Furthermore, new technologies have radically increased PC capabilities and available options. As prices have dropped, more and more households and individuals have purchased PCs, learned to decipher the "technology" behind the screen, and become savvy consumers of new products. These key changes have unleashed an important pattern—the collapse of the middle—in the PC industry.

COLLAPSE OF THE MIDDLE

As customers have matured, a "one size fits all" solution is no longer viable. Indeed, today's customers have polarized into two camps. At one end of the spectrum, sophisticated corporate customers demand tailored computer systems capable of solving increasingly complex problems. These customers need solutions rather than "stock" products. Off-the-shelf inventory from retail rarely meets their needs. They require dedicated technical support, systems integration, and custom-configured hardware, software, and networking solutions.

Specialized sales forces (e.g., Hewlett-Packard's Global Account Management teams) and systems integration specialists (e.g., Andersen Consulting, EDS) "got" the needs of this customer segment early, and they have created significant value in recent years as high-end, integrated solutions providers.

At the other end of the spectrum are tech-savvy customers (corporate and individual) whose primary goal is to obtain the PC they want at the lowest possible price and with the least amount of hassle. Armed with knowledge of the technical specifications of PCs (a body of knowledge easily learned because Intel, Microsoft, and others have established industry "standards"), these customers know what they want, what price they are willing to pay, and they are willing to sacrifice the "handholding" of traditional retailers to get it quickly and cheaply.

Michael Dell had these customers in mind when he founded his PC company from his freshman dorm room in 1984. Dell started by buying old IBM and DEC computers, refurbishing them with new parts and peripherals, and selling them at prices 10 to 15 percent below the market. Dell's business model—give the price-seeking customers exactly what they want as cheaply as possible—was simple. It was also extremely profitable. By 1988, when the Dell Computer Corporation went public, it was selling over $150 million worth of computers. A decade later, Dell generates $16.8 billion in revenue and nearly $1.3 billion in profit.

Early recognition of the strategic market conditions and changing customer needs in the PC industry enabled Dell to exploit the collapse of the middle pattern by focusing on these customers. To build a successful business, however, Dell recognized and exploited two other patterns—channel compression and deintegration.

CHANNEL COMPRESSION

Traditionally, PC manufacturers sold their machines through retail outlets that bought PCs wholesale and resold them at profit. Resellers offered convenient location and multiple brands, but they added little value, in products or services, for customers. Michael Dell "got" the pattern far earlier than his competitors. He recognized that customers would sacrifice face-to-face sales relationships in exchange for low prices and many product options. He reasoned that "seeing" a PC mattered little; rather, product specifications (e.g., memory, processor) were the real factor in a consumer's purchase decision.

Dell responded to these emerging customer priorities by "compressing" the value chain and bypassing the traditional distribution channel. The company began selling its computers exclusively by phone. Dell offered customers an added benefit—customization. Rather than purchase one of the preconfigured machines a dealer had "in stock," Dell gave its customers the ability to choose the features their PC would have.

The overwhelming success of Dell's direct sales model has been amplified by the explosion of Internet commerce. In 1996, Dell supplemented its telephone sales force with an online ordering center. Dell's Internet sales have grown rapidly; today, nearly $2 billion of its sales (16 percent of total revenue) are processed online.

Dell's sales model allows the company to undercut resellers' prices (no markup) and to upsell accessory products and service agreements to its customers. At the same time a customer chooses a PC configuration (either online or over the phone), he or she is offered a selection of printers, warranties, notebook cases, storage devices, and cables. In 1997, Dell sold nearly $800 million in options and accessories, and it will sell over $1 billion in 1998. By going directly to consumers, Dell has captured a large portion of the "add-on" dollars these customers traditionally spent at retail outlets.

More importantly, Dell's direct sales model has allowed it to completely control the "entire customer experience." Unlike its competitors, who are vulnerable to the weaknesses of their distribution channel (e.g., poor service, lost orders, lack of knowledge about products), Dell is able to control sales, service, and support. This allows the company to build and maintain superior relationships with its customers.

DEINTEGRATION

Dell's exploitation of the channel compression pattern has given it a sizable cost advantage over its competitors. At the same time, the company has strengthened this advantage by further deintegrating the PC manufacturing value chain.

In the 1970s and early 1980s, the leading computer manufacturers, IBM and DEC, operated across the entire manufacturing value chain, from component manufacturing, operating system design, and applications software development to assembly and distribution. By the early 1990s, however, a host of new players had created extraordinary value by specializing in specific pieces of the value chain—Intel in microprocessors, Microsoft in operating systems and applications software, Compaq in hardware manufacturing.

Dell recognized, ahead of the competition, the opportunity to further subdivide and deintegrate the PC value chain. Dell was the first company to focus solely on assembly and delivery of finished products. In reality, Dell is not a PC manufacturer—it is a PC "assembler."

By exploiting this second phase of value chain deintegration, Dell has developed a superior, low-cost production model. It buys off-the-shelf components (motherboards, processors, storage devices) from local suppliers on an as-needed basis. As a result of its close relationships with these suppliers, Dell has nearly eliminated the need to stock inventory. With only one week of parts on hand, Dell's inventory is "earmarked for a system" as soon as it reaches the assembly plant. This "virtual inventory" process enables Dell to turn its inventory fifty-two times per year. In contrast, Compaq turns its inventory 13.5 times, and IBM, 9.8 times.

Through its just-in-time manufacturing process, Dell has reduced its asset intensity and SG&A expenses. Its SG&A costs per dollar are nearly half those of IBM and 25 percent lower than those of Compaq. Similarly, Dell's revenue per fixed-asset dollar is roughly 30 times greater than IBM's. Such efficiency has driven results straight to the bottom line: the company's operating expenses/sales ratio is only 11.4 percent—3 points lower than Compaq's, 11 points lower than Hewlett-Packard's, and 16 points lower than IBM's.

Rather than stock finished-product inventory for shipment to resellers, Dell assembles and ships each of its computers within thirty-six hours of receipt of a customer's order. The production process begins once a buyer contacts Dell with an order, either through Dell's 800 number or its Web site. The order is routed immediately to one of Dell's plants: Austin, Texas; Penang, Malaysia; or Limerick, Ireland. From the time of their call or click, customers usually have their machines within a week.

By coupling superior supply-chain economics with the price advantage of a direct sales model, Dell has consistently beaten its competition to market with cheaper, higher-quality machines. Because it does not have outdated component or finished goods stocks on site, Dell can move faster to market with new chips, faster modems, and larger hard drives than its competitors.

This combination of rapid delivery, low prices, and customization has enabled Dell to attract the most valuable, tech-savvy customers and to build strong loyalty among its installed base of users. By outsourcing aggressively and exploiting the ongoing deintegration of the PC value chain, Dell has self-selected a highly profitable customer population and drastically lowered the cost of serving them.

Despite its superior business model of low-cost production, Dell, like other PC makers, is facing shrinking margins as prices plummet. However, Dell's ability to anticipate evolving customer priorities has enabled the company to recognize the further evolution of the collapse of the middle in the computer industry and to make changes that continue to fuel its exceptional growth.

Dell's continued success is largely due to its recognition that customer priorities among high-end corporate customers are also evolving.

These new customers demand the higher performance of top-of-the-line products, but they have become more like the low-end consumers as the PC market has matured.

Like their low-end counterparts, high-end customers have also become more knowledgeable. Rather than relying on Andersen or IBM to choose and integrate their systems, more and more corporate customers have sought to minimize costs by purchasing direct-order machines and performing in-house integration. They have readily embraced the opportunity to purchase top-quality hardware at the lowest possible prices, and they have benefited from Dell's technical support and superior customer service.

Once again, Dell "got" the evolution of customer priorities ahead of its competitors, and it has successfully responded to these customer needs. Building from its position as a leader in desktop/laptop PCs, Dell has become a leader in workstations and corporate servers; the company launched a major push into the network server market in 1996, and it introduced its first workstation units in 1997.

Today, Dell is the number-two vendor of servers in the United States. It generates over 10 percent of its revenue from the sale of servers and workstations to corporate and government customers. High-end products, the company's fastest growing segment, are expected to generate over 15 percent of revenues by 2000.

By taking advantage of three key patterns—(1) the collapse of the middle, (2) channel compression, and (3) deintegration—Dell has generated over $80 billion in shareholder value over the past decade. Dell's business design, focused on satisfying customer needs (low price and custom design) at the lowest cost possible, has enabled it to become a key player worldwide, with over 7 percent of the market. In the United States, Dell is now in a neck and neck race with Compaq for market leadership. More importantly, Dell has become one of the most profitable players in the PC industry.

Nevertheless, Dell is facing increasing competition, as well as imitation of its business model. Gateway, IBM, and Compaq are aggressively moving into online direct sales in order to improve their business economics and compete on price with Dell. To remain ahead of the curve, Dell will need to make new moves and exploit new

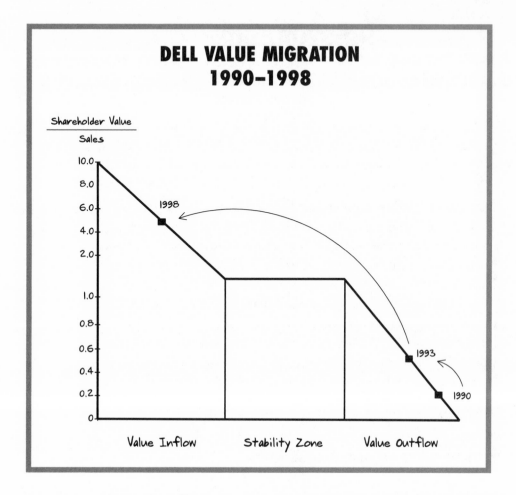

**DELL VALUE MIGRATION
1990–1998**

Shareholder Value
―――――――――
Sales

Value Inflow   Stability Zone   Value Outflow

emerging patterns in the PC industry. Indeed, the company is already anticipating the next pattern to transform its business; recently, Dell announced plans to bundle Cisco's DSL modems and service from U S West and other RBOCs with its computers to provide customers with complete solutions for high-speed Internet access.

Whether it further outsources assembly or microsegments its customer base, Dell will need to evolve its business design to sustain growth and profitability. Dell is leading the race at the latest post, but the dynamism of the industry will trigger a whole set of new patterns to be deciphered and exploited.

Amazon.com

Digital business design, microsegmentation, cornerstoning.

Where do you buy your books today? Chances are, if you are among the fifty million Americans online, you will say, "Amazon.com." The company was founded in 1995 by Jeff Bezos, a New York investment banker who "got it"—the potential of the Web as a medium for retail—far earlier than the competition. Capitalizing on the accelerating trend toward disintermediation of physical retailers via the Internet, Amazon has become the largest online retail business.

Amazon's Web-based approach makes its value proposition— better convenience, better selection, and better price than traditional retailers—possible. Amazon has been able to deliver on this proposition by exploiting multiple patterns (digital business design, microsegmentation, and cornerstoning) to become a major competitor to the incumbent superstore leaders, Barnes & Noble and Borders.

CONVENTIONAL TO DIGITAL BUSINESS DESIGN

Amazon's successful exploitation of the shift from conventional to digital business design has enabled it to meet consumers' emerging needs for greater selection, lower prices, and improved customer service. It has leveraged Internet and database technologies to address the inefficiencies that exist at both ends of the traditional retail channel spectrum.

Amazon's virtual store offers over two million titles to consumers, a selection magnitude that exceeds the offerings at even the largest superstores. It also addresses the key needs of both the shopper who prefers wide selection and the shopper who is deeply interested in a narrow topic area. Physical superstores feature a large selection of books, but they don't stock many titles for the serious reader or subject expert. Amazon, with its virtual storefront and single warehouse, is able to "stock" over ten times the number of titles on its "shelves" as its bricks-and-mortar competitors.

By replacing the entire bookstore infrastructure with a digital system, Amazon has drastically reduced its asset intensity and has negative working capital. Its inventory turn is twenty times that of superstores and over fifty times that of specialty stores. This operational streamlining has reduced expenses and enabled Amazon to undercut its competitors' prices by 20 to 30 percent. Even with the added cost of shipping and handling, most books are cheaper when ordered online from Amazon than when bought at a physical bookstore.

MICROSEGMENTATION

Amazon's digital business design has allowed it to take advantage of another pattern for building personalized relationships with its customers: microsegmentation. Recognizing that e-commerce necessitated the "giving" of purchase data and product preferences by the customer, Amazon has utilized this information to tailor its site on an individualized basis. As a result, Amazon is able to build one-to-one relationships with its customers.

To meet customers' growing need for advice and recommendations, Amazon allows each customer to create a personal virtual bookstore customized to individual book-shopping needs. A customer who logs on to the Amazon site is greeted with specific recommendations—not geared to a demographic segment, but tailored to the specifc individual. Amazon accomplishes this by tracking past purchases and comparing them against other customers who have purchased similar books. As it builds a profile of each customer, the recommendations become more and more refined. The more a customer shops, the more detailed the profile and the better the recommendations.

To a customer seeking personalized assistance, Amazon's value added is clearly above and beyond that provided by traditional bookstores. Specialty stores and independents offer relatively high levels of service, but at the cost of both lower selection and higher prices for customers. Superstores offer a larger selection, but are often impersonal and overwhelming. Indeed, the appeal of Amazon is so great that some consumers browse titles in a bricks-and-mortar store, but ultimately make their purchase through Amazon.com to ensure that all their purchase activity is captured and that their recommendations are enhanced.

In the future, Amazon may continue to exploit this pattern throughout its Web site. One might expect a completely personalized store, where the colors, fonts, bestseller lists, reviews, and chat rooms are all tailored to each individual customer. At that point, customers will truly have their own personalized bookstore, and the costs of switching stores will be far higher than in the traditional retail world.

Amazon's exploitation of the conventional to digital business design and microsegmentation patterns has allowed the company to grow extremely quickly. From 1995, when Amazon.com was founded, to 1997, sales grew to nearly $150 million, and they continue to grow rapidly. Amazon went public in May 1997; its market capitalization went from around $400 million to over $10 billion in November 1998.

CORNERSTONING

Having capitalized on the digital business design and microsegmentation patterns to become the leading online book retailer, Amazon is now seeking to expand the scope of its business. Rather than envisioning itself only as a bookseller, Amazon is aggressively moving to become a *total* Internet retailer. In preparation for the expected boom in e-commerce and "remote shopping," Amazon has begun to exploit the cornerstoning pattern (building from a company's base position to the next most profitable position) by expanding its offerings beyond books. Visitors to Amazon.com can now choose from over three million books, CDs, or audiobooks, multiplying the size of the market that Amazon can serve.

Despite the success of these moves, Amazon continues to seek new cornerstoning opportunities. Its acquisitions of Internet Movie Database Ltd., a comprehensive repository for movie information, and Junglee Corporation, a one-stop commerce Web site, hint at Amazon's future intentions. Junglee is a particularly interesting piece of Amazon's cornerstoning strategy: the company's online product databases allow shoppers to compare prices and products in a number of categories. Its technology could become the springboard that enables Amazon.com to become the portal for all of its customers' online transactions, regardless of product category. Indeed, Amazon's latest additions—videos, consumer electronics, and holiday gifts—clearly indicate the company's intentions to leverage its online brand name to become an e-commerce superstore.

In spite of its success and winning moves, Amazon is far from emerging the victor in e-commerce. The need to invest in marketing and in building scale means that Amazon will not turn a profit for several years. Meanwhile, it faces at least two new, very well financed competitors. Within the past year, the two dominant book chains, Barnes & Noble and Borders, have set up similar Web sites and have invested heavily in advertising them, so future positions are far from resolved. Barnes & Noble has locked up the preferred bookselling position with *The New York Times'* online Book Review section, and its financial resources dwarf those of Amazon.

Recently, Barnes & Noble's strategic position was further reinforced when Bertelsmann, the German publishing giant, bought a 50 percent position in barnesandnoble.com. Perhaps more importantly, Barnes & Noble recently paid $600 million to acquire Ingram Book Group, Amazon.com's largest supplier.

In addition, Amazon faces competition from a host of new Internet players. One of those is Cendant's Books.com. As part of NetMarket (an online members-only shopping service), Books.com allows members to buy books at greatly discounted rates. Since NetMarket's value capture is based on the membership fee it charges rather than the products it sells, it may be able to undercut Amazon's discount prices. In addition, online music players such as CDNow and N2K have achieved sufficient scale to appear on Amazon's radar screen as key competitors.

A second threat to Amazon is the emerging electronic book, a concept created to remove the bits from the atoms. Customers buy only one piece of hardware, but they can download thousands of electronic stories to read at their leisure. Readers will be able to carry favorite selections with them on vacation, without the usual book bulk. Amazon can begin to supply the software for these e-books, but will face competition from several of the hardware creators who plan to replace retailers with their own electronic bookstores. Nevertheless, Amazon could be well positioned to become the central clearinghouse for e-books in the future.

To date, by leveraging a digital business design and exploiting the microsegmentation and cornerstoning patterns, Amazon has made a long series of "on-target" moves to become a household name and an Internet power. In the future, Amazon.com may find the convergence pattern to be the most important factor transforming its strategic landscape; as the company moves into online retailing of multiple product lines, it will find itself coming up against multiple "bricks and mortar" powerhouses: Circuit City, CompUSA, and others. Ultimately, Barnes & Noble may not be Amazon's largest competitor. It could be Wal-Mart, Macy's, or even the shopping mall itself. The game is just getting started, but Amazon must anticipate the next key patterns in its evolution, or else it will be unable to retain its current momentum and trajectory.

Bang & Olufsen

Customer redefinition, product to brand, reintegration.

By the late 1980s, consumer electronics was rapidly becoming a no-profit zone. Stiff competition, coupled with commoditization of products as the price of technology declined rapidly, made it increasingly difficult for manufacturers to create value in that space. Moreover, with the product-centric mindset typical of most manufacturing companies, the consumer electronics players ceded control of the customer relationship to the channel, which cared little about which products it sold, since margins were universally low for nearly all equipment.

In this "declining profits" world, Bang & Olufsen was a high-end niche player in the consumer electronics market. It manufactured sophisticated, feature-laden stereos targeted at the high end of the market. However, despite its machines' higher pricetag and superior performance, Bang & Olufsen found itself confronted with the same declining (if not disappearing) profit margins as its lower end competitors, Sony, Panasonic, and Kenwood.

Over the past seven years, however, Bang & Olufsen has managed to separate itself from the competition through strategic anticipation and exploitation of the patterns transforming its business. Bang & Olufsen has successfully exploited three patterns—customer redefinition, product to brand, and reintegration—to return to profitability and create meaningful value growth.

CUSTOMER REDEFINITION

The key to Bang & Olufsen's success has been its ability to see and exploit the customer redefinition pattern. In the 1980s, Bang & Olufsen's customer was, by and large, the European audiophile. While this customer cared about style, he or she did so only within the limited world of high-fidelity audio equipment. This customer's primary interest was not the "image" or prestige of owning a luxury product, but rather knowing that the system's technical specifications and sound quality were unsurpassed.

To reach these customers, Bang & Olufsen advertised in niche publications aimed at audiophiles (*Stereo Review, Audiophile Voice*), and it sought to differentiate itself from its competitors based on technology, product specifications, and performance. Each of its ads contained a black box listing the specific performance features of the product in painstaking detail. Like other high-end consumer electronics manufacturers (e.g., Nakamichi, Bose), the company sought to appeal to its highly knowledgeable, highly focused customer base by focusing its marketing efforts on its products' technological superiority (real or perceived).

Despite Bang & Olufsen's technical superiority, the market valued the company on par with other consumer electronics manufacturers; in 1991, its market value to sales ratio was 0.3, similar to that of Sony, Pioneer, and Kenwood.

Unlike these traditional competitors, however, Bang & Olufsen anticipated the opportunity to create significant value by redefining its selected customer base. Recognizing that its products could be more appealing to luxury goods consumers (the same people who buy Moët & Chandon champagne, Gucci leather goods, and Rolex watches) than to customers who also bought expensive VCRs, camcorders, and high-end PCs, Bang & Olufsen set out to serve the image-conscious, luxury goods consumers. As Bang & Olufsen's CEO, Anders Knutsen explained his company's new focus: "The Bang & Olufsen philosophy consists of the synergy . . . of emotional appeal and technical excellence. What Bang & Olufsen wants to achieve with its products is to help make each of our customer's lives full of experiences."

To reach these "image" customers, Bang & Olufsen pulled its audiophile magazine ads and placed ads in *GQ, Esquire, Cosmopolitan,* and other upscale "lifestyle" magazines. Whereas its customers were formerly older, narrowly focused consumers, Bang & Olufsen's new target population does not fit into traditional demographic groups. Rather, its new customers are part of an "attitudinal" group of high-income, lifestyle-purchasing individuals who are willing to pay high prices for a high-style, "image-building" product. These customers buy

BANG & OLUFSEN'S COMPETITIVE RADAR SCREEN:
Focusing on Those That Matter . . .

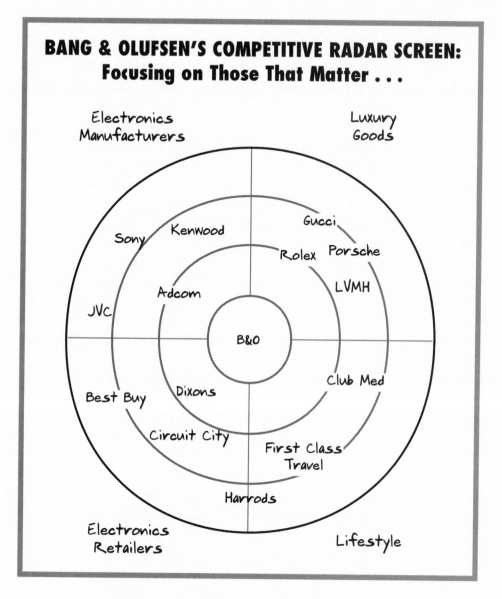

Electronics
Manufacturers

Luxury
Goods

Gucci

Sony   Kenwood

Rolex   Porsche

LVMH

Adcom

JVC

B&O

Club Med

Best Buy   Dixons

Circuit City

First Class
Travel

Harrods

Electronics
Retailers

Lifestyle

Bang & Olufsen equipment as much for what it says about their lifestyle (and wallet size) as for its high-end sound quality and technical specifications. While they may only listen to CDs once a week, these customers purchase Bang & Olufsen's equipment for the same reason they buy LVMH products or Gucci handbags: because it is "the best that money can buy."

PRODUCT TO BRAND

In order to fully exploit the customer redefinition pattern, Bang & Olufsen needed to take advantage of a second pattern: the product to brand pattern. In the 1980s, the company had a strictly product-centric mindset. It poured its efforts into designing and manufacturing every piece of its equipment, from components to finished products. Bang & Olufsen did this very well—its products were built to exacting specifications and led the industry in high-performance standards. However, while the company was renowned in the industry as a designer of premium quality products, it lacked name recognition with all but the most informed and dedicated audiophiles.

After Bang & Olufsen redefined its customer population, it moved aggressively to build its brand and differentiate its products on style and image. As mentioned earlier, the company drastically altered its advertising strategy from a specifications-based "sell" to an image/lifestyle message. At the same time, Bang & Olufsen drastically reduced the number of stores in which it placed its products, thereby creating and cultivating an image of "scarcity" and exclusivity for its products.

By exploiting the product to brand pattern, Bang & Olufsen has created an extraordinary price premium over its competitors. Because its products are now seen and sold as "luxury goods," Bang & Olufsen is able to command as much as 1000 percent price differential versus its competitors. For example, a typical Sony television costs roughly $500, a Bang & Olufsen system runs nearly $5,000. Customers are no longer purchasing Bang & Olufsen's products based on technical excellence or features; rather, they are buying the brand because they "need" (and "want") to have it.

Indeed, Bang & Olufsen has further exploited the product to brand pattern by broadening its line of equipment from stereos to televisions, phones, and speakers. Its products are now as much pieces of design "art" for display as they are equipment for performance. Whether the products actually outperform Sony or Panasonic is incidental. They send a message about the owner's lifestyle, taste, and wealth, just like expensive champagne, $10,000 dresses, or $75,000 sports cars.

REINTEGRATION

In order to fully exploit the product to brand pattern, Bang & Olufsen capitalized on a third pattern that enabled it to further strengthen its name and transform the company's image: the reintegration pattern. In the 1980s, despite its products' high-end reputation and specifications, Bang & Olufsen received the same low margins as lower-end electronics manufacturers because it was dependent on the same retailers for distribution. Anchored down with a weak brand and a manufacturing mindset, Bang & Olufsen had no special relationship with its channels; to them, it was just another vendor. Consequently, its products were not differentiated on the retail floor from the hundreds of other pieces of equipment available.

The end result was that only the knowledgeable, high-tech audiophile was aware of Bang & Olufsen's performance excellence; the uneducated customer did not even get past the higher price tag on Bang & Olufsen equipment to learn about the product's features, because that customer could not "see" any difference between a Bang & Olufsen product and a less expensive Sony. As a result, the customer was not willing to pay more for Bang & Olufsen equipment, and the company's products fell prey to the same low margins as its lower quality competition.

In order to further strengthen its brand name and appeal to its new customer group, Bang & Olufsen reintegrated the value chain by asserting more control over its distribution channels. Today, Bang & Olufsen's products are no longer found on the same shelf as Panasonic, Sony, Kenwood, JVC, and the other mass electronics companies. Rather, Bang & Olufsen's products are positioned only with high-end exclusive shops and Bang & Olufsen-owned distribution stores. By separating its products from the competition, Bang & Olufsen is able to market them as "status symbols" and luxury goods, rather than as consumer electronics devices. With its stereos, phones, and televisions lavishly displayed next door to LVMH and Gucci boutiques in Paris (as well as in a franchise shop in the electronics department of Harrods), Bang & Olufsen has completed the transformation from electronics manufacturer to luxury good provider. Just as its advertising strategy

and customer population support the "Bang & Olufsen image," now the channel strategy does as well.

By exploiting the customer redefinition, product to brand, and reintegration patterns, Bang & Olufsen achieved extraordinary results from 1991 to 1997. Revenues grew at 6 percent annually; profitability (EBIT margin) rose from 6 percent to 10 percent. The company also significantly reduced its asset intensity, from 0.72 in 1991 to 0.5 in 1997. Projected profit growth for 1998 was 25 percent. Bang & Olufsen's performance is even more striking when compared to its key rivals, whose asset intensity (0.9), EBIT margins (5–6 percent), and projected earnings growth (~10 percent) are far less impressive.

Most importantly, Bang & Olufsen is now valued on par with other luxury goods companies. Its 1997 market value/sales ratio was 1.5, closer to that of LVMH (2.4), Ralph Lauren (2.2), and Gucci (2.8), than to the valuations of its consumer electronics competitors: Sony (0.8), Pioneer (0.8), and Kenwood (0.3). The company's ability to anticipate and exploit several key patterns in its industry has enabled it to redefine its customers, reshape its business design, and create a new "value space" at the intersection of electronics and luxury goods. In doing so, Bang & Olufsen has also created significant value for its shareholders.

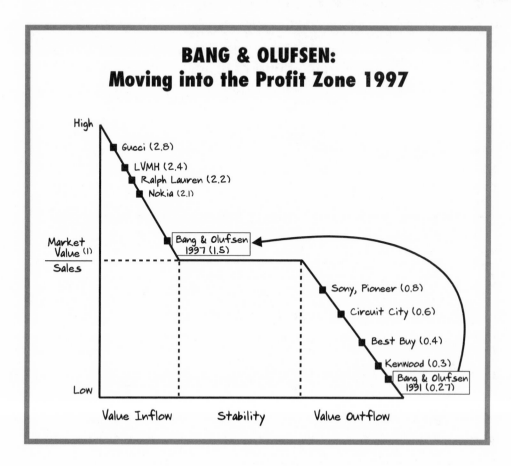

BANG & OLUFSEN:
Moving into the Profit Zone 1997

High

Gucci (2.8)

LVMH (2.4)

Ralph Lauren (2.2)

Nokia (2.1)

Market Value [1]
_____
Sales

Bang & Olufsen 1997 (1.5)

Sony, Pioneer (0.8)

Circuit City (0.6)

Best Buy (0.4)

Kenwood (0.3)

Bang & Olufsen 1991 (0.27)

Low

Value Inflow   Stability   Value Outflow

Nevertheless, Bang & Olufsen cannot afford to rest on its impressive economic accomplishments. Companies that depend on image and lifestyle appeal for sales are always susceptible to the next wave of styles and "fads." If Bang & Olufsen is to maintain its growth trajectory, it must continue to anticipate its customers' evolving priorities and invest astutely in its brand. Furthermore, it must continue to look for ways to extend control over the distribution channel and streamline its manufacturing process in order to maximize profitability. Only by anticipating the future patterns of change transforming the electronics and luxury goods industries will Bang & Olufsen sustain its value growth in the coming years.

ACCELERATED PATTERN DETECTION

Learn the Patterns

↓

Map Your Strategic Landscape;
Mindshare Overlay

↓

Map Leading Indicators and Pattern Triggers
- extreme variations
- dysfunctionality
- rapid movement

↓

Ask yourself, what's wrong with this picture?
(State A)

↓

(CHAPTER 13)

Ask yourself, what would fix this picture?
What are my strategic response options?
(State B)

↓

CHAPTER 12
ACCELERATED PATTERN DETECTION

How to "Get It" One Year Sooner

T HE PREVIOUS CHAPTER illustrated the most fundamental method of identifying future profit patterns: understanding the key stories that have reshaped your industry, and thinking through the stories that will redefine its future. To apply this method to your own business, write down the past 10-year history of your industry and company. Develop its story in the language of patterns. Let patterns help you exchange your mental "still camera" for a mental "video recorder," enabling you to shift from still pictures to moving frames. Then let this video carry you into the future. Anticipate how long the current pattern(s) in your industry will define competitive advantage, and what future pattern(s) will replace it.

Once you have completed this exercise, you will be challenged by a new set of perspectives that will help you manage your business or investments more successfully. However, there are numerous occasions

> # Chance favors the prepared mind.

when additional methods of pattern identification and analysis can also be helpful. This chapter describes three of those methods. They should be used as supplements, not substitutes, for the strategic story telling method of pattern identification.

These additional methods offer several benefits. First, they may help you identify patterns that would otherwise remain hidden, particularly when you are facing a very complex environment. Second, they create a focus on more specific moves and actions. These methods get to the level of naming names—competitors, customers, potential partners, pieces of the value chain—that strategic story telling treats at a higher, more general level. As a result, the specific moves that come from pattern thinking—action implications for your company or your investments—become more precise and more urgent. Finally, because they focus on preconditions and early indicators, these methods can help you anticipate the emergence of a new pattern sooner—sometimes as much as a year sooner—than your competitors might.

These three additional methods are:

1. *Mapping your strategic landscape,* and the business designs of those who inhabit it.
2. *Measuring mindshare*—exploring which business designs are winning mindshare with customers, investors, and scarce talent—and why.
3. *Deciphering the conditions and triggers* that will signal the start of the next patterns in your business.

Knowing patterns prepares the mind.

THAT "CHILLING MOMENT"

At least once in every executive's career, he or she experiences a "chilling moment": an icy sensation of fear caused by the sudden, terrible realization that they have "gotten it"—the strategic pattern transforming their industry—*too late.* Later than their competitors, later than their customers, later than their suppliers. That chilling moment can be triggered by multiple signals indicating that a new pattern has already started to play out, leaving your organization behind:

- Your largest customer has just taken all of its business to the competition.
- Your largest competitor and your most innovative competitor have agreed to merge.
- One of your major distributors has filed for bankruptcy.
- A key customer refused your last two price increases and got away with it.

In contrast, an externally hypersensitive management team would be acutely aware of the changing strategic market conditions in its industry because they are constantly searching for even the subtlest signals of fundamental change in the market. The team would suspect the pattern even before it is triggered, define the new opportunity, and adapt the corporation's business design to exploit the opportunity.

Spotting patterns while there is still time to lock in the polarization premium can be extremely profitable. In most companies, however, the traditional planning process is not tuned to the type of strategic anticipation that is required to see potential patterns early, clearly, and actionably. Creating this capability requires shifting the mindset from yesterday's data to tomorrow's, from static to dynamic views, and from linear to nonlinear assumptions. It means moving from internal measures to external ones, and from a budget-oriented ritual to a process intensely focused on anticipating the three or four critical patterns that will reshape your business.

Exhibit "Pattern Detection Spectrum" points to the level of clarity and conviction required for early action. Strategic anticipation is not about prediction; it is about understanding enough to make the right moves. The challenge of strategic anticipation through superior pattern recognition is not a one-time exercise; it is a new way of thinking that is designed to increase the odds of creating sustained profit growth. A good way to begin is to understand the strategic landscape that defines the economic context of your business.

MAP YOUR STRATEGIC LANDSCAPE

Pattern detection is an outside-in process that requires monitoring not only your competitors' business designs, but the broader strategic landscape—seeing the *entire* business chess board. It means moving beyond a well-developed competitive radar screen to sketching the entire economic field around your own position. Your strategic landscape is shaped by all of the key players and unfolding events that will trigger and define the profit patterns that will affect your company. These players include: customers, prospects, traditional channels, new channels, investors, media, sources of talent, sources of innovation, and competitors, both traditional and nontraditional.

The strategic landscape for most companies has become increasingly messy. The number of relevant competitors has grown (from five to fifty, in many categories), and the types of customer buying behavior have multiplied as well. Moreover, the continual blurring of

PATTERN DETECTION SPECTRUM

"I know for sure"

"I see it coming"

STRATEGIC ANTICIPATION

"I think it might happen"

"I have a sneaking suspicion"

"I'm totally oblivious"

traditional roles and boundaries has made the landscape a crowded and confusing place.

This complexity increases the need to create an accurate rendering of today's strategic landscape, including an accurate and sufficiently detailed perspective on its past and future evolution. By forcing yourself to construct a comprehensive visual representation of your true playing field, you can identify all of the conflicts, dysfunctionalities, inconsistencies, gaps, and troubling elements that will help you find emerging patterns and keys to value growth in the future. Exhibit "Strategic Landscape" shows in schematic fashion what such a rendering might look like. Start with customers and potential customers. Include all the channels, influencers, innovators, competitors (no matter how different their business designs might be), and types of suppliers ("potential forward integrators") who play in the system.

Fine-tuning your view of the landscape can be a very helpful element of this process. Look for ways to simplify sections, make other parts more detailed, or iterate the picture through several variations. Search for openings, conflicts, and opportunities. Be certain to include all the newly important unconventional players, such as investors, media, and talent sources. An exercise designed to help you systematically fine-tune your landscape is provided in Chapter 14.

As you further fine-tune, realize that limited dimensions create shortcomings in landscape sketches. Among the particular issues to address are: momentum, opportunity space, and time.

The strategic landscape contains many customer groups and many competitors who, if drawn to scale, are quite small. Relative size, however, can be enormously misleading. Twenty years ago, size was often the most important variable. In a market share world, the biggest player had the lowest costs and the highest profits. In a value migration world, where value shifts rapidly from old business models to new, we are more interested in momentum than in mass. Small customer groups that are highly profitable and growing at 30 percent are enormously important. Small competitors who have 30 percent margins and 30 percent growth are enormously important. (Quite often, these two groups are linked.) Therefore, it's important to amend the sketch of the strategic landscape with some indication of momentum.

STRATEGIC LANDSCAPE

Sources of innovation
- R&D
- Venture firms
- Universities

Influencers
- Media
- Investors
- Securities analysts
- Regulators
- Interest groups

Sources of talent

Alliance partners from other industries

Customers	Distribution Channels	Competing Value Chains/Business Designs	Suppliers

Profit-impacting observations:

The second shortcoming of a strategic landscape sketch is a lack of perspective on the opportunity space available to the different business designs competing on the landscape. Calculating the opportunity space for a particular business design can help to estimate how long the momentum behind that business model will last. Will a competitor who is capturing most of the value growth in our industry *hit the ceiling in three years, or in ten?* The answer will tell us whether our current business model is a victim of the current pattern, or whether there is enough unchallenged space in the system for us to build a protected and profitable position. Better yet, it will tell us whether there is enough time left to build a new business design that could participate profitably in the new pattern.

Momentum and opportunity space are difficult to measure and understand, but neither is as difficult to understand as time. Opportunity space, momentum, and time are, of course, related. If the opportunity space for a particular business design, in terms of revenue, is $2 billion and a $300 million business is growing at 45 percent per year, it will fill that space in five years. If the opportunity space is $80 billion and a $1 billion business design is growing at 35 percent per year, it will fill that space in fifteen years (as Wal-Mart did between 1980 and 1995).

Having drawn the strategic landscape of your business, ask whether the company's management team can:

- Identify all of the new entrant customers.
- See all of the variations in profitability along the value chain.
- Spot a value chain squeeze emerging.
- Spot the weak links in the system that impair your ability to create value.
- See the full range of problems and dysfunctionalities in the system that can trigger the next pattern.
- Identify the new, emerging profit zones in the system.

This might have been the kind of strategic mapping that Charles Schwab did, in leading up to his financial planner move (making independent financial planners collaborators rather than competitors), his OneSource move (providing investors with the ability to buy and sell the funds of different mutual fund companies), and his insurance move (offering discount insurance to his customers, to better serve the full spectrum of their needs). Similarly, we can develop our own observational method that will lead us to this kind of thinking.

By developing a visualization and an in-depth exploration of the interdependencies among all the actors in the system (customers, prospects, channels, investors, influencers, competitors, sources of talent, externalities, and value chain neighbors), managers can begin to detect the patterns that will change the fundamentals of their own business.

MEASURE MINDSHARE

In Chapter 3, we discussed the growing importance of mindshare in determining business success. An understanding of mindshare has the power to take managers beyond today's market share, and beyond today's market capitalization, to see tomorrow's opportunities more clearly. As you search for opportunities and emerging patterns along the strategic landscape of your industry, use mindshare thinking to help further fine-tune your rendering of the strategic landscape. The mindshare dynamics of key constituents—customers, influencers, investors, and talent—are leading indicators of the next opportunity shifts in the marketplace.

Develop a mindshare overlay for the strategic landscape by asking:

- Who has won the *customers'* mindshare today?
  - —Where are the most profitable customers or customer segments voting with their dollars?
- Who has won mindshare with *investors*?
  - —Where are early-stage investments being placed?
  - —Where are the IPOs occurring?

- Who has won mindshare with the best business *talent*?
  —What does an analysis of the turnover of the industry's top-decile performers show? Who is attracting them?
- Who has won mindshare with media, other influencers, and alliance partners?

Accurate, quantitative responses to these questions will allow you to highlight the most dynamic "hot zones" across the strategic landscape. More specifically, they should allow you to identify future defining customers, competitors, and talent, all of which are important clues to emerging patterns and value creation opportunities.

But simply understanding where mindshare is headed is not enough. The next step is to understand *why* certain players are winning mindshare. This involves digging beneath the surface to unearth the factors that are driving those attitudinal and behavioral shifts. The next section outlines some of the leading indicators that cause shifts among key mindshare constituents in the strategic landscape.

DECIPHER CONDITIONS AND TRIGGERS

An in-depth understanding of the full dimensions of your strategic landscape is the first step to pattern detection. The next step involves developing a system for monitoring the underlying conditions and triggers that catalyze patterns in your industry (Exhibit "Pattern Conditions and Triggers"). Profit patterns do not happen in a vacuum, nor do they happen without being provoked. Rather, they develop over time and out of sight. Like the roots of a tree, the preconditions leading to a new pattern expand invisibly beneath the ground. Over the course of years, the fundamental realities of an industry evolve in a certain direction and at a certain rate (both of which may vary over time). Eventually, several change variables drop into place, and the conditions are ripe to set new patterns in motion.

Many shifts in the fundamental nature of the strategic landscape are subtle and hard to see. These slow, often imperceptible changes are the root cause of pattern evolution. They alter the strategic landscape of an industry and prepare the way for discontinuous change, for a shift from A to B. These shifts weaken the existing structure—the foundations—of the business or industry and make drastic and widespread change possible (and profitable for those who excel at strategic anticipation).

These shifting foundations in a business or industry create the potential for new business designs, because they shape new customer priorities, rearrange value chain relationships, and disturb the current competitive equilibrium. Ultimately, a combination of conditions and triggers creates new opportunities for creating value growth and capturing strategic control. By recognizing, measuring, and tracking these conditions and triggers, a forward-looking management team is in a better position to anticipate the next wave of value growth and to seize the initiative.

Leading indicators of patterns manifest themselves in many forms, as shown in "Pattern Conditions and Triggers." At their root, many of them tend to fall into three categories:

1. *Variability*—a widening in the range of customers' priorities, competitors' relative performance, or economics (cost position, shareholder value creation, profitability).

2. *Rate and direction of change*—an acceleration in the rate, or a shift in the direction, of change in customer priorities, economics, technology, infrastructure, or business designs.

3. *Dysfunctionality*—emerging friction, inefficiency, or mismatches in the value chain, the organization, or the customer population.

The presence of any of these conditions can signal an important opportunity. High degrees of customer variability in a world of homogeneous business models signal opportunity. Change, particularly in a world of static and similar business models, can also signal opportunity. Dysfunctionalities, mismatches, or inefficiencies related to the value chain, the channel, the product, the organization, or the customer (in terms of systems economics, satisfaction, or preferences) can also signal opportunities for new business models.

PATTERN CONDITIONS AND TRIGGERS

"signals and clues pointing to the emergence of a new pattern"

- Changing customer priorities
- Customer sophistication
- Business design innovation
- Technological change
- New infrastructure
- Variations in customer preferences
- Changing economics (costs, prices, asset intensity)
- Customer receptivity to new options
- Customer boredom

- Redistribution of power
- Changes in level of wealth or distribution of wealth
- Business design lethargy
- Non-economic motivation
  - Irrational competition
  - Externalities
- New access to information
- Rising expectations
- Regulatory change
- New actors (new competitors, customers, investors)
- Media focus

- Poor performance
- Mismatch between current options and required functionality
- Combination of two or more factors
- Commoditization
- Specialization economics
- Extreme variation in profitability (along the value chain, among customer types, etc.)
- Oversupply
- Moving bottlenecks

Typically, no single condition or trigger will set off a pattern. Rather, multiple elements will combine to catalyze the change. At times, a specific condition or trigger can spark multiple patterns, depending on the other conditions or triggers with which it combines. For example, increasing variability in customer preferences can lead to both the product pyramid pattern and the microsegmentation pattern. Similarly, rapid technological change can spark both the digital business design and the channel multiplication pattern. To best anticipate which patterns are emerging in your industry, map the full array of key conditions (variability, rate of change, dysfunctionality) that are transforming the strategic landscape of your business (see "The Abridged Patterns Workbook," Chapter 14, for a template for mapping key conditions and triggers).

The challenge to detecting the next pattern is to maintain an unusually strong external orientation within the management and investor team. When you understand the array of conditions and triggers that can catalyze the next major shift, you can dramatically improve your ability to spot the current pattern and to anticipate the next one (see Exhibit "Always Look for the Next Shift").

PRACTICE

Pattern detection is a bit like watching a movie. After so many minutes or so many plot twists, we start anticipating the possible outcomes. Many films give so many clues that little is left to the imagination. Today's business landscape is more complex, but the response is the same: as you learn the basic plot twists and turns, you improve your ability to anticipate outcomes.

Be active, rather than passive, in the process. Be especially proactive in looking for new examples of well-defined patterns as you read the business press. Ask what makes these examples similar to or different from the patterns you already know.

Put yourself inside the game. Debate your views with a colleague or even a customer. Be honest with yourself about facts that you don't know (but could find out). Focus on reducing the amount of guesswork and risk in the process.

Be prepared for ambiguity and confusion, especially when faced with multiple patterns. Be comfortable with the reality that two, three, or more simultaneous patterns will usually be in play within a complex business situation.

Always keep in mind that pattern recognition is not about prediction. We cannot predict the future. The goal is to increase your odds

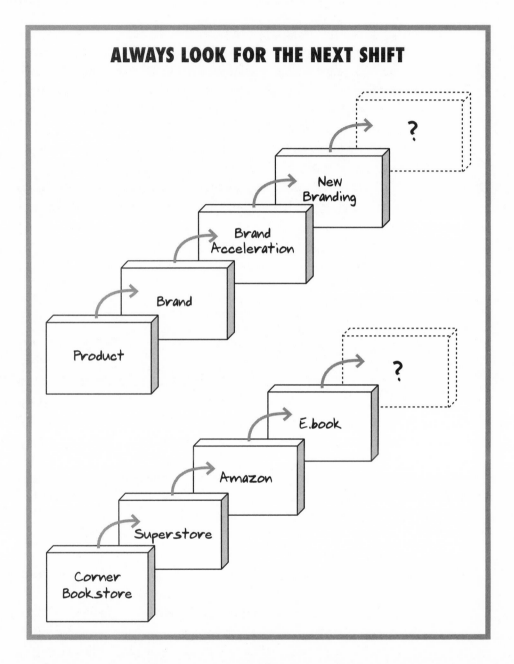

ALWAYS LOOK FOR THE NEXT SHIFT

of success by minimizing the unknown and undetected realities that are transforming your business. Some patterns are, of course, random. They are triggered by unexpected events that suddenly alter an industry. However, most patterns are probabilistic. They are the outcome of identifiable and measurable conditions affecting the strategic landscape. Honing your pattern recognition skills will enable you, and your company, to detect these patterns first and respond sooner than others do.

Above all, be insistent on asking questions about where the *next* shift will occur. Constantly seek out new patterns and new potential moves. If your competitors have beaten you to the best move, identify the best possible countermove.

Ask the questions and see the patterns. Raise your odds of winning the next cycle.

CHAPTER 13

PUTTING PATTERNS TO WORK IN YOUR ORGANIZATION

MOVING FROM "GETTING IT" TO "ACTING ON IT"

PATTERNS ARE PROVOCATIVE. More often than not, they challenge the status quo. They help companies move beyond answering the question "What does our management team *need to know?*" to address the question "What is our management team *afraid to find out?*" Only those companies, management teams, and investors gutsy enough to face the implications of the patterns reshaping their industry will profit from the knowledge that patterns can provide.

Patterns can help companies recognize and respond to the discontinuities altering the strategic landscape of their business. Despite the necessity of "acting on" these patterns, dealing with discontinuity and change in business invariably causes extreme tension and discomfort. Past experience, natural human resistance to change, and clashing personalities often prevent even the most effective leaders from successfully dealing with discontinuity. In this situation, many managers are unable to overcome the organizational inertia and internal resistance to change that prevent their company from fully exploiting the value growth opportunities created by the next cycle of change in their industry.

In order to address this set of issues, the effective leader must be aware of the tension and discomfort inherent in a major shift of organizational focus and strategic direction. In every case, there will be predictable concerns from those who would vote for the comfort of incremental change, those who have been raised in the school of product superiority, and those who would like to avoid rocking the boat.

The patterns thinker can anticipate the arguments that this group will use against acting on the next pattern. There are patterns of internal organizational behavior that can be anticipated as effectively as the external patterns reshaping the outside world. These patterns arise again and again, in meeting after meeting, in company after company. These reactions are rooted in human nature, not in industry dynamics. This natural preference for avoiding the challenge of dealing with discontinuity manifests itself in many ways. In general, however, these objections pertain to issues such as risk, type of move considered, timing, sticking to the traditional playbook, and profit protection.

The following table summarizes the key issues that stand in the way of dealing profitably with discontinuity, and the sections within this chapter that begin to address these issues.

Issue	Section That Addresses Issue
"Business design change is too risky"	"Understand Strategic Risk"
"We don't want too many choices"	"Multiply Strategic Choices"
"We have enough time—we'll wait to see how things evolve further before changing"	"Understand and Exploit Time"
"Let's just stick with the playbook of moves we already know"	"Develop an Action Repertoire of Moves and Countermoves"
"Why make this move? There is too much uncertainty. Besides, others will imitate and take profit away"	"Create Strategic Control"

In order to overcome these objections, the astute manager must combine one part economics, one part political skill in building coalitions, and one part sheer persistence and determination. The best argument does not always win—but it can prepare you to deal with the issues you will need to address in making the journey from "getting it" to "acting on it."

This chapter sets forth a series of ideas for thinking through and addressing these issues. The ideas are designed to help create organizational energy and enthusiasm for achieving excellence in strategic anticipation, crafting the right moves, and devising new means of profit protection. After reading it, we hope you will be equipped to contribute more effective leadership in helping the organization meet these challenges. Leadership can make the difference between achieving the first, second, or last place in the value polarization environment that is affecting a growing number of businesses in the economy today.

UNDERSTAND STRATEGIC RISK

Companies face many different types of risk: operating risk (machines break down), financial risk (currencies fluctuate), product liability risk (the unexpected lawsuit), and natural forces risk (floods destroy the factory) are but a few.

There is a new risk that is much more expensive than those above and that needs to be added to the list: *strategic risk*. In a world of Value Migration and value polarization, business designs lose their customer relevance and profit power more quickly than before. Strategic risk manifests itself abruptly and dramatically. Value collapse, value stagnation, and the silver medal in a polarization game are merely one or two bad decisions (or missed decisions) away. (See Exhibits "Value Collapse," "Value Stagnation," and "The Silver Medal in a Polarization Game.")

In many organizations, the first objection to "acting on" patterns is that changing the company's business design is "too risky." Often, managers are concerned that significant change in the company's strategic direction could risk hurting its existing business and operations.

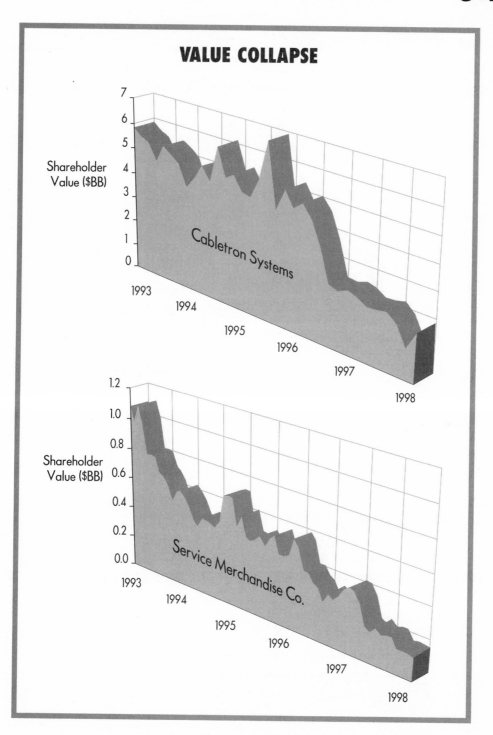

VALUE COLLAPSE

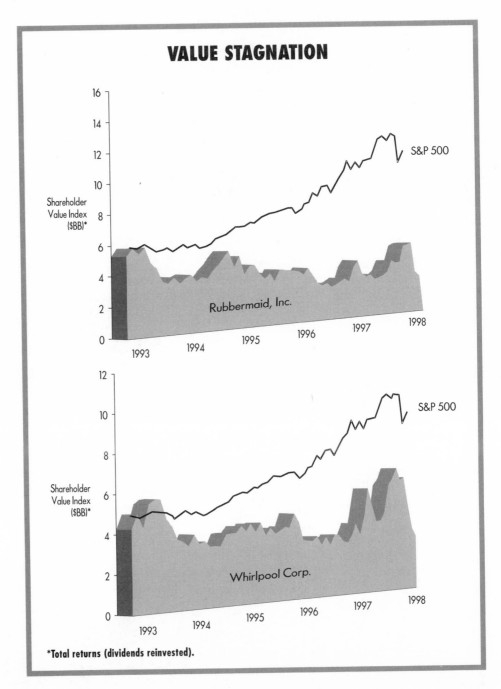

VALUE STAGNATION

*Total returns (dividends reinvested).

THE SILVER MEDAL IN A POLARIZATION GAME

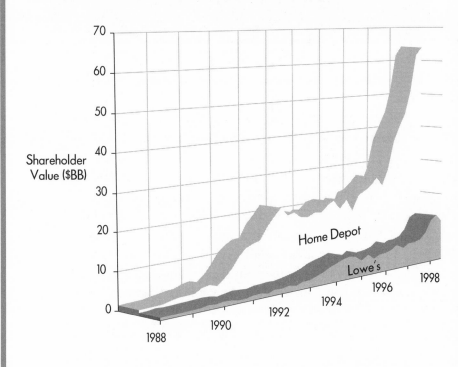

Shareholder Value ($BB)

Home Depot

Lowe's

1988 · 1990 · 1992 · 1994 · 1996 · 1998

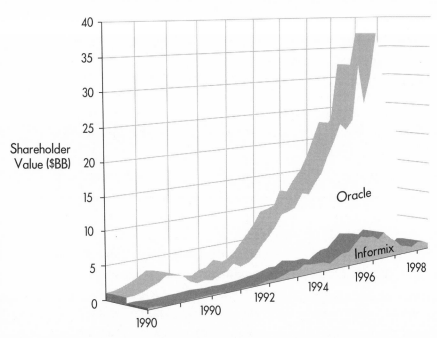

Shareholder Value ($BB)

Oracle

Informix

1990 · 1990 · 1992 · 1994 · 1996 · 1998

The reality is that not "getting" the patterns, or not acting on them quickly is often far riskier to a company's strategic position. Indeed, an organization's failure to reinvent its business design can severely damage its existing profitable operations, and raise its level of strategic risk.

Strategic risk is a little bit like asset intensity: who needs it? You don't want a business model with high asset intensity; you don't want one with a lot of risk intensity either.

The paradox is that much of the risk intensity in many companies' business models is unnecessary. The risk is there because, at a strategic level, *the customer remains unknown.* There is no reason to be caught in that situation. Great business chess players like Bill Gates, Jack Welch, or Percy Barnevik radically reduce the risk of their business by interacting directly with customers ten times more often than many of their peers. Every hour spent in dialogue with the right customer drives down the level of risk in your business. Dialoguing with the toughest and most forward-looking customers is the most profitable habit that managers can create, for themselves and for their management teams.

And it is habit-forming. Once you've experienced the advantage of taking action based on the right customer information, you'll never want to operate in the dark again.

Other major sources of strategic risk are:

- Lack of clarity, within the organization, about *the firm's profit model.* A company needs to understand exactly how high profits occur in its business.

- *Target fixation*—continuing to measure the wrong variables even after the market has shifted and a new pattern is in play.

- *Premature "scenario planning"*—modeling the future before nailing down the available facts and their implications. Many exercises in scenario planning build models around "uncertainties" that should be known quantities, because additional effort in strategic detective work can get the right facts into the decision process. The ratio of "uncertain" to "known" is often 80 percent to 20 percent. Through a deeper understanding of the strategic landscape and of newly unfolding patterns, those percentages could be reversed.

- *Excess modeling*—Why overuse models when you can test many innovations directly with the customer? Microsoft's method is "planning for failure." When you design your first move, assume that it probably won't work perfectly, or at all. Have your second and third moves ready to go. Microsoft's magic sequence is:

  Move—fail
  Move—fail
  Move—win big

- *Inadequate competitive intensity,* early in the life of a new pattern. Competing hard *early* is cheap and low risk; competing hard later is expensive and high risk. The combination of "getting it" early, and competing most intensely just as the new pattern begins to unfold, dramatically reduces the risk of your competitive position. It also increases the odds of achieving spectacular success (revisit the polarization examples in Chapter 2 to see how dramatic that competitive success can be).

In summary, it's important to realize that your next move and your next business can be *designed* not just for customer relevance and high profitability, but for risk minimization as well. Failing to carefully minimize strategic risk can lead to value collapse, value stagnation, or the silver medal in a polarization game.

The table below tries to capture the spirit of the key differences between designing for high and low strategic risk:

DESIGN DIFFERENCES

Design for High Risk	Design for Risk Minimization
"Sort of know the customer."	"Really know the most important customers, how *fast* they are changing, and *how* they are changing."
"Fuzziness around what the profit model is."	"Absolute clarity about the company's current and likely future profit model, based on a robust understanding of patterns, and how they play out."

Design for High Risk	Design for Risk Minimization
"Target fixation."	"Actively look for the next major shift."
"Scenario planning."	"Constantly deepen the company's understanding of the evolving strategic landscape and its implications for action."

"Build models."	Adopt the strategic experimentation approach:
	    "Move—fail."
	    "Move—fail."
	    "Move—win."

"Compete."	"Compete most intensely at the outset of the new pattern, to lock in the polarization premium."
"Target 90 percent of mindshare on how to optimize today's model."	"Target 90 percent of management's mindshare on seeing the next pattern and inventing tomorrow's business design two years before others do."

* * *

- Is my company on the verge of:
  - Stock price collapse,
  - Value stagnation,
  - The silver medal in a polarization contest, or
  - The gold medal in a polarization contest?
- Is the level of strategic risk in my company increasing or decreasing over time? Why?
- How does my level of strategic risk compare to that of my strongest competitor?

MULTIPLY STRATEGIC CHOICES

In their planning processes, many companies consider only three or four major alternatives or strategic choices. Typically, these choices are conservative and represent only a fine-tuning of the current business design. In a static world of happy customers, high profits, and little business design innovation, that might be just fine—for a while.

Other companies might weigh seven or eight choices, three or four of which are "out of the box." Successful business leaders typically work with a dramatically expanded set of choices (twelve or fifteen major options or combinations), of which three or four are truly revolutionary.

Consider the history of Coca-Cola. The early 1980s were a time of intense strategic experimentation: divestitures, Columbia Pictures, New Coke, bottler acquisitions, expansion abroad, and so on. Roberto Goizueta was creating a spectrum of a dozen choices for his company, not two or three.

The effects of a broader and more creative option set are striking. Enlarging the choice spectrum will dramatically expand the value that can be created and compress the time frame required. (That's why the polarization curves for the winner are so steep.)

How can we create a revolutionary portfolio of choices? As in the old joke about how to get to Carnegie Hall, the answer is: Practice. We chronically do not spend enough time expanding our set of options. Spend an hour, or a half-day, thinking through what your options *really* are. What's the next major move to be made, and what choices are available to pick from?

Some options will be marginally feasible, or may seem outright crazy. Radically expanding our option set, however, can have two subtle, yet powerful, effects on our thinking:

1. It causes us to improve our primary options.
2. It causes us to develop new alternatives that aren't so crazy.

Expanding the choice spectrum inevitably leads to another result. An organization begins to look beyond the first move to the next one, and the next. By expanding the time horizon to two or three moves ahead, you may see that choice "eight" is far better than choice "twelve." (See Exhibit "Choice Spectrum—Three Moves Out.")

Great decisions come from the interaction of several types of thinking. When we create an interaction between sophisticated pattern recognition and astute option multiplication, the probability of making a truly great, uncopiable move increases tremendously.

In many companies there exists the strong belief that the organization needs only to find a "good enough" answer to its strategic issues.

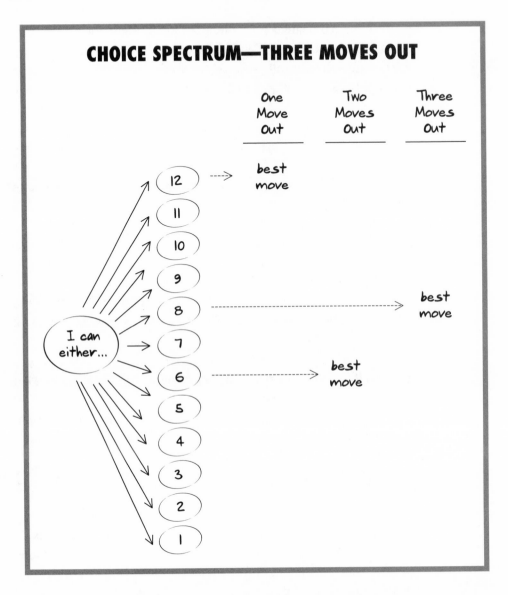

CHOICE SPECTRUM—THREE MOVES OUT

Opponents to change are reluctant to engage in extended exploration, because it produces "too many options." Rather than identifying multiple growth ideas, they want to find a workable idea and move rapidly to the implementation phase. All too often, even the best strategy teams stop thinking too soon—too few options, too few moves into the future.

In reality, a decision maker's power increases when he or she deals with the full range of relevant strategic options. While a multiplicity of options often requires greater thought and care in choosing, the only way to identify the highest value opportunities for your company is to understand the complete set of strategic moves available to a player in your position. This is especially true when some of the best competitors in the business are also actively expanding their choice sets. Unless the organization reflects on its full range of options and evaluates the potential value of these options several moves into the future, it runs the risk of missing out on the most valuable opportunities. In the long run, a series of repeated "misses" will not only prevent sustained value growth; it may lead to value collapse.

Think of your own company. Is it a 4×1 company (four options, evaluated one move out)? Or a 7×2 company (seven options, evaluated two moves out)? Or a 10×3 company (ten options, three moves out)? How does it compare to its key rivals?

(Place a check on the appropriate line)

Type of Strategic Thinking: Number of Options, Number of Moves Out	My Company	My #1 Competitor Today	My #1 Competitor Tomorrow
4×1	_____	_____	_____
7×2	_____	_____	_____
10×3	_____	_____	_____

A 10×3 company will systematically trump a 7×2 or a 4×1. It's not just about resources anymore. It's about the quality of *choices* that your team creates.

UNDERSTAND AND EXPLOIT TIME

The reinventors profiled in *The Profit Zone* offer some of the most instructive examples of the highly sophisticated use of time in strategy development and execution.

For these business leaders, time is a much more complex, subtle, and powerful variable than is commonly recognized. They know that time is not absolute, that it works in very different ways, depending on the customer and the economic landscape confronting their organization. Their use of time contributed to their extraordinary legacy of sustained value growth in a chaotic, nonlinear business world.

The conventional view is that time in business is about speed: "Be faster, and win."

Is it always better to be faster? Is it always possible to be faster? Does time move at the same rate?

Faster *is* better, sometimes. But speed is just one dimension. Other aspects of time matter more in different customer circumstances: moving more slowly; moving in the right sequence; seeing a decade ahead.

To broaden your perspectives on business time, read Alan Lightman's delightful and provocative little tome, *Einstein's Dreams.* It

DALI TIME

Decisions in Months

presents thirty-three different ways that time works, or could work, in physics: examples include forward, backward, circular, slow, erratic, and not at all.

It blows up the notion that time is linear, constant, or unidirectional.

Time in business can be as complex as time in physics. The best players in business can help us understand how time really works, and how we can use it, shape it, and twist it to our advantage.

CONVENTIONAL TIME

Decisions in Weeks

DIGITAL TIME

10^h : 24 : 37 : 79	10^h : 24 : 37 : 80	10^h : 24 : 37 : 81
10^h : 24 : 37 : 82	10^h : 24 : 37 : 83	10^h : 24 : 37 : 84

Decisions in days, or hours

How fast is market time? How does time work in your own industry? How does time work in your company? How does time work in your own thinking? What kind of time flow are you dealing with?

Time does *not* move at the same rate, even within a single market or a single industry. To get a sense of the unconstant, nonlinear nature of this key strategic variable, it is useful to glimpse inside a brief history of computing, which can shed light on how time can work in funny and unexpected ways, and can provide us with some clues as to the nature of time in our own business.

The Nature of Time in Computing

Two years is an eternity in computing. Or is it?

It is widely accepted to speak of steel, chemicals, and utilities as very long cycle industries, and consumer electronics, computing, and fashion as very short cycle industries. "It takes five years to plan and build a steel mill" goes one view. "A product is obsolete twenty-four months after it's introduced" goes the other. Time moves quickly in computing; time moves slowly in steel.

Is this really true? Consider three distinct periods in computing and make your own determination.

The first period is 1979 to the start of 1984. Five full years. In 1979, several things were true:

1. There was an Apple computer.
2. There was VisiCalc.

3. There was Wordstar.

4. There was a very small installed base of personal computers.

5. Total revenue from all personal computers and peripherals and software was less than $500 million.

6. Intel was king of memory chips, but not king enough. It was about to initiate a major sales campaign to capture the lead away from Motorola.

There was tremendous excitement about computing—inside the very small group of people who actually used the Apple. Their excitement was so intense that, like the density of gas inside a star, it radiated energy for great distances, causing everyone to believe that the world would change radically and forever—and soon.

1979 came and went. Then came 1981. Even more excitement greeted IBM's launch (and more importantly, its blessing) of the PC. Yet, in 1981, if you were a bit of a Neanderthal, and, overhearing a conversation about PCs, asked: "Why is this a big deal? What do you do with the PC that's very useful to you? Or just useful?"—you would likely have received little more than a sheepish stare.

Then 1982 came and went; millions of PCs were sold; corporations were convinced that this technology had to be important because IBM supported it. But what did the PCs do differently? Word processing? IBM's MTST machines were extremely efficient word-processing devices. Users could make corrections, additions, changes, and so on. Power users of word processing (say, at law firms) could buy a Wang system that did an amazing job on word-processing projects, large and small.

"The world would change," experts had said in 1978. It was 1982, and the world hadn't changed.

In 1983, Lotus introduced its 1-2-3 spreadsheet. The world changed, finally. Unlike VisiCalc, which was not optimized to the PC, Lotus 1-2-3 was designed to take full advantage of the PC's capabilities. In essence, the combination of Lotus 1-2-3 and the PC created a sophisticated calculator, plus grapher, plus report-writer. The business world had a reason to use the PC and a legitimate brand (IBM) to buy from. In 1984, Lotus sales were $157 million. IBM's PC sales had increased to $5 billion. Several million new PC users joined the ranks. All the hype of 1978 became reality—in 1984.

Fast-forward the timescope to 1995, the year of the Internet. There is no end to the number of articles being written about its capabilities. As in 1978, there are some very tangible events, signs, and companies: Netscape, UUNet, millions of users, the World Wide Web. There's some culture, too. If you don't have an Internet address, you must be antediluvian. Once again, imagine a Neanderthal intruding upon a superheated "the-Internet-is-*it*" conversation.

He asks: "Why is it *it*?"

The reply is simple: "You can send e-mail."

The Neanderthal presses on: "But you can do the same with voice mail, which everyone's had for years. And you can fax documents."

"Not big ones," comes the reply. "People still need Federal Express to send a 50-slide presentation."

"Hmmm . . . Is that all there is?"

"You can surf for Web sites."

"And then what do you do with them?"

"You can access data."

"True enough."

The Internet, in 1995, made it possible to enjoy a sort of large-scale Lexis-Nexis opportunity as the gold-rush psychology around the Internet caused thousands of organizations to make their knowledge available for free.

But access speeds for most users were still incredibly slow, and the knowledge structure of the information on the Net was incredibly chaotic. Peter Drucker complained that there was no classification system for organizing the information, for making these vast mountains of data into a system that was efficiently searchable. In terms of "gotta have it," there were few compelling reasons for most people to be on the Internet. In terms of business, there were no real models for how to make a profit from this sea of information.

All this—the bandwidth, the compelling reason, the profit models—will change completely, in 1999 or 2000. But four or five years will have passed since the supernova of hype in 1995. In early 1999, we are more than thirty-six months into Internet mania, and the sun has not yet exploded. Computing leaves you with a funny sensation. It doesn't "feel like" a two-year-cycle industry if, after 10,000 articles, conferences, demos, and discussion groups, we are still one to two years away from the real Internet supernova.

The third time period to reflect on is 1982 to 1990. Eight long years. Not an eternity, but two or three eternities in computing. How did the world—to be specific, the computing world—give Bill Gates eight years to make Windows happen? This will always remain one of the great enigmas in the drama-packed first half-century of the history of computing.

The spark for Windows happened at Comdex in 1982, when Bill Gates saw the first demo of VisiOn. He was shocked, then paralyzed, then ignited into action. He began what would be a crusade to bring a graphic user interface (GUI) to the world of the PC. His march to the holy land would claim hundreds of casualties and last the better part of a decade. His vision and willpower, in combination with the passivity, indulgence, and forbearance of the rest of the computing world, were the primary reasons for the spectacular success of Windows 3.0.

Now change the perspective, from software and operating systems to microprocessors. Andy Grove built a profit model for Intel, which recognized that profit in microprocessors was a function of four factors: (1) building the fastest new chips first, (2) maximizing the period when the fastest chip is the only one on the market, (3) encouraging fragmentation in the channel, and (4) introducing new generations of processors so quickly that slower competitors have little chance to earn a return on their investments in design and fabrication.

Grove didn't build his business design around "time to market," but around "a two-year lead." The difference is crucial. Many firms pursue a time-to-market strategy. They try to shorten cycles in their portfolio to get to market faster. Yet, as the typical time-profit curve shows, it is not time itself that matters, but *relative* time to market. Better a two-year lead on *one* important product than a two-month lead on ten. Intel knows this. That's why its profits have been so high for so long.

Same sector, two timescales. Grove and the team at Intel raced day and night to literally push the newest and fastest chip through the channel. Gates took eight years to make Windows happen. It makes you scratch your head and ask: "What is the true nature of time in this industry?"

The honest answer is: Who knows? A partial answer is that time in computing is not unitary; it has many components, like the gears inside a finely crafted Swiss watch. The gears are nested in a very precise and complex way. Some are very large and rotate slowly. Others, rotating hectically, seem almost microscopic.

So too in computing. There are enormous gears and tiny gears. They are all connected by a complex mechanism that creates a system within which they influence each other in subtle, interdependent ways. The big gears are customer groups, the small ones are product and technology variations. True technology breakthroughs fall somewhere in between. That's an oversimplification, of course, because what matters most is not the components' relative size or relative rate, but how they interact and influence each other.

The Nature of Time in Business

Time moves differently in different industries. Even within the same industry, it moves at different rates within different circles.

The key strategy question is not "How can we be faster?" The key question is: "How can we use time to our best advantage?"

Among the great business players, the differences in how each used time to create the best next business design are striking. At Intel, time in the sense of being fast *and far ahead* is the essence of business design.

At Disney, moving quickly was also important, except when it wasn't. Moving quickly to implement a price increase in the U.S. theme parks would have led to a large-scale public relations and customer relations disaster. Time was slow, not fast. Michael Eisner implemented the required price increase in carefully structured intervals over four years, creating high profit and avoiding customer disaster. The rule was not "Be fast." It was "Be slow, be measured." Navigate within the bounds of a narrow window and protect the delicate balance between the customer-centric and the profit-centric points of view.

At ABB, time was different yet again. Speed was important; sequence was even more important. Percy Barnevik was famous for converting six-month tasks into six-week completions. But any image of

Barnevik as a conventional time compressor would be deeply mistaken. Time, in the ABB system, requires a profound understanding of the many different *economic* time zones across which the system operates. The economic time zone of Germany, or the United States, is very different from that of Spain or Greece, and different again from that of Poland or Ukraine, or India or Malaysia.

ABB's "global network of specialists" business design is constructed to adapt to economic time zones and to take advantage of the differences among them. To ABB, being fast is still important, but being different in different economic time zones is more important. When the nature of time is staggered and staged, the business design needs to operate in stages as well. In that sense, ABB's business design of "being local" is not just having a presence in the customer's region, but having a business design *that fits the economic time zone* in which the customer is operating.

In Nicolas Hayek's case, time had stopped in the Swiss watch industry, and he restarted it. Hayek moved quickly, but being quick to reach the wrong target would have failed completely. Hayek took the time, up front, to perform two critical tasks: (1) define the real customer issue with his "three-price experiment" (see *The Profit Zone*, p. 117), and (2) define the magnitude of breakthrough required (in design, in cost, and in advertising). The year spent defining the targets determined the success of the next decade of execution. Being fast and incorrect about the target definition would have undermined all the value of the enormous hard work that followed.

The nature of time in business, and in the process of pattern recognition and reinvention, is highly complex. It is about speed but also about sequence. It is about appropriate slowness. It is about operating in multiple economic time zones. It is about how timing relates to customer readiness.

Being sophisticated about the use of time takes reflection, careful observation, and considerable time to think things through completely. Paradoxically, this last factor is completely missing from the schedules of many of the most talented managers today.

A striking characteristic of great business players is their grasp not only of how the customer thinks and of how profit works, but also of how time works in their industry. They have an ability to use time brilliantly in the early detection of patterns and in the nature, spacing, and rhythm of their business design reinventions.

* * *

- How well does my company understand and take advantage of time in its industry?
- How does our strategic metabolism and sense of urgency compare to others?

(Place a check on the appropriate line)

Time	Me	My Organization	Our Market	Our Toughest Competitor
Dali Time	_____	_____	_____	_____
Conventional Time	_____	_____	_____	_____
Digital Time	_____	_____	_____	_____

> "When the rate of change in the marketplace exceeds the rate of change in the organization, the end is in sight."
>
> - Jack Welch

DEVELOP AN ACTION REPERTOIRE OF MOVES AND COUNTERMOVES

A frequent obstacle to "acting on" patterns is reversion to the "tried and true" approach, the strong urge to stick with the company's traditional "strategic playbook." Mindful of their company's past successes, failures, and limitations, managers often advocate sticking to the existing set of options that have worked for the company in the past. They are reluctant to formulate new types of actions that may be necessary to exploit the high-value opportunities emerging in their industry. Rather, they prefer choosing from the "known quantities"—the narrow set of moves defined by past experience and traditional industry experts.

The reality is that expanding your playbook and repertoire is never a bad move. In every case, the player with the most options and moves is in the best position to adapt quickly to new economic realities and take advantage of the patterns altering the strategic landscape. By exploiting nontraditional options and approaches, the patterns-thinking organization can create extraordinary value and capture strategic control in its industry.

The value of an expanded repertoire is especially high in cases of late pattern detection. Even when one company recognizes a pattern and acts on it first, its competitors don't have to give up the game. Competitors always have the option of making a countermove, of responding to the pattern in a different way. The right countermove can enable the second player to maintain or regain strategic control.

The good news is that every pattern has a smart response, if not several responses. Every pattern can engender two, three, or even a half-dozen profitable countermoves. The repertoire is limited only by one's own strategic imagination, and the imagination of other strong players on your team. For example, a very good strategist recently developed the countermove repertoire for the value chain deintegration pattern:

Pattern	Potential Countermoves
Value chain deintegration	Specialize.
	Specialize in two cells.
	Look for second stage breakup (deintegration, phase II).
	Create a basis for systems integration.
	Figure out how to fence in the specialist and rebalance the power in the system.
	Anticipate where the *reintegration* will begin, and be there early.

The management team's challenge is to develop a variety of smart responses and assess their relative risks and advantages. Fortunately, in today's competitive business environment, several types of countermoves are used over and over again. The list is not endless. These strategic responses can be learned, and can form an initial "action repertoire" for managers:

Action Repertoire	Examples
Invent a new business design.	Coke, GE, Disney, others.
Accelerate: Execute your move faster than anybody else.	Starbucks, SAP, Cisco, Dell, HP (account management), Nokia (software engineers), Amazon.com (brand).
Hedge: Make a double bet.	Intel (486 *and* i86); Microsoft (OS/2 *and* Windows).
Emulate: Copy from someone else, or copy and improve.	Home Depot, SMH, Time Warner, Nissan, Office Depot, Gateway, Microsoft, Glaxo, Fidelity.
Block: Stop someone else from making their best move, and preserve your own opportunities.	TCI/Microsoft, Banks/Microsoft, Microsoft/ Auto-by-Tel.
Intervene: Take over an activity from someone else, or cause them to improve their performance.	Toyota, McDonald's.
Concede: Or, concede now to win later.	Sega, Nintendo, numerous others.

Invent a New Business Design

At the first sign of a new pattern, the most obvious (though not the easiest) move is to preempt competitors through the development of a new business design. This move can be made by players who are first to see patterns evolving and creating new areas of opportunity. Companies that have done this well (and repeatedly) include: Coke, General Electric, and Disney. Coke moved first to create an integrated business design and develop a significant international presence; Pepsi followed.

General Electric moved first to develop capabilities along the value chain beyond manufacturing, and has continued to innovate ahead of the competition. Disney preempted other film studios by being the first to realize the power of the blockbuster, and to build a profit multiplier system around it.

Accelerate: Execute Your Move Faster Than Anybody Else

Sometimes, opportunity can be captured through speed alone. By moving swiftly and decisively, a competitor can preempt, catch, or race ahead of other players, thereby capturing crucial mindshare, physical locations, or capabilities. Examples include Starbucks, Amazon.com, and SAP. Starbucks orchestrated a very fast rollout of its own stores and maximized availability in other distribution channels (restaurants, institutions, etc.). Ask yourself: "Who is number two to Starbucks?"

Hedge: Make a Double Bet

As some patterns emerge, their outcomes will not be obvious soon enough to make one definitive decision. The smart move then may be to place more than one bet. Companies that have done this include: Intel with the 486 and i86 chips, and Microsoft with OS/2 and Windows. Whatever direction the market took, they were ready.

Emulate: Copy from Someone Else, or Copy and Improve

The emulate response is straightforward and is built on the assumption that the first mover's business design is sound. The "category killer" concept has been emulated across a broad range of merchandise categories. Companies like Gateway and Fidelity also provide good examples of the emulate response.

The emulate response creates a foot race. The first mover is copied almost immediately, and the two opponents race neck and neck, each challenging the other, each responding quickly to the other's strategic moves. The earlier the emulate response is executed, the greater is its success.

For Gateway, the model to emulate was Dell. Because there was ample customer opportunity to address, the two were able to coexist: Dell in corporate, Gateway in consumer.

Another emulate move was made by Fidelity soon after Schwab created OneSource as a switchboard to facilitate the purchase of mutual funds. Fidelity countered with a switchboard of its own. And when Honda began manufacturing the high-end Acura, Toyota mimicked with Lexus, and Nissan mimicked with Infiniti.

Block: Stop Someone Else from Making Their Best Move, and Preserve Your Own Opportunities

Two examples illustrate successful execution of the *block* counterplay. The first is when Microsoft recognized the strategic control inherent in the switchboard it was helping Auto-by-Tel to build. Microsoft broke away from its partner and created its own switchboard, called Microsoft CarPoint. By doing so, it minimized the strategic impact of Auto-by-Tel's move. Auto-by-Tel did not have time to build a tremendous customer base or overwhelming brand recognition, or exclusive contracts with suppliers. These would have been potential means of strategic control, had Microsoft not mimicked the move.

Microsoft found itself on the receiving end of the "block" move when TCI blocked Microsoft from capturing the lead position for providing the operating system for the set-top box. TCI made certain that others (Sun's Java) stayed in the game, maximizing TCI's options for the future.

Intervene: Take Over an Activity from Someone Else, or Cause Them to Improve Their Performance

Another option is to intervene or to take greater control of an opportunity from someone else. Examples of this response include Toyota and McDonald's. Their strategic moves involved improving the capabilities of their suppliers in order to improve their ability to deliver value for the customer. For Toyota and McDonald's, this involved training, systems standardization, consolidating and upgrading the supplier base, improved information, and equity sharing.

Concede: Or, Concede Now to Win Later

A final option that is always available to a competitor is to simply *concede* the space. Resources (especially talent) are scarce and may be better invested in another arena. Sometimes, the best option is simply to "wait for the next bus." One excellent example of this type of countermove is the ongoing rivalry between two video game companies, Nintendo and Sega.

When Nintendo first came out with a successful 8-bit video game system, Sega did not contest Nintendo's domination of that market. Instead, Sega introduced the next generation 16-bit system, knowing that they could capture the entire market as users upgraded to new systems. Nintendo countered with a similar strategy and has been successful in the 64-bit market. Sega is again attempting to "beat" Nintendo by developing a 128-bit system. Rather than race to dominate all of the markets all of the time, each company employs a "concede now, preempt later" strategy to cannibalize its competitor's market.

Action or Move	What Moves Is Our Team Executing Now?	What Moves *Should* We Be Executing?
Invent		
Accelerate		
Hedge		
Emulate		
Block		
Intervene		
Concede		

CREATE STRATEGIC CONTROL

Because of the phenomenon of polarization, the value of early pattern detection is higher than it has been for over a hundred years. Companies that first detect the emerging pattern and capitalize on it by re-crafting their business design can be rewarded with significantly greater market valuation. Companies that are late to detect the pattern relative to their competitors can experience significantly lower market valuation.

In addition to gaining higher market value, companies that are successful at early pattern detection are in a position to generate significant strategic control to protect the profitability of their business design. Strategic control refers to a company's ability to protect its profit stream against *both* competition and customer power. The degree of strategic control is a critical determinant of the success of a business design. These early pattern detectors have the potential to develop strategic control points within their industry.

The intense business design innovation of the past decade has created a growing repertoire of strategic control points:

Strategic Control Point	Examples
• Ownership of the standard.	• Microsoft, Oracle.
• Management of the value chain.	• Intel, Coke.
• Superdominant positions.	• Coke internationally.
• Patent.	• Pfizer, Merck.
• Copyright.	• Disney.
• Ownership of the customer relationship.	• Schwab, GE.
• Control of sources of supply.	• Debeers.
• Control of talent.	• Microsoft, Cisco.
• Control of distribution/delivery mechanism.	• AOL.
• Brand.	• Yahoo, Amazon.
• Regulatory advantage.	• Starwood Lodging.
• Two-year product development lead.	• Intel.
• 20 percent cost differential.	• Nucor.

When a new pattern is triggered and a new value cycle begins, the opportunities to create strategic control are greatest in the very first year. As the pattern matures, those opportunities begin to constrict and by the third and fourth years of the value cycle, there are almost no opportunities for strategic control. If they still do exist, they do not have great value because the cycle will be over in a year or two.

Together, the financial and strategic benefits of early pattern recognition create a positive feedback cycle. Creating strategic control reduces the risk to the company's profit stream, which increases the company's market value-to-sales ratio, and furthers the polarization effect. The result is creation of a wide gap in value between the gold medalist and the second-place finisher, which often winds up "donating" its potential value to the gold medalist.

* * *

We've reviewed several of the key approaches that can help an organization to capitalize on change, rather than be hurt by it:

- Understanding the true nature of strategic risk.
- Constantly seeking the best move for your company (multiplying strategic choices).
- Exploiting how time works.
- Building and applying an action repertoire of key moves and countermoves.
- Building-in profit insurance (strategic control).

Now it's your team's turn. Based on your short list of patterns and long list of strategic choices, play out your moves, likely competitive responses, and countermoves. Play the game at least three or four moves out.

- Which pattern(s) are most likely to play out in your business? Why?
- What are the greatest strategic risks facing your company?
- Is time working for you or against you? How can you make it work for you?

- Which set of moves puts you in the best position? Why?
- How will your company make a profit in each situation?
- How will your company build strategic control in each situation?
- Is there a clear choice among the options, or does it appear you'll need to hedge?
- What more do you need to know to make yourself more certain?
- Is your organization ready to move?

Traditional organizations are accustomed to and comfortable with "product think" and "industry think." Today's successful organizations have moved beyond that to master "customer think" and "investor think."

Tomorrow's successful organizations will build on customer think and investor think. They will also master:

"Risk think"	"Choice think"
"Time think"	"Strategic Control think"

THE BANDWIDTH CRISIS

How many times in the past month did you devote four uninterrupted hours to strategy? How many times in the past month did your three best workers do so?

Hundreds of five-minute fragments do not solve a billion-dollar problem. Pattern thinking doesn't respond well to sound-bite schedules.

Therein lies both a dilemma and an opportunity. As competitors get "mailed" to death (with e-mail, voice mail, fax mail, FedEx mail, paper mail, and so on), and as their flood of messages erases every residual crumb of bandwidth, the player who creates (and protects) the space to decipher the industry's key patterns and to make the right moves will overwhelm the operationally distracted rival. However, reserving "bandwidth" for strategy is becoming increasingly difficult in our world of instant—and constant—communications.

Think for a moment: what would happen if you carved out some bandwidth just for strategy?

You'd have more time for seeing and analyzing patterns, for expanding your strategic choice set, for thinking three moves out, for more careful consideration of the need for and possibilities for strategic control.

You could actually begin to reverse the "no time for strategy" downward spiral. You could make better decisions and moves. You could develop a sense of what a good move is and how to craft it.

As this process progresses, one good move would lead to another, opening up a new opportunity space for your organization and creating new resources for your firm. Furthermore, it would create more bandwidth for you to repeat the process. Ultimately, it would create an upward spiral: more bandwidth, better moves, more opportunities.

Think for a moment: what would happen if you carved out some bandwidth for strategy?

THE STRATEGIC SHORTCUT

The bandwidth crisis is particularly tough when senior managers don't invest the time needed to find a strategic shortcut. Once you understand how time really works in business, you want to beat it. You want to figure out how to overcome the "slow motion" of the conventional approach.

Most strategic initiatives take years to accomplish. Building a brand, or an installed base, or a service capability, or a new product position, takes time, money, and more time. It takes thought, planning, investment, mistakes, corrections, and development.

It may take years and tens of millions of dollars to get from point A to point B, along the conventional path (see Exhibit "The Strategic Shortcut").

Occasionally, you can create a strategic shortcut—a unique, unconventional pathway that gets you to point B in a fraction of the normal interval.

The strategic shortcut is rare but invaluable. It is worth thinking about.

In theoretical physics, a wormhole exploits the curvature of space-time to get from A to B very quickly.

In real business, a strategic shortcut exploits the peculiarities of market time to get from A to B very quickly.

In 1983, for example, Swatch had neither the time nor the money to build a brand in the conventional manner. The Swatch team built a 500-foot Swatch, hung it from the headquarters of Commerzbank, the highest skyscraper in Frankfurt, built a public relations firestorm around that event, and created universal awareness for the product in weeks rather than years.

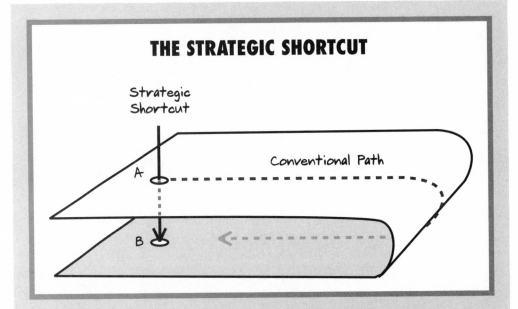

THE STRATEGIC SHORTCUT

In 1993, Starbucks had neither the time nor the money to build a brand in the intensely competitive, rapidly evolving gourmet coffee category. It triggered countless articles about itself and the idea that Starbucks represented. It used the event of its initial public offering (IPO) to multiply that publicity. Afterward, it continued to pull the public relations lever.

The conventional way to build universal awareness required five years and $100 million in advertising. Starbucks did it in two years, with virtually no advertising.

In 1992, Lotus had a potential winner in Notes, but the market was an e-mail market. Lotus could have spent five years developing a product and building an installed base of users.

Instead, Lotus bought cc:mail and achieved access to the best product and the largest installed base. It built *from* there, instead of taking years to build *to* there.

In 1998, Compaq's server business needed a world-class, globally deployed service capability. It would have taken years to build it. Compaq bought Digital Equipment Corporation (DEC), built *from* there instead of *to* there, and saved five years of market time in the process.

In the late 1980s, Charles Schwab was building a financial services brand, to get access to millions of customers. It was a slow, steady, cumulative process. To accelerate, Schwab developed an alliance with thousands of financial planners, providing them with processing services. With this move, Schwab gained access to millions of potential customers, years sooner.

In 1983, Microsoft launched Windows 1.0. The product was not ready, but Microsoft made the move. The launch preempted VisiOn, and it started an accelerated learning process for Microsoft.

Another company would have taken three to four years to perfect the product, with two results: (1) the product would not really have been "perfected" because it would not have been barraged with real user feedback, and (2) VisiOn would have owned the market anyway.

More examples of strategic shortcuts are developing every year. Build your own list. It will challenge your thinking and help you become significantly more profitable.

Patterns are a form of strategic shortcut. You can either spend six months doing bottom-up, inductive analysis to "get it." Or, you can use a pattern as a hypothesis, and spend two months to validate it or modify it. The four months saved can be the difference between winning a gold medal or winning a silver medal in your category.

Strategic shortcuts are not free. You have to pay. Swatch paid with extraordinary imagination. Lotus and Compaq paid with acquisition premiums and the pain of post-merger integration. Starbucks paid with exceptional public relations intensity. Microsoft paid with exposure to criticism and ridicule.

But, in each case, the price paid was a tiny fraction of the benefit received.

Strategic shortcuts are not unique to business. They are created in science and in areas as diverse as logistics, biology, and physical systems. In logistics, the Karmarkar algorithm, developed by Narendra Karmarkar at AT&T, optimizes scheduling and routing in a fraction of the time required by conventional methods. In biology, the "chromosome-jumping" methodology, developed by Dr. Francis Collins at the University of Michigan, dramatically reduced the time required to find a disease-carrying site. In physical systems, "fuzzy logic," invented by Lofti Zadeh and developed in Japan, dramatically improves the timing and performance of physical systems relative to methods based on binary algorithms.

These "shortcut" methods are far better developed in science than in business. But that will change in the next few years, as practitioners understand the incredible economic advantages that a strategic shortcut can create.

Strategic shortcuts bring the fun back to business. By creating a shortcut, you move your organization to a position that is one to two years ahead of the curve. The energy level rises. Confidence grows. Successes feed each other. The game is more fun when it's played from the leadership position.

CHAPTER 14

THE ABRIDGED PATTERNS WORKBOOK

rofit Patterns HAS outlined a new way of deciphering the rapidly changing business environment that we live in today. Chapters 1 through 3 discussed the changes taking place in today's business landscape. Not only is it becoming increasingly difficult to sift through the increasing chaos of the business world, but the penalty for failure has multiplied. Chapters 4 through 10 delved beneath that surface chaos, providing a library of pattern examples that have played out across various industries. Chapters 11 through 13 illustrated how to combine that library of knowledge with a skill set and mindset to create your own business strategy—how to "get it" early enough to realize a market advantage.

This final chapter is designed to solidify the knowledge and processes presented in the first thirteen chapters. The workbook offers in-depth exercises for learning *how* to detect patterns and *how* to create value from them.

The workbook is organized into five sections:

1. Learning Patterns
2. Understanding the Full Strategic Landscape
3. Strategic Anticipation—Deciphering Leading Indicators

4. Multiplying Strategic Options

5. Profiting from Patterns: "What's My Best Move?"

Working through this sequence will help you to develop and use this thinking process for your own company and industry.

One final note: This chapter is titled "The *Abridged* Patterns Workbook." A version that goes into further detail is located on the Profit Patterns Web site.

1. LEARNING PATTERNS

Having a great patterns vocabulary makes a difference. Revisit Chapters 4 through 10 at least once every two months. Add your own examples to each of the patterns; write them in the book's margins. Think about why the patterns happen, and what the early signals are.

Think also about the variants: Why are they important? Which ones might be most valuable to you?

Focus on the rewards of early detection, and the opportunity cost of missing it. As you re-read the patterns chapters, think hard about the companies that didn't "get it." Why did they miss it? What was it about their thought process, or how they were organized, that caused them to miss the signals and not recognize the next major profit opportunity? What would you have done differently? Why?

Debate these examples with your colleagues. Even better, debate them with your most profitable customers and your most longstanding investors. It's the best preparation for deciphering your own strategic landscape and the opportunities hidden within it.

2. UNDERSTANDING THE FULL STRATEGIC LANDSCAPE

Moving Beyond the Competitor Radar Screen to the Strategic Landscape

Value Migration challenges you to think creatively and differently about who your *real* competitors are. It uses the concept of the "radar

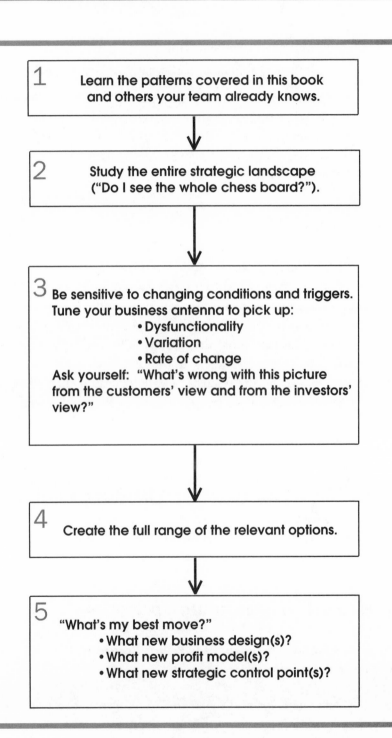

1   Learn the patterns covered in this book and others your team already knows.

2   Study the entire strategic landscape ("Do I see the whole chess board?").

3   Be sensitive to changing conditions and triggers. Tune your business antenna to pick up:
- Dysfunctionality
- Variation
- Rate of change

Ask yourself: "What's wrong with this picture from the customers' view and from the investors' view?"

4   Create the full range of the relevant options.

5   "What's my best move?"
- What new business design(s)?
- What new profit model(s)?
- What new strategic control point(s)?

screen" to push your thinking beyond the normal scope of: "My competitors are those companies that do what my company does." The radar screen forces broader thinking about who your competitors are. It combines traditional, customer, and future perspectives regarding potential threats. (See *Value Migration*, Chapter 2.)

This book asks you to apply that rigorous thinking to the multiple groups that impact your business; to move beyond the competitor radar screen to the entire strategic landscape. The challenge is to lay out your company and *all* the other players (customers, channels, media, talent, suppliers, third parties) in a way that allows you to step back and understand the relationships, points of control, and emerging profit zones.

Mapping Your Strategic Landscape

Chapter 12 introduced the concept of the strategic landscape and the basics of landscape mapping and fine-tuning. The exercise below complements that discussion and is designed to help you systematically create a representation of your entire relevant landscape.

But first, an example.

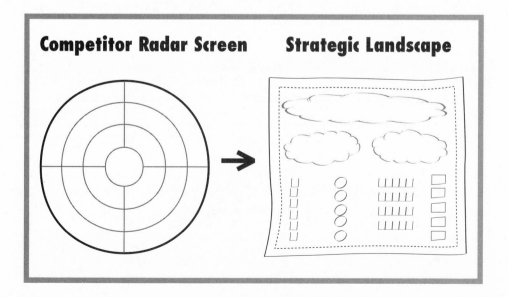

Competitor Radar Screen   **Strategic Landscape**

Recall the reference to Schwab's strategic landscape, in Chapter 12. The insights gained from a sketch of the strategic landscape are critical to explaining the company's success. Here is an example of Schwab's strategic landscape in 1991:

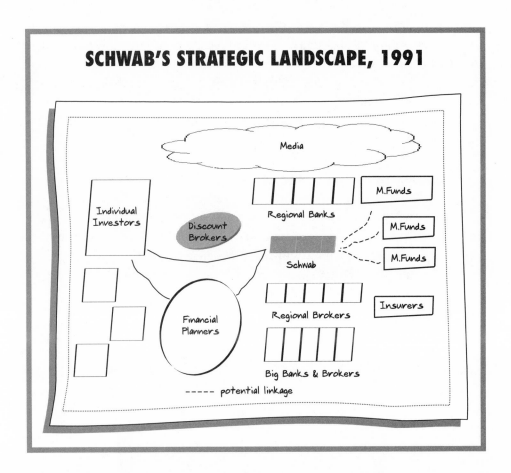

SCHWAB'S STRATEGIC LANDSCAPE, 1991

What can you learn from observing Schwab's strategic landscape? A variation of this rendering of the strategic landscape may have led to several profit-impacting observations confronting Schwab in 1991:

- Most customers are poorly served
- Financial planners are a key channel to customers, but are a neglected group

- The multiple mutual funds communicating to millions of prospects are incredible inefficiency
- Channeling mutual funds through one point would be an improvement for both customers and funds
- Major banks and brokers are not the same as regional banks and brokers and should be addressed differently

Now, Your Turn

Think about your own strategic landscape in its broadest sense. How many different customer types are there? An example to spark your thinking may be Coke's potential customer set, which included bottlers, grocers, fountains, vending machine location owners, consumers, investors, and the media. Don't forget to add in *potential* customers—those who are not served now but could be in the future.

Identify the different customer types for your business. Then think about what makes each customer type different, and jot down a one-liner that captures that difference. Focus especially on the differences in what's most important to each customer type.

Customer Type   **What's Most Important to Them?**

1. _____   _____
2. _____   _____
3. _____   _____
4. _____   _____
5. _____   _____
6. _____   _____
7. _____   _____

Now rearrange the order of the customer types you have listed. Array your customers from most important or most valuable (line 1), down to least important or least valuable. A customer may not be the most profitable, but can still be quite valuable. Are there such strategic customers for your business?

Rank Order of Customer Type by Value

1. _____
2. _____
3. _____
4. _____
5. _____
6. _____
7. _____

You've just built one dimension of your own strategic landscape, your own business chess board.

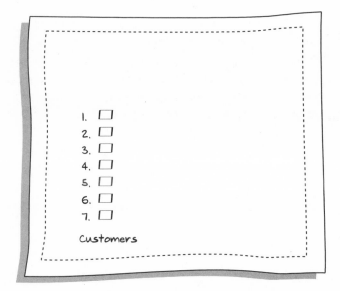

Next, fill in another dimension of the landscape. In the spaces on page 379, name the various channels through which customers in your industry buy. Go beyond the conventional channels to list all of the ways customers can access the offerings that you and your relevant competitors make available.

Channels

1.

2.

3.

4.

5.

6.

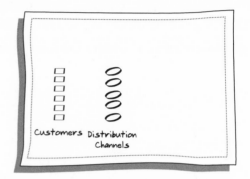

Given this information, write down each different type of business design/value chain that seeks to serve these customers and channels (for example, financial services may have a banking value chain, a mutual fund value chain, a brokerage value chain, a software value chain, an insurance value chain, and so on). Sketch out the value chains. Draw them unconventionally, beginning with the interface to distribution (closest to the customer) on the left, and adding product, component, and asset as you move toward the right.

Business Designs

1.

2.

3.

4.

5.

6.

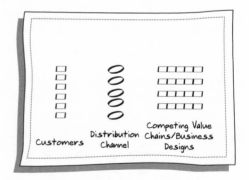

Is it important to fill in each step in the value chains? It depends. Is your intent to simply get a bird's-eye view of your industry? To understand how all the major parts interact? Then the details of each step are not as important. But, when you begin to search for the opportunity spaces and profit zones, knowing the details of each value chain will become significantly more important.

The last step is to fill in the rest of the picture by adding suppliers, sources of innovation, talent, media, investors, and so on. The result might look like this:

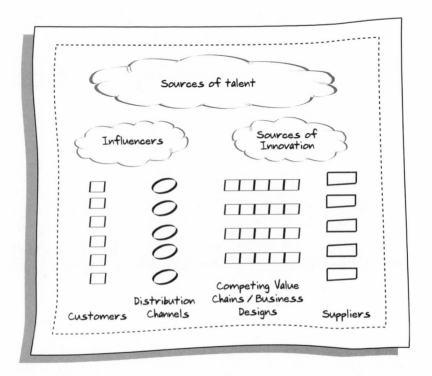

It might seem easy to assume that these last players are unimportant and leave them out of the sketch. Such a decision is dangerously wrong. Often, adding those players onto the landscape will provide important insights into the most profitable strategic moves your company might be able to make, and raise some of the most important questions you may want to address, such as:

- Who has a lock on the sources of talent?
- Who is the focus of the media and investors?
- Who has targeted the influencers?

The final, most important task is to identify your profit-impacting observations. Answering some of the following questions might help:

- Are any customer sets underserved in the current landscape?
- Are any channels, value chains, suppliers, or other players currently being ignored?
- Are there dysfunctionalities in the flow of goods, services, and information among all players?
- Who now occupies the strategic position(s) on the landscape?
- Where are the areas of high profit on the landscape?

3. STRATEGIC ANTICIPATION: DECIPHERING LEADING INDICATORS

After you have drawn the strategic landscape, you can begin to search for the patterns that are altering its topography. Recognizing the patterns reshaping your industry will place you in a position to "get it" early and take the lead, or to react earlier and shorten the lag behind your competitors. There are three key components to this process:

- Knowing your industry's past patterns (see introduction to Chapter 11)
- Identifying the conditions and triggers that lead to new patterns (see Chapter 12)
- Recognizing the magnitude of value at stake

Recognizing the Magnitude of Value at Stake

The stakes for winning and losing have increased dramatically. What is the magnitude of the value, and profit, at stake in *your* industry?

The table on page 382 provides a few examples from several industries. Think for a moment about the value differential between the gold medalist and the silver medalist in each industry. This is the benefit of "getting it" early—or, conversely, the cost of "getting it" too late or

Industry—1998	Gold Medalist	Silver Medalist
Semiconductors	• Intel—$180 BB	• AMD—$4 BB
Beverages	• Coke—$160 BB	• Pepsi—$60 BB
Retail	• Home Depot—$70 BB	• Lowe's—$14 BB
Your Industry	• _____ - $_____	• _____ - $_____

not at all. Fill in your own industry on the bottom line. Remember to think broadly about whom you define as your competitor.

What is the amount of value at stake in your industry? Take another look at your strategic landscape. Who else is competing for this value?

Are you the gold medalist in your industry? Do you understand why you are or aren't? Do you know the patterns that have shaped your industry's past?

Knowing Your Industry's Story

- What previous patterns have occurred in your industry?

  _____

  _____

  _____

- What patterns did the gold medalist in your industry exploit?

  _____

  _____

  _____

It is often said that those who don't know history are doomed to repeat it. Today, such a replay has become very expensive. What lessons can you learn from other industries that will help you in your strategic decisions? What predictions can you make about what is likely to happen in your industry?

In Chapters 4 through 10, we surveyed many of the gold medalists across numerous industries. These winners were among the first in their industry to "get" and exploit the emerging patterns, and they created tremendous value in the process.

Gold Medalist	Patterns at Work
• Microsoft	• Deintegration, de facto standard, cornerstoning
• Coke	• Customer redefinition, reintegration
• Cisco	• De facto standard, digital business design, solutions
• GE	• Solutions, product to knowledge
• Nike	• Outsourcing, brand
• Yahoo	• Brand, switchboard, cornerstoning
• Mattel	• Brand, product to pyramid
• The Gap	• Brand, reintegration

What can you learn from how the patterns you listed reshaped your industry? Answering the following questions will guide you through your response:

- When did you first suspect the pattern?   • _____
- When did you "get it"?   • _____
- What did you do?   • _____
- What could you have done?   • _____

What enabled you to first suspect that a pattern was occurring?

Think for a moment about the lag time between first suspecting it, "getting it," and then "acting on it." Was the lag time too long? Companies for whom that lag is extremely short will capture the most value in their industry. Time means value!

Being attuned to the conditions and triggers that are forming in your strategic landscape is a critical means of reducing the lag between suspicion and action. What conditions and triggers do you suspect are in motion in your industry today?

3. Identifying the Conditions and Triggers That Lead to New Patterns

From Chapter 4 on, you have learned about companies that have successfully anticipated and exploited patterns in multiple industries. Many of these companies continue to be keenly attuned to the conditions and triggers that cause new patterns to occur.

Examine the activity in your strategic landscape from multiple perspectives, using the following sequence:

1. Your customers (traditional).

2. Your customers (broad definition).

3. Your competitors (traditional).

4. Your competitors (multiple perspectives).

5. Your complementor/supplier/alliance partner set.

Recall the conditions and triggers listed in Chapter 12. Are any of these conditions and triggers manifesting themselves in your strategic landscape?

_____

_____

_____

Chapter 12 briefly introduced the major categories of conditions and triggers: dysfunctionality, variation, rate and direction of change. The three charts that follow expand on those ideas. The intent is to determine the nature of the conditions and triggers that are at work in your own strategic landscape.

* * *

What are the dysfunctionalities, sources of variability, and change vectors (rate and direction) in your strategic landscape? Ask yourself that question for each of the categories in the following pages. For example: What are the dysfunctionalities in my value chain?

VARIABILITY

Example: Profitability Across Value Chain

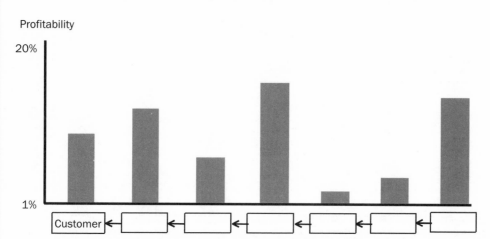

Profitability

20%

1%

| Customer |

What does a current snapshot of my economic neighborhood reveal?

- What variability exists in my customer base in terms of:

    –Sophistication

    –Power

    –Systems economics

    –Preferences (brands, products, or services)

    –Levels/distribution of wealth

    –Media usage

    –Satisfaction

- What variability in economics exists, e.g., profitability, cost position, asset intensity, shareholder value creation:

    –Along the value chain

    –Among customer types

    –Across geographies

- What variability exists among my competitor/ complementor/supplier/ alliance partner set?

    –Levels of operating performance (e.g., customer satisfaction, customer boredom, cycle time, response time, quality)

    –Levels of business design innovation (lethargy)

    –Levels of financial performance

What new ways of doing business could take advantage of this variability?

RATE/DIRECTION OF CHANGE
Example: Internet Bandwidth

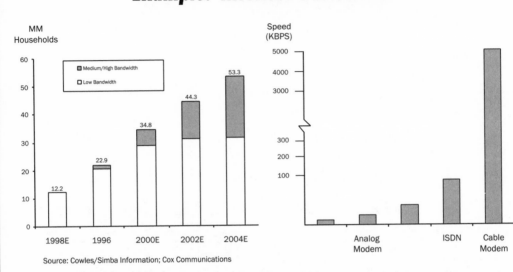

Source: Cowles/Simba Information; Cox Communications

**What changes have we seen over the past three years?
Will these movements continue/accelerate?**

- How are customers changing?
  - Key priorities
  - Our relative ratings vs. competitors on most important priorities
  - Rising expectations/ sophistication
  - Level/distribution of wealth

- How are the economics of my business changing?
  - Along the value chain
  - Among customer types
  - Across geographies

- Is a new infrastructure expected in the marketplace?

- How quickly and in what direction is technology or regulation changing?

- How quickly are competitors changing?
  - Business design innovation
    - New investments/ skill sets
    - Adjacent economic neighborhood
  - New actors or redistribution of power/status
    - Competitors; customers/ channels; investors/ analysts

**What new ways of doing business could take advantage
of these changes?**

DYSFUNCTIONALITY
Example: Home Project Supplies

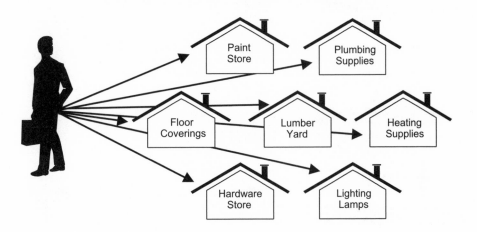

Where are the points of friction, inefficiency, or mismatch in my economic neighborhood?

- Are there mismatches between the customers' current option(s) and the required functionality?
  - Features, skills, inefficiency, slow response times, etc.

- Are there inefficiencies along the value chain (which the customer may recognize)?
  - Oversupply
  - Bottlenecks
  - Channel fragmentation

- Are the economics of this marketplace fundamentally unattractive? Are they deteriorating?
  - Commoditization
  - Irrational competition
  - Asset intensity
  - Regulation/other externalities

- Are major organizational dysfunctionalities at work?
  - Lack of leadership
  - Institutional memory
  - Wrong capabilities/ skill sets
  - Atherosclerosis in information flow

What new ways of doing business could address/ repair these dysfunctionalities?

What conditions and triggers are at work?	Value Chain	Customer	Channel	Product	Knowledge	Organization
Dysfunctionality						
• Inefficiency • Mismatch between form and need • Moving bottlenecks • Other						
Variability						
• In profit along value chain or customer types • In preferences • In distribution of wealth • Other						
Rate/Direction of Change						
• Of technology • Of business design innovation • Customer sophistication • Other						

In your strategic landscape, what are the three most important:

Dysfunctionalities	Sources of Variability	Change Vectors
1.	1.	1.
2.	2.	2.
3.	3.	3.

4. MULTIPLYING STRATEGIC OPTIONS

As you begin to anticipate the next patterns that will emerge in your industry, what actions will you take?

Before making your move, increasing your choice spectrum will dramatically expand the value that can be created, and will compress the time frame required for success. Financial options are used to reduce risk. They have value. Why shouldn't strategic options do the same?

How can you create an expanded portfolio of options? Begin by examining companies that have themselves aggressively pursued a greater choice set. For each company, it is important to understand:

- When were the critical strategic junctures in its value growth history?
- What options were available? Considered?
- What choices were made?

In 1987, Microsoft may have regarded Windows and OS/2 as its entire options set. But it could also have chosen among DOS applications, additional Macintosh applications, database software, etc. It considered an extremely broad spectrum of moves, and chose several of the most valuable ones. Today, Microsoft's choice spectrum is significantly broader. Choosing among applications, operating systems, the Internet, financial services, electronic appliances, and other strategic options allows Microsoft to improve its odds of success dramatically.

Turn to the experience of your company. What is your historic value growth curve? Take the time to identify the critical junctures, the options considered, and key moves actually made that have determined its shape. What were the critical decision junctures along the way? What options were considered? How broad was the set of options available? What choices were made? Why were they made?

Use this thinking to expand your own choice set. If you need ideas, examine the profit models discussed in *The Profit Zone*. The profit models are shorthand versions of business design options for your company. Find which ones are most appropriate and add them to your list.

Creativity is often a team sport. Get together a team of your strongest thinkers. Familiarize them with your company's strategic landscape. Then challenge them to design three new businesses that could take your most profitable customers away. Take their ideas seriously (many successful upstarts were founded by managers who once worked for incumbents). Are some of these options available to you?

List your options in the manner shown below. Begin with conventional options, then add the options that would be aggressive for your company. Complete the set with those that might be the most innovative or creative combinations of other options. What risks and advantages are associated with each set of options?

When you have compiled your list of options, array your full set of choices, from conservative on the bottom to revolutionary at the top. How sparse is the top of the page? Do you need to challenge yourself further?

What is the best move? Does the answer change depending on whether you think two moves out rather than one? Three moves out rather than two?

Conventional	Aggressive	Full-Range	One move out	Two moves out	Three moves out
		(9) _____			
		(8) _____			
		(7) _____			
	(6) _____	(6) _____			
	(5) _____	(5) _____			
	(4) _____	(4) _____			
(3) _____	(3) _____	(3) _____			
(2) _____	(2) _____	(2) _____			
(1) _____	(1) _____	(1) _____			

5. PROFITING FROM PATTERNS: "WHAT'S MY *BEST* MOVE?"

When you have an option set, you need to decide what will be your best move. Traditional thinking may look only at your next move. But, as in game theory and chess, the true value comes from looking two or three moves into the future.

Narrow choices, or thinking that is only one move out, deliver low or no value growth. With broader choices and thinking that looks two moves out, greater value growth can be achieved. The broadest choice set, together with thinking that looks three moves out, builds a foundation for creating the most powerful value growth for your company.

Using the options set you compiled in the previous section, assess each option one, two, and three moves out. Which option offers the greatest realizable value? One move out? Two moves out? Three moves out?

Which option creates the greatest strategic control? The greatest risk?

Now that you have chosen your move, how do you get there?

Activities Required to Implement Best Option

1. _____
2. _____
3. _____
4. _____
5. _____
6. _____
7. _____

Some final questions to keep in mind:

- How much bandwidth do you need to make this change happen? How much bandwidth do you have available?
- Is there a strategic shortcut that you can use to beat the time needed to implement?

- How prepared is your organization to create this change?

  —Does it have the necessary talent?

  —Does it have the right structure?

  —Does it have the right culture?

- What can be done to best prepare it?

- How long will the pattern last? Will you be able to recognize when the next pattern comes along? What are the questions that you need to keep in mind to do so?

"MONEY MAKERS": Questions To Translate Patterns to Profits

A different way to use patterns is to test your own situation against the ones found in Chapters 4 through 10. Are untapped profit opportunities for your organization suggested by the patterns that have played out in other industries? Here are two examples of "profit challenge" questions drawn from two categories of patterns: product and organizational.

Product Patterns

Product to Brand	• Do I have a brand?
	• What does my brand mean?
	• What does it stand for?
	• What price premium does it command?
	• What's the most efficient path for building the brand I need?
Product to Blockbuster	• Has profit gone from portfolio to blockbuster?
	• How do I create a system for producing blockbusters consistently?
Product to Profit Multiplier	• How many times do I reuse my product or assets?
	1
	2
	3
	4
	5
	6
	7
	• What system would enable me to reuse assets more frequently?

Product to Pyramid	• How many levels/price points does my product have? • How many could there be?
Product to Solution	• Do I know my customers' system economics? • How can I improve those economics—significantly? • Which customers will pay me for doing so?

Organizational Patterns

Skill Shift	• What skill mix do I have? (A) • What skill mix do I need? (B) • How do I get from A to B? • How fast can I get from A to B?

Pyramid to Network	• On a scale of 1 to 10 (10 is high), how much exposure do my people have to
	   —customers?
	   —profit accountability?
	   —investors?
	• How do I maximize that exposure? In the shortest possible time?

Cornerstoning	• Where am I A+? • What's the single best next space for my organization to pursue?
Conventional to Digital Business Design	• What are my company's most important business issues? • How much of my business activity related to those issues is bits rather than atoms? • What percentage of those bits do I manage electronically? • Where will the transition to managing bits electronically have the most positive impact on my most important business issues?

CHESS, A VALUABLE METAPHOR

Peter Drucker once suggested that every manager ought to learn to play the violin. This is certainly good advice for developing harmony and patience, both important skills for effective teamwork. But is there another activity that can help train your thinking for the strategic decisions that will determine the success of your business? You can learn to play chess.

Chess is an excellent metaphor for business strategy. This Appendix looks at chess through the eyes of a grandmaster. Four elements of chess mastery are highlighted: (1) position, (2) lines of force, (3) seeing the whole board, and (4) candidate moves. Understanding these elements will not only give you a much better sense of how a grandmaster thinks about a chess position, but will provide a new perspective on strategic analysis and strategic moves in business.

As each element of chess mastery is explained, it is followed by an example of how that element pertains to the successful strategy of a real business. Viewing different business strategies in relation to these chess ideas can help clarify the reasons for their success or failure. And just as the ultimate goal of studying chess is to increase your chances of winning future games, so the ultimate goal of understanding the success and failure of past business strategies is to increase your ability to grow your business more profitably in the future.

Even if you know almost nothing about chess, do not be intimidated! So long as you recognize each chess piece, and can remember (with some reminders) how each one moves, you will have no trouble understanding the lessons chess can teach about business.

There are, of course, countless aspects of business that chess doesn't address. But in a business environment where strategic moves and countermoves are happening much more frequently, the lessons chess can teach are more valuable than ever before.

THE FIRST ELEMENT: POSITION

Let's begin by understanding how a grandmaster sees each piece by itself.[1] In chess, the number of squares a piece can move to—think of this as the "raw power" of a piece—depends on where it sits on the chess board. The grandmaster knows instinctively that the power of any piece changes dramatically, depending on which square it occupies. Because of this, he never makes the mistake that beginners at chess often make: they think most about the queen (the most powerful of all the pieces). A chess grandmaster understands that the opportunity or threat that each piece represents depends entirely on the position it occupies—and the positions it can move to in the foreseeable future.

Do you want to see through a grandmaster's eyes? Let's take a look at how the number of squares each chess piece controls depends upon what square it occupies.

---

[1]The players and the grandmaster are designated as male to avoid the cumbersome "he or she" description at each occurrence.

Start with the knight, arguably the weakest of all the pieces.[2] When the knight occupies one of the four corner squares, it can move to one of only two squares.

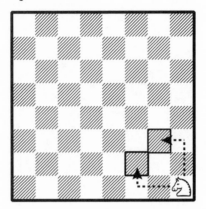

But when the knight occupies one of the squares in the middle of the chess board, it has a choice of eight squares, a fourfold increase in its power! The knight is much more of a force to be reckoned with when it is in the middle of the chess board.

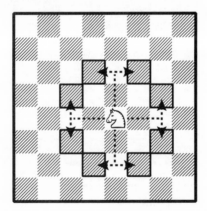

---

[2]For simplicity's sake, we won't bother with the pawns or the kings. To remind you of how they move: the king moves or captures one square in any direction. The pawn moves one or two squares forward on its first move, and thereafter moves only one square forward. The pawn is the only piece that captures differently than it moves: always one square diagonally forward in either direction.

The next piece to consider is the bishop. When it occupies one of the corner squares, its power is somewhat greater than that of the knight: It can move to one of seven squares.

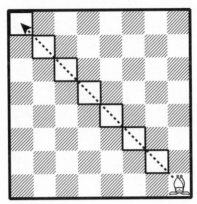

But, like the knight, its power is greatly increased when it occupies a center square. It can then move to one of thirteen squares.

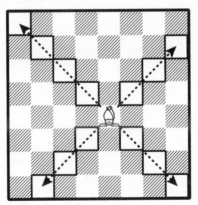

By the way, the bishop and the knight are considered to be equally powerful pieces (the knight has certain abilities that compensate for its lack of mobility), but notice that the knight gained twice as much power in the center of the board as the bishop did. Which piece do you think the grandmaster will try to get to the middle of the chess board as quickly as possible?

Next comes the rook. When it occupies a corner square, it can move to one of fourteen squares.

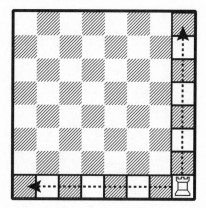

You've seen what happened to the knight and the bishop when they moved to the center. How much more powerful do you think the rook will be in the center of the board?

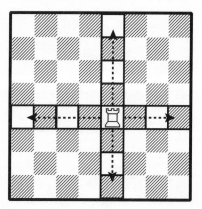

Surprise! The answer is, "No extra power." The rook controls just as many squares from the corner or the edge as from the center. And, not surprisingly, a grandmaster is often very happy to keep the rook in the corner or on the edge for many moves; other pieces have a greater need to reach the center.

A queen moves like a bishop and a rook combined. From the corner, a queen controls twenty-one squares.

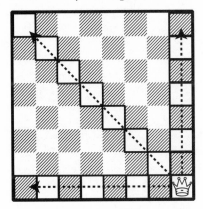

Thinking back to the examples of the bishop and the rook, how much more powerful do you think the queen becomes in the center of the board?

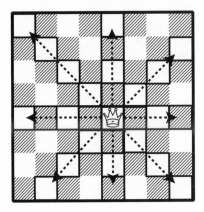

The queen is powerful no matter where it is, but in the center it is especially fearsome!

POSITION: ANALOGY TO BUSINESS

A chess piece can have a very different worth, depending on which square it occupies. A chess amateur often fails to appreciate this fact, and assumes that the most important thing is to keep as many pieces as he can. The grandmaster understands that *there is no value to a chess piece apart from where it stands within the totality of the chess game.* Some pieces are usually more powerful than others—a queen is more powerful than a bishop, for example. But the key to winning a game may be the specific position of a particular piece—sometimes victory depends on sacrificing the queen for the particular placement of a bishop. Although the queen is usually more powerful than the bishop, in a particular case the bishop may become the locus of value. The grandmaster recognizes such situations much more quickly than other players because he is not fooled by appearances. He knows that a chess piece's value depends on what it is *and* where it is located.

This analogy holds for business. Take lodging, for example. For decades, hotel franchisers ran their business according to the conventional understanding of their position in relation to the franchisees and the customers of the franchised hotels. Customers chose particular hotels over others because of the power of the brand or the quality of the service and the physical property. The franchisees were responsible for running the day-to-day operations of each hotel. The franchiser added value by building the value of the brand through advertising, raising the quality of the service and property through training and inspections, and maintaining the standards of the brand by eliminating franchisees who ran poor hotels. A hotel franchisee made money by running a good hotel, and a hotel franchiser made money by having many successful hotel franchisees contributing a percentage of their revenues.

Franchisers also contributed to the success of their franchisees in other ways. For example, they organized bulk purchase discounts on various hotel supplies. This bulk purchasing was considered simply one way franchisers helped their franchisees. But it also represented an advantage the franchiser held by virtue of its position in relation to hotel customers, franchisees, and its suppliers. It was an advantage that lay unexploited for many years.

In 1992, HFS (which merged with CUC in 1997 and is now Cendant) recognized this advantage and crafted a successful strategy to exploit it. HFS began a campaign of negotiating contracts on a scale never before seen, for just about anything hotel franchisees could use—phone service, hotel safes, or pizza delivery to rooms. Because the contracts were on such a large scale, HFS could negotiate a very good price for the franchisees, making it well within their interest to participate.

Because HFS had so many franchisees and so many hotel customers within its system, it was well within the interest of the suppliers to agree to the lower price in exchange for large volume. And because HFS was in the middle, it could capture a meaningful percentage of the savings. That money contributed straight to the bottom line.

No one had done this before, because a focused strategy was required to make it happen. HFS thought very carefully about how to organize its business so as to maximize its efficiency in communicating these deals to the franchisees. It also launched a massive campaign to purchase many hotel brands in order to build up the size of its system. By 1996, that campaign made it the largest hotel franchiser in the world. It was well worth the effort. By the end of 1997, about 20 percent of the total EBITDA from lodging came from these purchase agreements, and the revenue from the purchase agreements came with a 98 percent profit margin!

HFS did not start from an advantaged position. Had Holiday Inn (sold from 1988–1990 to the giant British conglomerate, Bass PLC) understood the value of its position, it could have undertaken the same strategy. The difference is that HFS, like a grandmaster, understood the potential of its position and organized a strategy to exploit it. (Later, the merged company, Cendant, experienced a market value crisis due to serious accounting irregularities discovered within CUC, but this does not affect the merit of the strategy HFS employed.)

THE SECOND ELEMENT: LINES OF FORCE

By now you should have some appreciation of the difference in the power of a chess piece, depending on what square it occupies. But we were considering only the simplest positions, with only one piece on the whole board. In an actual game, the grandmaster has to perceive the different power of all the pieces on a board, when many pieces occupy a variety of different squares. How does he do it? The answer is that he doesn't really "see" a piece at all. He sees beyond its physical shape or color and perceives its power directly. By seeing immediately where each piece can move—its "lines of force"—he can anticipate what moves can play out in the chess game.

The best way to appreciate the difference in the possibilities is to look at the same chess position through your own eyes and then through the eyes of a grandmaster.

Let's start with a position that looks completely even. Each player has the same number and kind of pieces, except that White has a bishop and Black has a knight. A bishop and a knight are equally powerful, so it would seem that neither player has an advantage.

But a grandmaster sees the position very differently. By immediately recognizing where each piece can move, he sees that Black's rook and knight are attacked at the same time.

Even further, he sees that the rook could protect the knight by moving to one of the highlighted squares (below), but this defense would be to no avail because the bishop would then capture the rook. Black must lose the knight, and should quickly lose the game thereafter.

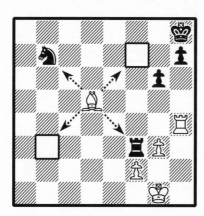

The next position is even more dramatic. At first, it seems that White must be hopelessly lost, because Black has the enormous advantage of a queen over a knight.

But look beyond the pieces to see where they can move, and another picture emerges. The player who is hopelessly lost is Black, not White! The knight puts Black's king into check, and there is no defense except to move it. When he does so, White will capture the queen and have a winning advantage.

One last example: Is anything special happening here?

It's checkmate! A grandmaster sees this instantly because he perceives the power of each piece.

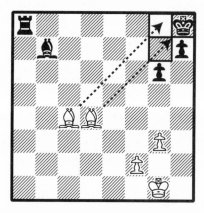

LINES OF FORCE: ANALOGY TO BUSINESS

When an amateur chess player sees a chess piece, he sees a piece of wood or plastic. A grandmaster sees a chess piece very differently. He sees right through the physical object to perceive its power directly. Show a grandmaster a rook, and before he can describe to you what it looks like, he will tell you exactly what squares it can move to. You should look at your business environment exactly the same way. Before you see what your customers or competitors look like, you should see exactly where they are going and what they can do.

Had General Foods (the maker of Maxwell House), Procter & Gamble (the maker of Folgers), or Nestlé (the maker of Nescafé) perceived its business environment the way a grandmaster sees a chessboard, any one of them could have captured enormous value. It took several years for a small, independent café called Starbucks to reach its present position of power. Had one of the three giants seen beyond the traditional definitions of the situation and perceived the real power of the players, it could have created billions in shareholder value.

Imagine yourself as the CEO of General Foods in 1988. Coffee is a commodity. It is distributed through grocery markets, and is sold based on price. You know that customers won't respond to quality, because, three years earlier, Maxwell House introduced a premium brand under the "Private Collection" label, and the product failed. Unpleasant as it is to admit, years of experience have taught you that there is no way to raise margins on your product. And the price wars continue.

One day, you hear that a café named Starbucks, in Seattle, has been very successful. People living there talk about it a lot. Starbucks has great coffee, and charges high margins. Lots of people go there on the way to work and pay $2.00 for a cup of coffee. Many others go there on the way home and buy a $9 bag of premium coffee. Should you care?

If you see Starbucks as a local café, and its customers as merely Seattle residents, the answer is, of course, "no." It's a different business. You are a national giant with shelf space in groceries across the country; Starbucks is a local café in one city.

Had you as the hypothetical CEO seen through appearances and perceived the lines of force emanating from the respective players, you would have seen something entirely different: a business design that could be replicated around the country. If Starbucks could generate this kind of success in Seattle, why not elsewhere? If Seattle residents would pay such a premium, why wouldn't other customers? Maybe the reason the premium brand failed wasn't that people wouldn't pay for high-quality coffee, but rather that people desired it in a setting apart from the supermarket. Maybe they even needed a completely different brand association. Look beyond the physical aspect of a small café in a single city, and you can see the potential threat it represents.

But a threat often carries with it an opportunity. As CEO of General Foods, you occupy a position of tremendous advantage. You could buy out Starbucks, and then use your economies of scale to execute the same business design more efficiently. Or you could start your own string of cafés (learning from close observation of the Starbucks business design), sell your own premium coffee, and win the race before Starbucks could take over even one more city.

None of the three giant coffee players did any of these things. For years, they saw Starbucks for its appearance (a local café) rather than its potential power (local market leader in coffee cafés around the country). In doing so, they ceded enormous value to the once-small café.

By the way, do you think Starbucks has reached its peak? Look beyond the appearance of the local market leader in cafés. What is the limit to the power of its brand equity as it uses other distribution channels to sell more products?

THE THIRD ELEMENT: SEEING THE WHOLE BOARD

A corollary to perceiving the power in each piece is that you must see *every* piece's power. In the examples on pages 403–405, the critical pieces were in the center of the board. In chess, as in anything else, we tend to give the most attention to whatever is in the middle of our line of sight. But the grandmaster understands very well that the crucial piece might not be in the center of his line of sight. He considers every piece on every square of the chess board, to make sure that not a single one escapes his notice.

Let's look at some positions where it might not be at all obvious which piece is the crucial one to notice.

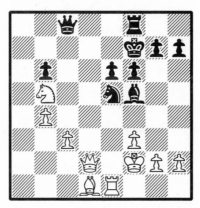

There are a lot of pieces to take into consideration here, but White can gain an overwhelming advantage if he makes the right move. Which is the critical piece to see?

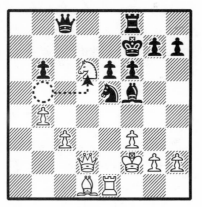

The White knight would certainly not escape the notice of the grandmaster. And, by bringing it closer to both the king and the queen, it gives a deadly check. Black must move the king out of harm's way, leaving no escape for the queen.

Here is another example, more difficult than the previous one.

Both sides have the same number and kind of pieces, and neither side seems to have a knockout punch. But Black is going to checkmate White in just two moves! A grandmaster would already have seen how to do it. Do you? Remember, look at ALL the pieces.

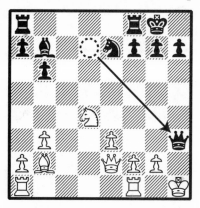

This check is the key. At first, it looks as though White should just be able to capture the queen. But that's not possible because of Black's bishop: If White were to capture the queen, Black's bishop would capture the king.

White has no choice but to move the king out of the check. But now Black has a killer move. Do you see how? Remember to use the queen and the bishop together.

Black's queen is protected by his bishop, and White has no way to move the king out of check, so he is checkmated and the game is over. It's all very simple—as long as you don't overlook the power of the bishop, on the other side of the board.

SEEING THE WHOLE BOARD: ANALOGY TO BUSINESS

Seeing the whole board is similar to perceiving the lines of force of all the chess pieces. Perceiving the lines of force translates into seeing beyond the appearance of the pieces and understanding their potential power. When you see the whole board, you see *all* the crucial components, not just the obvious ones.

In chess, the grandmaster will never allow himself to forget about a piece on the periphery. He won't miss the fact that a knight on the edge of the board can give a deadly check, or forget that a bishop buried deep in his opponent's position might be the crucial piece in attacking his opponent's king. Always considering the entire board is crucial for winning at chess.

The same skill is crucial for winning at business. You must not let your perception of the world be defined or limited by the set of your current customers, competitors, suppliers, and other players within your central vision. The most important player might be just outside of this field of view. You must constantly challenge yourself to see beyond the middle of your strategic landscape to see the entire board.

Seeing the whole board can have a tremendous impact on the course of the game. The year 1995 provides us with a sharp contrast between "seeing the whole board" and "not seeing it." Two very different industries (software and book publishing/selling) were faced with the very same phenomenon. Something happened at the periphery of both their playing fields, something so small, so remote that it was very hard to see. Worse, even if you did see it, this event was hard to take seriously. And these peripheral developments were not taken seriously. These developments were Netscape and Amazon.com.

Windows 95 had just been released. Microsoft had won the desktop software game. Won in a very big way. However, far from the vicinity of the desktop realm, the Internet was beginning to emerge. The "Net" was in its very early stages and it was incredibly difficult to assess its strategic and commercial importance. There was a tremendous tendency to focus on developing desktop software and winning the PC battle.

Yet a few individuals within Microsoft were incredibly focused on the Internet, and even more focused on Netscape. They argued repeatedly that this "minor" development would move from "peripheral" to "central" within a few quarters, not a few years.

They persisted. And they were heard and understood. In one of the most dramatic reversals of corporate focus and attention, Microsoft, in December of 1995, acknowledged and announced that the "Net is it." Microsoft immediately began to concentrate completely on developing a leadership position in that space.

Same year. Different industry (books). Same employee phenomenon. A handful of employees working within the structure of a major bookseller also began to see the Internet on their periphery, and began to narrow their focus on Amazon.com. Admittedly a tiny, peripheral player with almost no revenues. But a player that might transition from "peripheral" to "central" within just a couple of years.

In stark contrast to the case of Microsoft, the employees' arguments were not heard, and were not acted upon. The institution that employed them ended up "not seeing the whole board." As a consequence, Amazon.com was allowed to move from the periphery to the center of the book world. By November of 1998, Amazon had reached a market value of over $10 billion. A rapidly growing percentage of all books purchased in the United States are bought through the once "peripheral" Internet start-up.

One can only speculate as to what the configuration of the booksellers' "board" would be today, if the book industry incumbents had responded as vigorously to a "peripheral" Amazon as Microsoft had to a "peripheral" Netscape.

THE FOURTH ELEMENT: CANDIDATE MOVES

A grandmaster understands that a chess piece has very different value depending on what square it occupies and its relationship to other pieces on the board. A grandmaster "sees" value by looking beyond the physical appearance of the piece to perceive its power. A grandmaster always searches the entire chess board to understand every piece—not a single one escapes his attention. But even after all that, a grandmaster will not know what the best move is at first glance. How does he push himself to find the best move? He considers several "candidate moves," and then calculates the consequences that would result from each move. Only after carefully considering the consequences can he work backward to decide which of the candidate moves is the best one to play. Any grandmaster will tell you that pushing yourself to consider all the reasonable candidate moves, and their consequences, is the linchpin of playing good chess.

You can see the power of candidate moves for yourself by reading through the analysis of the following position.

What do you think White's best move is here? The most obvious pieces to look at are the queens. By studying the lines of force, you can see that one potential move would be for White to capture Black's queen. What could be wrong with that?

White did not think through the consequences of this move. He didn't see how anything could be wrong with making such an enormous profit without any obvious loss. After all, Black's queen was not defended by another piece, so it appears that White has simply won the queen. But had White carefully considered all of Black's possible replies, then thinking *one move ahead* would have alerted him of the consequence.

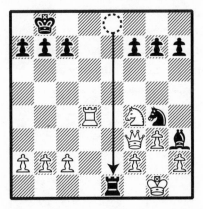

White has no defense to the check, so the king is checkmated and the game is over. White has been punished for taking the quick and easy profit without thinking one move ahead.

Let's try again. Can you find a better move for White?

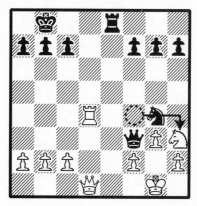

Suppose that White had foreseen the danger of capturing the queen. Looking for a better move, and making sure to look at all the pieces on every square, he might decide to capture the bishop instead. In fact, there is nothing wrong this move. After Black captures White's queen with check—

. . . and White recaptures . . .

. . . the position is completely level. White might conclude that he had done as well as he could for himself; he reached a satisfactory position by correctly calculating the consequences of his move. The only problem is, in safely arriving at an even position, he has missed an opportunity to win the game. You may stay in business by playing like that, but you won't perform like a grandmaster.

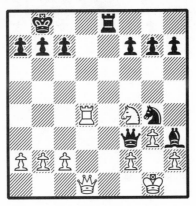

Let's give it one more try. Look beyond the obvious moves to find all the possibilities in the position. Search every reasonable candidate move. What should White play?

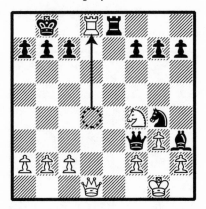

You should probably always look at a check, since that's at least a direct threat to the king. But what is the point of this move? Can't Black simply capture the rook?

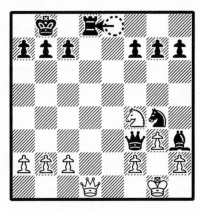

Never play a move just to make a single threat. But, at the same time, always calculate the consequences of making a threat, because who knows what possibilities lie behind it? White has found the key to the position, because he anticipated Black's response and saw that he would have a killer move to follow.

By recapturing the rook with the queen, White puts Black back into check. This time, however, there is no defense, and the game is over: Checkmate. Now that you have seen this possibility, it should be obvious that the rook check was the best move. But would you have seen it on your own? Or would the possibility of capturing one of Black's pieces prevented you from even considering it?

AN EXAMPLE OF A BUSINESS CHESS GAME: LOTUS

The following story is presented to complete the analogy between chess and business. It is a true drama, with winners and losers. In a difficult position, the winner played like a grandmaster and was rewarded. The loser was not. Imagine that you were one of the CEOs in the following story. Would you have been able to win this game of business chess?

It's December 1990, and times are good for PC software companies. Sales are strong. What was a $500 million industry in 1983 has grown to become a $6 billion industry. Profits are high for most major players. Lotus has some of the highest profits of any software company—in 1990.

Does Lotus have reason to think the good times will continue? Certainly! Its spreadsheet program, 1-2-3, is terrific, and it is widely accepted as the industry standard. People have been willing to pay a premium for the enormous gain in utility that 1-2-3 provides. True, challengers are trying to gain a share in the market: Borland has gained 10 percent of the business with its spreadsheet program called Quattro Pro, and Microsoft has introduced a spreadsheet program called Excel (which, at this time, is mainly a Macintosh product).

Challengers are to be expected in such a profitable market. Every market leader has to deal with challengers. If the leader stumbles—moves away from what it does best, or loses touch with its customers—the challengers might gain ground. But so long as Lotus stays focused, there should be nothing to fear and everything to gain. After all, more and more people are using computers, and they will need a first-rate spreadsheet program. If Lotus keeps doing what it does best, its commanding share of such a profitable, growing market will carry it ever upward.

Or at least, that's what a traditional evaluation of the situation would have suggested. If you think of business as a football game, you tend to think in terms of short bursts of activity followed by long periods of standing around. The players line up in one of a few familiar formations; they run the same set play that was practiced over and over again, and most of the effort goes into the execution. In the old days, when business was simpler, that approach was appropriate. This world has changed. The world has become more complicated. These days, you have to play your business situation like a grandmaster plays a chess game. The moment you think you're winning the game may actually be the moment when you're in the most danger.

Jim Manzi was CEO of Lotus. He understood the importance of position. He looked beyond the appearance of the players in his business to see their full potential. He realized that this situation required him to consider every possible option very carefully. He calculated the consequences of every possible move. While others around him were enjoying the company's apparent success, he took a very hard look at his situation. What he saw scared him.

What did he see? To begin with, there was some disturbing evidence that customers' priorities were changing. When personal computers were first introduced, people used them for only one or two applications. In that world, people wanted the single best product for a particular application, in terms of both productivity and ease of use. But as people put more and more programs on their machine, it became critically important for those programs to work well together. Lotus 1-2-3 exploited the old circumstances superbly. But Manzi had to wonder whether Lotus was positioned to take advantage of the emerging circumstances with equally good effects. Was there a pattern of profit shifting from product to solution that was about to play itself out in the industry?

Furthermore, there was reason to believe that Lotus was losing power with the customer. The list price of a shrink-wrapped software product like 1-2-3 had been $495 from 1983 up to 1990. But the real, "street" price had fallen dramatically from 1985 onward, as customers were able to get upgrades and "competitive upgrades" for less and less money. True, the reduction in real price was compensated for by greater efficiency and higher volumes. Nevertheless, beneath the surface of ever-increasing profits, Manzi saw an important weakness. What was forcing Lotus to accept lower and lower prices?

The answer: the point of strategic control was shifting. Driven by changing customer priorities, the character of the winning business design of the future was different. The marginal benefit derived from each new upgrade was declining, leading customers to expect a basic level of service. The value of having all these programs work together efficiently, and with as little bother as possible, was rising. Before, the winner had been the company able to offer the premier spreadsheet program. Soon, the winner would be the company able to offer a low price for basic applications while guaranteeing seamless integration and communication among all software products.

There was an even deeper reason for concern. Lotus was not unique in seeing price erosion. Other products (word processing, graphics, etc.) were experiencing the same erosion. Was there a no-profit pattern in the offing for all the major players?

The value of the pieces on the business chess board had changed. Suddenly, Manzi had to take account of very different pieces. Which ones were most critical?

Traditional business strategy would say that the leader in a growing market has a huge advantage, whereas new entrants with tiny market share can be discounted. But a chess grandmaster never overlooks any piece, regardless of its distance from what looks like the main theater of action. At the end of 1990, it became clear to Manzi that Microsoft held a dominant strategic position because the Windows operating system would defeat OS/2 in the marketplace.

Lotus had been part of a group of software companies—along with WordPerfect, Harvard Graphics, and IBM—that put their resources behind the OS/2 operating system. They all decided to make their programs compatible with OS/2, rather than Windows, because they wanted to block the growing power of Microsoft. The group believed that the combined appeal of their software applications would make consumers prefer OS/2 to Windows. But OS/2 experienced difficulties in development and customer acceptance. It never fulfilled its promise. Windows 3.0 came out ahead of OS/2 and was immediately successful. Furthermore, with Windows, Microsoft launched MS Office, which included Excel, Word, and PowerPoint. With the competition committed to the wrong operating system, Microsoft had a clear opportunity to dominate the desktop application market as the PC operating system shifted from DOS to Windows.

Manzi had made the first move in committing his program to OS/2. Microsoft countered with the release of Windows. Now Manzi had to deal with a new position on the business chess board. He could see the beginning of the de facto standard pattern being put in motion. What should he do?

One option was to stay the course and throw more resources into OS/2. Bet that the brand equity he had built with consumers would compensate for his late start in the marketplace. That would be the easy move, but Manzi calculated that it would lose the game. Microsoft's ability to preload applications on the PC was a winning advantage: it constituted an entirely new sales channel that consumers preferred. It was theoretically possible that consumers would bypass the opportunity to have a bundled MS Office and would hold out for the Lotus 1-2-3 product, but it did not seem likely. The convenience to the consumer was too important, as was the time advantage

Microsoft had (over a year) to build its position before 1-2-3 for Windows would be ready.

Another possibility was to expand Lotus's position in desktop software and produce new applications, diversifying away from the core spreadsheet product. But would that address the key issue? Manzi decided that it would not. If Windows could use the operating system to win in spreadsheets, it could do so in other desktop software products as well. And any market that was large enough to be of interest to Lotus would be of interest to Microsoft as well.

Was the position hopeless? A grandmaster searches every chess position to find not just the dangers but also the possibilities. Manzi did the same. He realized that since he couldn't do anything about Microsoft's dominance of the new strategic control point, he had to find a customer priority Lotus could service that was not threatened by Microsoft's development of Windows. He found it in the growing demand for network communications, a solution that was potentially more important to the customer than the bundling of the traditional desktop applications. Manzi decided to bet the company by focusing the company on communications offerings: groupware and electronic mail. He acquired cc:mail and licensed Notes—a radical redirection for the young spreadsheet company.

It was a hard decision. What made the decision so hard? Manzi had to:

- Radically change the distribution channel from retail to direct sales and value-added resellers
- Design a completely new marketing strategy
- Acquire networking expertise to develop and promote the new products and solutions
- Motivate people who had built their careers on being the best in the desktop software game to start over again in the network software game
- Convince everyone (employees, the board, Wall Street) that all this pain was necessary in a year of record profits

It was an incredibly difficult move, but making it saved the company. Another company in a similar situation was Borland, the desktop software company that made Quattro Pro and Paradox, the database software program. Borland bought Ashton-Tate to strengthen its position in desktop databases. According to old-style business strategy, it was a logical move. But Borland failed to consider all of the candidate moves and to calculate the consequences of each one. The "logical move" sealed its doom. It became the leader in the quickly shrinking DOS-based database market.

At first, Wall Street rewarded Borland ahead of Lotus. Borland's stock went up while Lotus's went down. Wall Street saw only the new profits Borland could create by rationalizing Ashton-Tate, and the new costs Lotus was incurring. Nobody likes to see the value of a company go down, and it would have been all too easy to listen to the Street and placate it. But Manzi knew he was doing what he had to do. He had looked ahead, seen the key patterns, and knew what was coming. He evaluated his options looking several moves ahead. He stayed the course and continued his strategy.

Sure enough, the game played itself out the way Manzi had calculated. Customers appreciated the convenience of having MS Office preinstalled on their computer. The market for non-Microsoft desktop software applications shrank dramatically. Lotus was ready; Borland was not. Lotus created a whole new future with Notes and cc:mail. Wall Street finally saw where the value was: Lotus's stock went up, Borland's went into free-fall. Eventually, IBM bought Lotus for $3.5BB. Borland sank to a tenth of its previous value and never recovered. It had lost decisively in the challenging game of business chess.

Photo credits:

INDEX